Monographs & Bibliographies in American Music

Number 19

Series Editor

Michael J. Budds, University of Missouri-Columbia

From The College Music Society

MONOGRAPHS & BIBLIOGRAPHIES IN AMERICAN MUSIC

No. 1 Charles Schwartz – George Gershwin: A Selective Bibliography and Discography

No. 2 Hans Nathan – William Billings: Data and Documents

No. 3 Donna K. Anderson – Charles K. Griffes: An Annotated Bibliography-Discography

No. 4 H. Earle Johnson – First Performances in America to 1900: Works with Orchestra

No. 5 Irving Lowens – Haydn in America

No. 6 Wilma Reid Cipolla – A Catalog of the Works of Arthur Foote, 1853-1907

No. 7 John G. Doyle – Louis Moreau Gottschalk (1829-1869): A Bibliographical Study and Catalog of Works

No. 8 James R. Heintze – American Music Studies: A Classified Bibliography of Masters Theses

No. 9 William Phemister – American Piano Concertos: A Bibliography

No. 10 Edward Brookhart – Music of American Higher Education: An Annotated Bibliography

No. 11 Ernst C. Krohn – Music Publishing in St. Louis

No. 12 Thomas E. Warner – Periodical Literature on American Music, 1620-1920: A Classified Bibliography with Annotations

No. 13 Kenneth Graber – William Mason (1829-1908): An Annotated Bibliography and Catalog of Works

No. 14 Clayton W. Henderson – The Charles Ives Tunebook

No. 15 David P. DeVenney – Source Readings in American Choral Music: Composers' Writings, Interviews, & Reviews

No. 16 James R. Heintze and Michael Saffle, eds. – Reflections of American Music: The Twentieth Century and the New Millennium

No. 17 Michael J. Budds, ed. – Jazz and The Germans: Essays on the Influence of "Hot" American Idioms on 20th-Century German Music

No. 18 James Mack Burk – A Charles Ives Omnibus

CMS SOURCEBOOKS IN AMERICAN MUSIC

No. 1 Larry Starr – The Dickinson Songs of Aaron Copland

No. 2 Neil Minturn – The Last Waltz of The Band

No. 3 Gene H. Anderson – The Original Hot Five Recordings of Louis Armstrong

No. 4 Paul R. Laird – The Chichester Psalms of Leonard Bernstein

No. 5 Frank Tirro – The Birth of the Cool of Miles Davis and His Associates

No. 6 Mark Zobel – The Third Symphony of Charles Ives

MUSIC IN AMERICA 1860-1918

✻ ✻ ✻ ✻ ✻ ✻ ✻ ✻ ✻ ✻

Essays, Reviews, and Remarks on Critical Issues

Selected, Prepared, and Introduced by

BILL F. FAUCETT

Edited by Michael J. Budds

Pendragon Press • Hillsdale, New York

MONOGRAPHS & BIBLIOGRAPHIES IN AMERICAN MUSIC

Reprinted by permission of New England Conservatory of Music:
George Whitefield Chadwick, "Musical Atmosphere and Student Life," *New England Conservatory Magazine* 9/4 (May 1903), 138-41.

Reprinted courtesy of the publisher:
From "The Phonograph," *Scientific American* 38/13 (30 March 1878), 193.
From "The Phonograph Wins a Victory," *Scientific American* 38/25 (22 June 1878), 384.
From Hiram K. Moderwell, "On Acquiring New Ears," *The New Republic* 4/44 (4 September 1915), 119-21.
From Hiram K. Moderwell, "Ragtime," *The New Republic* 4/50 (16 October 1915), 284-86.
From "Music of the Nation: Mrs. Thurber's Plan for Maintaining Her Conservatory," *Washington Post* (20 April 1890), 10.

Material (pp. xi-xii and 245-49) from Tom Quirk (Editor), Gary Scharnhorst (Editor). *American History Through Literature 1870-1920*, 1E © 2005 Gale, a part of Cengage Learning, Inc. Reproduced by permission. www.cengage.com/permissions

The fourteen photographs facing the chapter title pages are reproduced courtesy of the Library of Congress. Specific details, including the Library of Congress call numbers, are supplied with the photographs.

The cover for this volume was designed by Sarah E. Loberg.

Library of Congress Cataloging-in-Publication Data

Music in America 1860-1918 : essays, reviews, and remarks on critical issues / selected, prepared, and introduced by Bill F. Faucett ; edited by Michael J. Budds.
p. cm. -- (Monographs & bibliographies in American music ; no. 19)
Includes bibliographical references and index.
ISBN 978-1-57647-141-8 (alk. paper)
1. Music--Social aspects--United States--History--19th century. 2. Music--Social aspects--United States--History--20th century. 3. United States--Social life and customs--1865-1918. 4. United States--History--Civil War, 1861-1865--Music and the war. I. Faucett, Bill F. II. Budds, Michael J., 1947-
ML3917.U6M88 2008
780.973'09034--dc22

2008027131

* *

For Colleen, Billy, and Adam

* *

❋ Table of Contents

❊ Table of Illustrations

❊ Editor's Foreword

The historian's toolbox is loaded with useful implements. There are various strategies for creating a historical narrative, an assortment of lenses and prisms through which the past may be understood, a host of filters to sift and organize details for justifiable interpretation. And yet, according to G. M. Young, author of the magisterial study of Victorian England *Portrait of an Age* (1936), the "real, central theme of History is not what happened, but what people felt about it when it was happening." In the present volume, a thoughtful anthology of writings by participants and observers addressing issues related to music in the United States between 1860 and 1918, Bill F. Faucett might well be regarded as a disciple of the eminent British historian. Young's emphasis on identifying the concerns and responses of contemporaries is precisely the spirit guiding the even-handed efforts of Dr. Faucett, who has likewise moved beyond the once-automatic biases of his discipline.

In spite of notable pathbreakers, the goal of constructing a history of American music in all its splendid totality is a relatively recent phenomenon. The traditional orientation of musicologists favored the investigation of conspicuously European connections; indigenous or popular musics often attracted the interest of folklorists, sociologists, and other dedicated aficionados. Although the musical traditions of European settlers have been addressed in the documents of American civilization since the earliest days of colonization—the *Bay Psalm Book* (1640) being but one of its sterling cornerstones—it was only as the twentieth century began to wane that music scholars demonstrated a willingness and, indeed, an eagerness to embrace the remarkably rich evolution of musical thought and practice on what became American soil. One might aptly argue that American musical scholarship reached maturity in this quest. Thanks to the Internet, unprecedented access to the almost limitless raw materials for such studies has conditioned this development. By painstakingly collecting, carefully considering, and preparing for publication this sampling of significant commentary and criticism, Bill Faucett has made, I believe, a genuine contribution to a greater understanding of the American musical past. No other comparable collection concerning this particular subject exists.

Dr. Faucett's focus—the musical life between two traumatizing wars—is a worthy one. By 1860 practices transplanted by European colonists had taken root across the spectrum of American culture—whether it be the concert music of the elite and the aspiring middle class or the entertainment music of both urban and rural citizens. By that time, moreover, traditions identified as distinctively American in origin or flavor—ones typically percolating up from the least prestigious sectors of society—were already well seasoned. The fruits of the Industrial Revolution—notably cheap paper, mass production of instruments, and ultimately preservation and dissemination of performances via sound recording and radio—transformed musical life in all spheres. Between the onset of the Civil War and the armistice of World War I the United States experienced watershed developments in music-making and music sociology that consolidated its past, gave expression to currents and crosscurrents of the time, and provided the foundation for the near future when American musicians, American musical institutions, and American music business would exert great influence beyond national borders.[1]

Like all examples of fine music scholarship, this volume will encourage and entice its reader to seek out the music addressed or described in its pages and to hear and consider that music from a better-informed perspective. This will be the case no matter the level of familiarity or knowledge of that individual. The merely curious, the intrepid student, and the specialist will all be nourished with tasty food for thought. The cogent ideas, the passionate arguments, and even the writing style of our ancestors may surprise some or may exact revelations in others, but the overview provided by these readings may alter the perceptions of many. This is Dr. Faucett's achievement!

Michael J. Budds
Columbia, Missouri

I gratefully acknowledge the assistance of my associates Charles L. Turner, Jason D. Lozer, and Sarah E. Loberg in the preparation of this volume.

[1]Language in this paragraph first appeared in the editor's article on "Music," *American History through Literature 1870-1920*, 3 vols., ed. Tom Quirk and Gary Scharnhorst (Detroit: Charles Scribner's Sons / Thomson Gale, 2006), II, 721-30. 1E © 2005 Gale, a part of Cengage Learning, Inc. Reproduced by permission. www.cengage.com/permissions

⁂ Compiler's Preface

Because this book is a "reader," I have made every effort to modernize the selected passages to make them easier for contemporary readers to consume. I have also tried to make this book more easily readable by non-scholars and therefore have dispensed with some scholarly conventions. This has been attempted with the hope of retaining the character and spirit of each excerpt. I have not tried to impose a consistent prose style on these diverse writings, nor have I tried to clarify the writers' remarks with the excessive use of brackets. Rather, I hope that I have offered selections that are clear and to the point.

The writing and editorial practices of the era represented here are wildly inconsistent. Grammar, spelling, capitalization, and punctuation were more often a product of the background of the respective writers and editors than of attention to contemporary scholarly and journalistic convention. So as not to interrupt the flow of the texts most changes have been made without comment. Ellipses are kept to a minimum; I use them very sparingly within a paragraph, and somewhat more frequently to denote separation after a paragraph or the continuation of the text beyond what has been included here. I have also minimized the use of "[*sic*]." While these tools are useful in their place, they can be disruptive to the eye and inelegant if too numerous.

Additions to the texts are minimal and will be found in square brackets. My intent in such instances is to complete the names of unfamiliar persons, to define or replace archaic words or spellings, and to provide information about compositions (i.e., opus numbers, translations of titles, etc.) and other such details, as deemed necessary. Titles of large musical works and songs have been have been regularized with italics and quotation marks, respectively. Books and magazines of the period contain many simple typographical errors, and I have corrected them without comment. I have not imposed any parentheses; all are found in the original documents. Some words have been modernized or Americanized (i.e., "Leipsic" to "Leipzig"; "technic" to "technique"; "programme" to "program"; "Strawinsky" to "Stravinsky," etc.). I have also added and adapted diacritical marks to names of individuals and composers to make them more musicologically acceptable ("Schönberg" to "Schoenberg; "Dvorak" to "Dvořák," etc.). The use of hyphens has been regularized to conform to modern practice (i.e., "to-day" to "today"; "moving-picture" to "moving picture," etc.) wherever appropriate. Subject-verb agreement (i.e., "the orchestra are. . . ." to "the orchestra is. . . .") and plurals (i.e., "Brahms' " to "Brahms's") have been changed to reflect current English usage. First names are usually omitted for well-known individuals (i.e., Beethoven), but I have tried—not always successfully—to complete the names of more obscure references. Unfamiliar and antiquated abbreviations are tacitly replaced with their modern equivalents (i.e., "&c." to "etc."). Foreign words, especially Latin and German, were commonly used in this era. I have left them in their original cases (regular or italics) but have translated those terms or phrases that one is unlikely to find in a standard English dictionary. Because I have made no attempt to draw the reader's attention to any particular lines of text, all italics appear here as they do in the original documents.

Punctuation, often a thorny issue, has remained largely unedited in an effort to maintain the integrity of the writer's literary pacing. In instances where alterations have been made, they are applied without comment.

Bibliographic information is found at the beginning of each entry. Although I have attempted to call attention to the most pertinent portions of a given entry, musicologists and serious students will wish to go to the sources and read for themselves the selections in their entirety. I have reprinted a number of unsigned articles, mostly from the editorial pages of newspapers. I have not cited unsigned articles when the reputation of the publication is generally considered low. When unsigned editorials are reproduced, they usually reflect an opinion that the publication expressed more than once. A brief selected bibliography will direct readers to works that have been especially important to the construction of this book.

Furthermore, I have made no attempt to conceal the biases of the day. Racism and an open contempt for women were simple realities, and their expression is unavoidable, especially given the emphasis on musical nationalism during this era and the patriarchal tenor of the times.

I would like especially to thank Professor Michael Budds, general editor of The College Music Society's *Monographs & Bibliographies in American Music* series, for his good advice and kind encouragement, and Professor Douglass Seaton of The Florida State University, who read an early draft of this book and provided valuable insights on both substance and style. In addition, Professor Seaton and Professor E. Douglas Bomberger of Elizabethtown College read the penultimate version of this text, and I am the grateful beneficiary of their expertise and generosity.

Sincere thanks to Marian Wilson Kimber, Professor of Music at The University of Iowa, for alerting me to articles written by David Bispham and retrieving many others for me; Jean Morrow of New England Conservatory for permission to use materials from the manuscript journals of George Whitefield Chadwick and from *New England Conservatory Magazine*; Linda Gerth, rights and permissions manager at *The New Republic*; Linda Hertz, permissions and rights manager at *Scientific American*; Charlotte A. Kolczynski, music reference specialist at Boston Public Library; Gary Johnson of the newspaper and current periodical room at the Library of Congress; and George Boziwick of the New York Public Library.

Special thanks to my family—Colleen, Billy, and Adam—for not only putting up with my many unusual hobbies but for encouraging me to pursue them.

Bill F. Faucett
Tampa, Florida

* * * * *

An American fairly conversant with the musical life of Europe will find it by far easier to survey acceptably music in Germany, France, [and] Italy, than music in his own country. Indeed, I defy anybody to survey the musical life of America with accuracy.

Oscar G. Sonneck, 1913

* * * * *

It is always necessary to wait for the winnowing process of time before we can see the true proportions of an age.

Daniel Gregory Mason, 1918

* * * * *

Thanks to the vitality of music publishers, initially successful in regional centers and ultimately centralized in New York City, amateur musicians filled American parlors with sheet music. As a result, popular song—sentimental, patriotic, or humorous—flourished as a beloved and characteristic mode of American musical expression. The elaborate sheet music cover above was engraved by H. F. Greene for a Boston firm (ca. 1865).

Courtesy of the Prints and Photographs Division, Library of Congress: LC-USZ62-89328.

⁂ 1 — Introduction

In this volume I identify seminal documents in the history of music in the United States written between 1860 and 1918, the most formative musical period in our nation's history. By presenting and examining writings by those composers, performers, and observers who were actual participants or witnesses, I hope to add a few patches to the great quilt that is the history of music in America, ones not usually proffered by the writings now available on the subject.

Among the documents collected here are essays, personal observations, and reviews. Their characters are diverse. Most are thoughtful and well planned, while a few are spontaneous. Some are reasonable; others are less so. Naturally, each reflects only a passing glimpse of an individual, a composition, or an event; each is but a snapshot of a very specific point in time. When considered *in toto*, however, they can reveal larger patterns of thoughts and beliefs that shed light on the era and, perhaps, even bring it to life. Although this is not intended as a manual of quotations, I have also taken the liberty of reprinting pithy ones if they encapsulate an important issue.

Documents can lend light and life to a modern-day discussion of American music history for two main reasons. First, our picture of the individuals engaged in music-making between the Civil War and the Great War is somewhat shadowed. This era is shrouded in an uncomfortable conventional wisdom that, more often than not, portrays serious American musicians and composers as "prim and proper," that is, Victorian in dress and manners and puritanical in morality. As a consequence, their music is assumed to have been unexciting or at least predictable and derivative. Like much conventional wisdom, these images do not completely hold up under close scrutiny. Several of the "Boston Classicists," as the New England composers of the age have been called, were fiery-tempered, opinionated, interested in money and possessions, and willing to argue energetically for a just cause. George Whitefield Chadwick was charming in polite society, but only the brave few dared to alter his music or cross him on a bad day; it was widely known that he did not suffer fools gladly. And when it came to losing money because of the lack of adequate copyright protections, he was downright vituperative. That these facets of our music history are terra incognita is a situation that has perpetuated the belief that all was perfectly dignified in musical circles of the time.

Second, music writings in newspapers and magazines proliferated during much of this period, not only in the larger cities but also throughout the nation, due in no small part to the tremendous expansion of the postal service. These periodicals breathe life into the music itself and into the age. Through elegant description, lucid analysis, and lively argument the best writings of the period illuminate the activities, propensities, and hopes of musical society. Furthermore, the best critical reviews of compositions help present-day arbiters better understand the music of the times, providing a more accurate cultural lens through which to view the past. For instance, it was not unusual for some newspapers to publish music excerpts alongside a concert preview or review. (For any reader who has ever written for a newspaper, take a moment now to imagine yourself asking your editor if you may do this!) Many reviewers also elaborately detailed form, harmony, and other technical aspects of music. While we cannot be sure how many read and understood these reviews, it would seem to reflect quite favorably on the general level of music literacy among the readership.

Because one cannot include everything in a single book, I have endeavored to illuminate the most critical and interesting topics in American music history as I find them. Besides documents that are widely recognized as crucial, I have attempted to introduce many that have thus far escaped the notice of scholars. Naturally, writings about the great issues—Dvořák's thoughts on how to forge a truly American music, for instance—are found here. I have also made every effort to incorporate important topics that are rarely addressed, such as copyright issues, patronage, and the many famous and infamous performers from the era. Some will wonder why matters of seemingly less importance appear here, such as the chronicle of Patrick Gilmore's jubilees or the Karl Muck scandal surrounding the performance of "The Star-Spangled Banner" in 1917. While small in hindsight and perhaps now evanescent, at the time these events occupied musicians and audiences both in thought and in print.

When discussing compositions and performances, scholars often rely on writings by professional musicians and critics, but some of the most remarkable reporters on great artistic and musical issues and events were not themselves musicians. To limit this book to writings solely by musicians would be to neglect several broad cultural concerns of the times. A case in point is novelist William Dean Howells, who penned some of the most fascinating and eloquent commentary about the Great Peace Jubilee of 1869; nowhere have I read a better account of the music and spectacle at that event.

It must also be noted that I have not hesitated to include an author more than once, nor have I shied away from breaking up larger documents that address a variety of topics. As for the former, I consider W. S. B. Mathews and Carl Van Vechten two of the best writers on music of their time, and both produced substantial bodies of work; I have drawn on their diverse writings for several chapters here. Regarding the latter practice, Oscar Sonneck addressed more than a handful of topics in his important essay, "A Survey of Music in America"; accordingly, his most cogent thoughts on critical issues are presented in several chapters of this book.

The chronological scope of this volume is not merely convenient, book-ended as it is by two major military conflicts; the period witnessed many changes that are vital to understanding ourselves and our musical culture. An elderly person living in the 1920s would have been affected by the Civil War, the Spanish-American War, and World War I (called at the time "The Great War"). That individual would have seen the rise of technology in the form of the electric light, the earliest stages of radio development, the gramophone and phonograph, automobiles, airplanes, and countless other inventions—some renowned, many forgotten. Events like Chicago's Columbian Exhibition of 1892 may also have introduced him or her to other technologies, perhaps most notably George Ferris's wheel, but more importantly it made the planet a much smaller place by importing exotic indigenous peoples from around the world and offering what was for most Americans a first glimpse at cultures not native to their own shores. Musically, the 1860s witnessed a remarkable self-awareness in music that had been lacking up to that point. Journals devoted to music became more widespread, many of our greatest cultural institutions were founded, and America's first classical music superstar (often referred to as a "matinee idol"), Louis Moreau Gottschalk, was at his zenith. The Great War era marked the end of an innocence that Americans had long harbored, although at the same time it presented new possibilities for the future. While America's reliance on Germany as the model for all things musical—instruction, composers, and conductors—was clearly ending, French music and musicians were becoming better known, modernism and sophisticated popular musics were embedding themselves in the national consciousness, and the possibilities of music at the movie theaters were just beginning to stir imaginations.

Lastly, I must note two personal conceits that affect this book. My own research in American music has focused primarily on Chadwick and his works. Besides crafting many wonderful compositions, he was also an engaging writer, accurate in most of his assessments and fearless in the face of controversy. I have drawn on his thoughts, perhaps, more than I would were I not so well acquainted with him. And while the issues must always be the historian's first concern, I am personally drawn to writers whose remarks are tinted with humor. Therefore, I have given special preference to writings that are not only essential and enlightening but also delightful.

American composers of the nineteenth century sought to write music that would provide moral uplift and educational enlightenment. This scene, a "Grand Concert of Public School Children at Boston Music Hall," is a wood engraving printed in *Frank Leslie's Illustrated Newspaper* (30 December 1871).

Courtesy of the Prints and Photographs Division, Library of Congress: LC-USZ62-79265.

⁂ 2 — Being an American Musician

1884 – George E. Whiting
From "An American School of Composition"

1894 – Anton Seidl
From "Wagner's Influence on Present-Day Composers"

1896 – Rupert Hughes
From "Music in America–The Women Composers"

1896 – Henry Edward Krehbiel
From "The American Composer of the Future"

1902 – W. S. B. Mathews
From "The American Composer in This Progress"

1903 – Arthur Elson
From *Woman's Work in Music*

1907 – Arthur Farwell
From "The Struggle toward a National Music"

1913 – Oscar G. Sonneck
From "A Survey of American Music"

1914 – John C. Freund
From "The Young American Artist and the Critic"

1917 – Philip H. Goepp
From "The Rise of the American Symphony"

1917 – Carl Van Vechten
From "The Great American Composer,"
Interpreters and Interpretations

1918 – Henry F. Gilbert
From "Composer Gilbert on American Music"

Audiences, musicians, and critics in the era between the Civil War and the Great War faced innumerable questions about the nature of music in the United States. What musical materials reflected Americanness? Was it necessary, desirable, or even possible to write American music? What was the role of women in the field of composition? Why did America's musical culture lag while industry surged? Answers to these seminal questions were posited throughout the period.

❊ 1884 — GEORGE E. WHITING, ORGANIST, TEACHER, AND COMPOSER

From "An American School of Composition," *MTNA Official Report of the Eighth Annual Meeting* (Cincinnati: Music Teachers National Association, 1884), 33-37.

In remarks to the members of the Music Teachers National Association George E. Whiting (1840-1923) addressed the possibility of forging an American school of composition. His plea—"try only to compose beautiful and interesting music"—reflects a Universalist approach that, although it had its proponents, received far less coverage and support than that which proposed the use of "native" materials to provide a basis for American music.

In writing down a few thoughts on "An American School of Composition" my remarks will mostly be addressed to young composers. . . . If I were called upon for a few words to young would-be composers, I should be strongly tempted to quote Punch's advice to those about to marry: "Don't!" Success in composition seems to me so uncertain; the way is so long; there are so many and such almost insurmountable difficulties in the way, that it is not strange many are frightened from even attempting the first steps, to say nothing of persevering until a reasonable amount of success is attained. And then the young composer is so hopeful. He naturally thinks that his own first ideas are so fresh, so bright, so new, that if he can only get them before the musical public, either by having them printed or performed, they will be sure to "set the Thames on fire," or at least be greatly admired. But what is the actual result, supposing he is fortunate enough to find some means of getting his compositions "brought out"? He finds, in nine cases out of ten, that the general public (if not the musicians) are almost totally indifferent to new works by unknown composers. He will probably find if he watches his hearers closely, that they listen with only half an ear; or with a smile, if not a sneer, of disdain; or "with wonder impressed on every feature" that a fellow mortal could be guilty of writing such inconceivable stupidity. Most of his best points will pass totally unnoticed. His pet idea, that was going to carry all before it and "make his reputation," attracts scarcely any attention. His wonderful melodies are voted copies of those by other composers, and to make a long story short, the general public is disposed to consider the whole thing a bore.

That is not an attractive picture, I am well aware; but let me ask any composer of experience who has brought out works of some magnitude, if I have overdrawn it? . . . But to come to the main subject of this paper, "A School of American Composition," I think two questions are before us. First, is it possible or desirable to have such a school? To which I answer unhesitatingly, yes. And second, should American composers endeavor to produce works distinctively national in character, or, on the other hand, should they only try to compose beautiful music without seeking to introduce local color to any particular extent into their works? Composers, especially young composers, are very much influenced in their productions by the literature of their country; by poems, ballads or dramas of their best writers.

Now, let us see how much our best known writers have relied on national subjects for their most successful works. . . . Now, if the American composer cannot draw to any great extent on the literature of his country for subjects wherewith to introduce local color into his works, where shall he look for them? In our national airs? "Hail Columbia," "The Star-Spangled Banner," "Yankee Doodle"—that most vulgar and idiotic of tunes? If not in them shall he look to our "folk songs" for material? The Negro minstrel melodies, written by white men like Stephen C. Foster? What is there here to inspire an educated musician? I answer, absolutely nothing. There is, however, one field of local color in this country, and which has been but little used, which I would like to call to the attention of composers. I refer to the melodies of the Creoles of the South and Cuba. [Louis Moreau] Gottschalk is really the only American who has ever succeeded in producing compositions founded on subjects from his own land, that have passed the ordeal of Parisian criticism, and have been accepted as something original and unique, and adopted into the repertoires of French pianists. I, for one, greatly admire Gottschalk's works, and fully believe that his compositions will be much better known in the future than they are now. . . .

And now for the especial points for our young composers to reflect upon and take seriously to heart: Try only to compose beautiful and interesting music; imitate in your style only the best models; be not in too great haste to get your compositions before the public; think of the years of preparation the great composers went through before their works attracted the ear of the musical public; write a great deal, but be contented with the publishing and performing of but few works; publish nothing until you are sure you have produced something that in workmanship and material will compare favorably with the best foreign work. In this way, and in this [way] only, can we have a school of American composition worthy of the name.

Other helps will come. This association [the Music Teachers National Association] can do much in the way of influencing the public mind as to the great importance of encouraging native composers. But care should be taken that the standard be set high. We do not want cheap work. It should "set its face like a flint" against all attempts by whomsoever made to foist on the public poor workmanship or poor material. Then whatever it sets its seal of approval on, the public will accept as genuine, and be accordingly grateful for, fearing no deception.

* * * * *

1894 — ANTON SEIDL, OPERA AND ORCHESTRA CONDUCTOR

From "Wagner's Influence on Present-Day Composers," *North American Review* 158/446 (January 1894), 86-93.

The opinion of Anton Seidl (1850-1898), the Hungarian-born conductor of both the Metropolitan Opera and the New York Philharmonic Orchestra, was similar to Whiting's in that he believed that a composer should strive to compose good music without regard to a nationalistic point of view. His preferred model for composers was Richard Wagner, whose music dramas, Seidl thought, provided the best vehicle for the expression of American ideas in music.

And this brings me to a consideration of the influence of the higher music in this country. Americans have shown a fine appreciation of the music of Wagner, though the American composers have not as yet given evidence of a disposition to imitate him in the composition of operas. Their abilities seem to lie in the writing of oratorios and concert music, and in this field there are several promising workers; indeed, workers who have already achieved brilliantly. But I know of no reason why Americans should not write grand operas expressive of their own life. Of course, this country is so young that its history does not afford material for great conceptions as do the European countries, rich in legend and tradition. One might go for material back to the Indians, but it would be pretty thin; it would be lacking in those majestic elements which Wagner found in the Norse legends. But if an author like Mr. [William Dean] Howells were to write a book for an American grand opera, it seems to me that it would afford an opportunity for a composer to achieve something really great in music. But, however American the theme and treatment might be, the music could not be considered distinctively American; for it would possess qualities that might belong to almost any other nation. Moreover, it might be written by a French, or a German, or an Italian composer living in this country. For there is a great deal that is absurd in the distinctions so often made between the music of different nations. All music belongs to the same art, and all musicians have certain fundamental qualities in common.

It must be borne in mind that the conditions by which art is surrounded in this country are peculiar. Here is a conglomerate people, made up of those who have brought from their native countries their native traditions. These traditions have their peculiar influence, and if one were keen and had patience enough to give the study necessary to detecting these, they could no doubt be traced to their sources. Dr. [Antonín] Dvořák, for example, has called attention to the Negro melodies; but his theory with regard to them has been generally misunderstood. I have no doubt that these melodies came originally from Europe; they were probably modified, however, by the influence of the new environment upon those who brought them here. It is quite possible that the servitude of the Negroes, or the laziness of their dispositions, gave to the melodies the melancholy cadence, the slow movement, that is characteristic of them. But this, of course, is only a surmise. It serves simply to illustrate my point that America has no national music, and is not likely to produce music free from European traditions.

This fact, however, cannot be considered in the least as a discouragement to American composers. The best they can do is to go on working according to the highest rules of art that have been discovered, and expressing their own individuality; for in every art there is a vast difference between nationality and individuality. . . .

That grand opera is destined to become a permanent institution and an educational influence in this country I have no doubt whatever. It has already been compared to a college; but it is really more important, for it educates the whole people, whereas a college educates only the few. Without it any system of civilization is incomplete. In Germany, the leading cities have each its own opera house; in America, we must begin with one only, and that, of course, should be in the chief city. But an opera established in New York could exert its influence in several of the other leading cities by giving adequate performances in these at different periods during the season. Later, such cities as Boston and Chicago should have operas of their own, just as Leipzig and Dresden have at the present time.

Until a movement in this direction is inaugurated we cannot expect American composers to achieve in grand opera; for, under the conditions in which they are now working, they receive practically no encouragement whatever to make such artistic endeavor. The labor of writing an opera is enormous; the rewards should be proportionate; but so far as this country is concerned, they are so meager that they might as well be left out of account altogether. This is a disheartening fact, but we might as well face the truth. . . .

To those Americans who are ambitious to undertake the writing of grand opera I can only reiterate the great lesson which Wagner has given them . . . that is, the fundamental importance of making the music the natural expression of the drama. In other words, the libretto must be regarded as the basis of the work; and as this is essentially a play, as much a play, indeed, as any that is spoken and acted, it must be treated according to the laws of dramatic construction. For this reason, the composer, before putting pen to paper, before even conceiving a harmony, must catch the spirit of the *libretto*, and study it in every detail from the point of view of the drama. To do this adequately, he should be thoroughly acquainted with the inner workings of the theater; everything should be regarded in its effect as passing from the stage to the auditorium. Of course, the composer who writes his own words knows best just what kind of music fits them; but even he must look at his work as a dramatic whole. He who, on the other hand, composes to words written for him must assume the same point of view that the librettist has taken in developing the plot.

As a preparation for such work, nothing can be finer than the study of Wagner's operas, representing as they do the perfect blending of the drama and music. They should be examined in every detail, for in all their minute parts this quality is evident. The danger of such study I have pointed out; but by those who are warned against this danger beforehand and appreciate the significance of the warning, it can be avoided. Its existence is in no sense a reflection upon the master's genius; on the contrary, it is a tribute to the overwhelming power of that genius. And at the present time, to American musicians who have shown a love for Wagner, but who have as yet refrained from imitating him, he offers at once an example and an incentive.

* * * * *

1896 — Rupert Hughes, Composer, Novelist, Film Maker, and Writer on Music

From "Music in America—The Women Composers," *Godey's Magazine* 132/787 (January 1896), 30-40.

As the nineteenth century came to a close, women composers began to occupy the attention of a number of writers because of their growing participation and prominence. Author and critic Rupert Hughes (1872-1956) commented on this development and noted that many women were extremely able composers. These remarks were published in a popular monthly directed to American women.

When an intimate friend of mine had attained the pomp of college Seniority he wrote a most exhaustive (not to say exhausting) thesis on the philosophical justification of the advanced woman. With Norn-like calm he denied all possibility of feminine genius in the Professions, the Sciences, and the Arts. He proved most conclusively that She could never attain any real, permanent, or high success. Especially in music did he ridicule Her pretensions.

In the usual course of post-graduate diminution the struggle of installing a little wisdom has dispossessed a vast amount of knowledge. Though less profound and content, he has come to see the error of his way, and now, with more appreciative humility, he admits that in the Arts as well as at home a woman will have whatever she sets her mind on, if you will only give her a little time.

While I must confess my blindness to the existence of any downright and exalted genius among the women who write music . . . a few of them are doing so much better than the great majority of men, and most of them are so near the average, that it is simply old-fashioned bigotry and empty nonsense to deny the sex musical recognition.

'Tis pity, but 'tis true, that women still write too little from their own souls, too few love songs in which the woman speaks, too few lullabies, and too few feminine moods. Yet Art knows no sex, and what they write in man-tone is at times surprisingly strong. The vast majority of our pianists and singers and music teachers are women, and now they are flooding the market with a snowstorm of sheet music. The time has evidently quite vanished when women, like Mendelssohn's sister, deem it a brazen disgrace to publish their compositions under their own names.

The Atlanta Exposition has promulgated the woman composer with great thoroughness, and the number of those who have written music, either good enough or bad enough for publishers' approval, is astounding. . . .

* * * * *

✻ 1896 — HENRY EDWARD KREHBIEL, MUSIC CRITIC AND WRITER ON MUSIC

From "The American Composer of the Future," *Church's Musical Visitor* 25/4 (April 1896), 98.

Henry E. Krehbiel (1854-1923) applied the "melting pot" theory to American composition. According to that theory, the finest characteristics from all the varied cultures represented in the United States would find a single place in American composition.

The characteristic mode of expression which will be stamped upon the music of the future American composer will be the joint creation of the American's freedom from conventional methods and his inherited predilections and capacities. The reflective German, the mercurial Frenchman, the stolid Englishman, the warm-hearted Irishman, the impulsive Italian, the daring Russian, each will contribute his factor to the sum of national taste. The folk melodies of all nations will yield up their individual charms, and disclose to the composer a hundred avenues of emotional expression which have not yet been explored. The American composer will be the truest representative of a universal art, because he will be the truest type of a citizen of the world.

* * * * *

* 1902 — W. S. B. MATHEWS, ORGANIST, MUSIC JOURNALIST, AND TEACHER

From "The American Composer in This Progress," *The Great in Music* (Chicago: Music Magazine Publishing Company, 1902), 423-24.

> **By the turn of the century Chicago-based W. S. B. Mathews (1837-1912) could sound the theme that, in comparison to continental Europe's musical accomplishments, "we are not there yet," but he maintained a positive outlook. Mathews argued that American composers would one day make the contributions to the art form that the American public expects.**

It is to be regretted that as yet we are not able to speak of our American composers in the same connection as the great geniuses of musical art. This will not always be so; but it takes a long experience before a country produces a master along any line. There is a heredity into which such a master must be born; and there must be an environment for shaping and coloring his youthful years; a sympathetic environment for appreciating his early efforts.

These elements are now in preparation. America is growing in musical culture; we are producing many good players, and fine music is being played within the hearing of all classes of people. Musical education is improving; we have schools as good as the best abroad, and teaching which is often more productive and painstaking. Our composers have illustrated almost every style of composition, often with talent. We have as fine art songs of American production as Europe is producing. Our popular music pervades the world. [Ethelbert] Nevin, [John Philip] Sousa, [Victor] Herbert are names well known to every European band master. Creditable efforts are made in the higher departments of music; but as yet, apparently, no masterwork. Later it will come. Even now our position is not inferior to England, where musical cultivation has been of longer and more persistent growth. Yet England has still to produce one single composer of a high class.

Sooner or later, perhaps very soon, some composer will arise whose compositions will of their own attractiveness take possession of American ears, and the composer will be assigned a high position as of right. When this takes place it will be through the good fortune of such a composer in so voicing American moods, American ideals and energy that his accents appeal to the American public without any efforts toward cultivating a taste for his works or undue lauding [of] the composer. His music will make its own way. Conductors will play it because it means something; because it is a new voice in the world concert. This is what we have a right to expect.

* * * * *

✻ 1903 — ARTHUR ELSON, MUSIC HISTORIAN

From *Woman's Work in Music* (Boston: The Page Company, 1903), 234-43.

> Arthur Elson (1873-1940), who authored this pioneering monograph documenting the participation of women in the history of Western music, also noted the recent rise to prominence of women composers. He also felt obliged to report that among their ranks there were still none of lasting merit.

The question of allowing women to compose, if they wish to do so, is hardly one that needs any extended debate. Yet it is only in the last few decades that woman's inalienable right to compose has been fully established. . . . The time has gone by when men need fear that they will have to do the sewing if their wives devote themselves to higher pursuits. . . .

Whether women are in any way handicapped by the constitution of their sex is a point that is still undecided. It would seem that composition demanded no great physical strength, and no one will deny that women often possess the requisite mental breadth. The average sweet girl graduate of the conservatories, who is made up chiefly of sentiment, and hates mathematics, will hardly make a very deep mark in any art. But there are many who do earnest work, and who lead lives of activity and production that afford them equal rank with men in this respect. . . .

It is often claimed that women study music merely as an accomplishment, with the object of pleasing friends and relatives by their performances. This horrible accusation the writer can attempt neither to palliate nor to deny. But why should it be denied? If music is to be regarded as one of the feminine accomplishments, why should this debar the more earnest students from doing more earnest work? The very fact that all cultivated women are expected to know something of music ought to result in a better chance for the discovery of woman's talent in composition. . . .

As yet there has been no woman composer of the very first rank, comparable to the tonal giants among men. But in explanation of this is the fact that women have not been generally at work in this field until the last century, while men have had considerably more time. And after all, there are not so many really great men among the composers. . . .

* * * * *

✻ 1907 — ARTHUR FARWELL, COMPOSER, MUSIC CRITIC, AND MUSIC EDITOR

From "The Struggle toward a National Music," *North American Review* 86/625 (December 1907), 565-70.

> Arthur Farwell (1872-1952), who founded the Wa-Wan Press to publish American compositions by American composers, was among the first to notice the establishment of a genuine school of American composition. He discussed American music in terms of finding a "solution" to a problem—a very American way to put it—rather than simply helping composers to identify avenues for self-expression. Farwell's goal of imbuing original "art music" with American "popular music," while already accomplished by many composers, was beginning to gain ground.

To one tracing in detail the progress of American music, the present is probably the most interesting and exciting epoch through which our nation will pass. For with this generation, and only with this, our composers have bent themselves to the task of genuinely mastering the technique of musical composition, and are thus for the first time gaining a medium through which American spirit and individuality may freely speak. From now on, we are not merely to observe how cleverly the American can imitate European modes of expression; we are to see what the American has to say for himself, for this nation, for *us*, through the medium of his art. Does he still reflect the pessimism, the melancholy, the artistic desperation of modern Europe; or does he voice the youthful, optimistic, heroic spirit of a new land? Has he found himself and us in his art?

It must be confessed at once that but few of our composers have awakened to the vitalizing knowledge that they must in some sort reflect the humanity about them, they must in some measure reflect the American spirit, or perish in their artistic pride. America will never retain what is not true to herself, and Europe will forever reject what is merely imitative of her. But it is the presence of a few composers who have realized the truth of this, consciously or unconsciously to themselves, which marks the significant evolutionary point in our American musical development. . . .

The exclusively European musical culture of America has retarded the growth of American music among Americans, except among the people, who have cared precisely nothing for that culture. Nor is this "popular" American music a growth to be disparaged by the culture. It is fresh in melody, and unprecedented in the history of popular music in its remarkable rhythms; and one day it will exercise a greater influence upon American musical culture than is dreamed of at the present time. No less a composer than Dvořák has said that American street music is the most interesting in the world. It is the music of our Folk, given us almost as by a miracle in default of a racial folk music, and it cannot be ignored, because that Folk is ourselves–is America. Beethoven demonstrated, and Wagner both insisted and demonstrated, that the greatest music must eventually arise from a Folk, through an individual who fundamentally touches and voices that Folk. Not only is that what will happen in America, but the time is ripe for the beginning of the particular work which shall lead to that end. For American popular music has now assumed a definite character (involving several styles); the other forms of folk song peculiar to American soil, chiefly the Negro and Indian, are now becoming well understood, and can lend to future work what force and color they possess. The American composer is equipping himself, and the nation's questioning attitude toward it all is driving the composer into the consideration of these problems, so that there remains but one step more—and that an inevitable one—namely, the solution of them.

This solution can take place only along one line; that is, a line which brings the composer closer to his Folk, to his own people. He must, in some way, be the apex of that structure of which they are the base. His art is to be a refinement of that which they process in a crude state. It can never be that which some other nation owns. Therefore, he must ask, What is that which they possess? But music is both body and spirit: that is, it is this or that kind of melody or harmony or rhythm, and it is also a particular feeling, a particular kind of spirit, which is the result of the manner of combining and using those three elements. . . . The composer to come, therefore, if he is to be in every fiber a product of America, as Lincoln was a product of America, must stoop to conquer; he must come down from the clouds of European refinement-imitations and understand the crude but inexhaustibly vital realities of his people which, for him, are their music and their independence. The composer must supply, on his part, brains and ideals. . . .

Probably no American composer is closer to the heart of the American people than Stephen Foster, who gave us "Swanee River," "Old Kentucky Home," "Massa's in de Cold Ground" and so many more songs which America can never forget. . . . Many of us, listening to the tickling strains of American comic opera melodies played by a cafe orchestra, will have noticed the magical effect upon those present of the appearance of a Foster melody on the scene. It scatters the feeble emotions aroused by the emasculated writers of our comic operas as the rising sun scatters the mists of the night. The inattentive diners seem to wake up, they forsake their small talk, and the vanities of life give place to sweeping and genuine emotions of the heart. They join in the song in a manner which convinces us that this music and their souls are made of the same stuff. What Stephen Foster has done, our composers of culture must learn to do; they must come close to the people. They may write symphonies instead of songs, but the symphonies must hold something which the people grasp as their own, something which they have been hungering for—a breadth, a simplicity and directness which they cannot find in the symphony concert halls of America today. Music which most deeply touches America must rise up from our own soil. Wagner understood the spirit of America, and very seriously thought of coming here at a time when his own land repudiated him. He was more of an American than many of our own composers, for he worked with the primal forces of man and nature, and not with the over-refined and predigested delicacies of a decadent culture; and Americans, however they may have rivaled Europeans in misunderstanding Wagner in the whole scope of his ideals, have nevertheless taken much of his work deeply to heart. Perhaps there is a hint for us here; it may be that only in the drama, the music drama, with its concrete presentation of human life, will Americans be most deeply touched by music. This result, however, will not be gained by imitating Wagner, but by exalting popular forms of American opera already in existence.

* * * * *

❋ 1913 — OSCAR G. SONNECK, MUSICOLOGIST AND LIBRARIAN

From "A Survey of American Music," *Suum Cuique: Essays in Music* (New York: Schirmer, 1916), 137-38. [Based on a lecture delivered in 1913]

Polymath Oscar Sonneck (1873-1928) contended that American citizens shared many traits despite their diverse heritages and insisted that the most serious hindrance to the creation of an American music was the dearth of American music teachers. A central point of Sonneck's discussion is that Americans must teach Americans and that Americans must learn from other Americans.

One of these European prejudices is that against the American composer. If our European critics merely contented themselves with stating the undeniable fact that we have not yet produced masters of the first rank, we should have no ground for complaint.; but it is just a little galling to be told *ad nauseam* that "commercial" America never can produce great creative musical artists, that even our best composers are but weak dilutions and imitations of an inferior European article, and that our only noteworthy contribution to music has been "ragtime." Such shortsighted nonsense is not dictated by a spirit of fair play, but by prejudice. As a matter of fact, we have composers of real merit in America, and more gratifying still, we have American composers. I mean composers whose musical idiom is permeated with a recognizable American aroma, whose works carry with them an American atmosphere because they reflect in some definite or indefinite manner the character and the temperament of the American Nation.

Some people deny to this composite nation of ours telling national characteristics, but this is another prejudice which we need not take seriously. No matter how, by looks or accent or temperament, we Americans may betray our different ancestry, yet [in] back of these distinguishing features we possess a more or less pronounced common something in appearance, in speech, in thought, in mental attitude, which stamps us everywhere as Americans. Whether acquired by contact, one might almost say by contagion, or inherited, the American characteristics cannot but make themselves felt in the utterance of the American musicians as well as of any other type of American. Nature demands that they come to the surface, and they do. I am deliberately refraining from mentioning names of the living in this lecture, so I must use [Edward] MacDowell's rather exceptional case as a concrete illustration. Deduct from his art everything that smacks of the "Made in Germany," deduct his indebtedness to [Edvard] Grieg, [Joachim] Raff, and others, deduct even his own powerful individuality, and there remains, especially in his mature works, the subtle, yet unmistakable atmosphere of the New World. His music could never have been composed by a European master of equal technique and genius. Psychologically, it is in the last analysis American music. It is of us and ours, and therewith you have the explanation, why Europeans do not share with us that impression of MacDowell's music which goes deeper than the mere appeal of beauty, originality, and mastery of technique. What is true of MacDowell is also true of lesser American composers in varying degrees. Indeed, the mode of musical speech of certain of our most representative composers of the "Made in Germany" or "Made in France" era is sounding a more and more sympathetic American undertone the more distant their early surroundings become.

If identical art-economic conditions prevailed here and abroad, this theory of an *inevitable* Americanism in music would be too obvious for discussion. As a matter of fact, however, they differ in one very important point. Nothing interferes with the ripening of a European composer in the soil in which his nature roots. A German composer, as a rule, is trained by Germans in a German atmosphere, a Frenchman in France by Frenchmen. Thus such national characteristics as add zest and sap to every artistic utterance, permeate his music unobtrusively and without external hindrances. It is German music made in Germany by Germans; not necessarily good music for that reason, of course, but at least homogeneous. Not so with the American composer. Conditions forced him to seek his musical education abroad at an age when his mind was [as] impressionable as wax. He would be influenced not merely by the powerful personality of his teacher—let us say, for instance, [Josef] Rheinberger—but also by Rheinberger as a German, and his innate Americanism would become atrophied. Hence, the music by American composers now in their prime so often sounds like German music made in Germany by Americans, not necessarily poor music for that reason, of course, but somewhat incongruous and heterogeneous in its fundamental racial psychological elements. At any rate, if nothing else can be said against the music of an American composer, it is quite customary to level criticism against his German or French accent. He is condemned as an imitator, without fair consideration of the fact that he is the victim of circumstances.

Unfortunately, this outpouring into Europe of our students of composition continues unabated, though no longer necessary. I am not advocating an educational boycott of Europe—far from it; but I do believe that the American student of music and especially of composition should now be sent to Europe, not at the beginning or in the middle of his training, but at the end, when his character is likely to have passed the formative period and when his horizon is likely to be widened, rather than narrowed, by a sojourn in Europe at the feet of one or more masters of different nationality. Once the present tendency of expatriation of adolescent Americans with all its unavoidable consequences stops, once the American composer has practically become a home-product, then his Americanism will inevitably assert itself. It will assert itself, moreover, spontaneously and without recourse to artificial, much less to chauvinistic, means. . . .

* * * * *

✻ 1914 — John C. Freund, Music Critic and Publisher

From "The Young American Artist and the Critic," *Musical America* 20/24 (17 October 1914), 60.

> John C. Freund (1848-1924), the founder of *Musical America*, referred to industrial accomplishments in his discussion of American achievement in music. A music critic and an influential publisher of music magazines, he argued that America's nascent musicality required validation from a reliable press that could be trusted to protect musical standards.

It is generally conceded, particularly by those Americans who have traveled abroad, and have come directly in touch with conditions in the musical world there, that one of the great differences between the attitude of foreign peoples to young and ambitious talent, and the attitude of the public in this country, is, that whereas the French encourage their young singers and composers, and are glad to give them opportunity, while the Germans and Italians do the same, and the English, in large measure, the same, we Americans are either indifferent or antagonistic to our own artistic children, and are ever ready to accept and prefer the foreign artists and musicians. . . .

Various explanations have been given of this situation. Perhaps the best is, that, as a young country, years ago, while we were solving the physical problems that faced us in the construction of towns, factories, matters of transportation, etc., we were compelled in all that concerned music, art and the drama to look to older nations and get our supply of talent from them.

That this would be an influence which would continue is reasonable to suppose. It is also reasonable to suppose that, after a time, we would reach such a standard of knowledge and culture, particularly in music, that we should develop talent of our own, and consequently, the time would come when this talent would demand recognition on its merits. Logically, it would follow that our young people would have to meet and overcome a national prejudice in favor of foreign musicians and artists, and be forced to make their way as best they could.

In this situation it is also clear that a very potent influence would be exercised by the writers for the press who dealt with musical matters. Upon their knowledge, their power of discrimination, as well as sense of justice, would depend, in large measure, the forming of public opinion, not only with the main issue involved, but with regard to the merits of any particular aspirant for fame.

It should be evident that one of the duties of such writers or critics would be to protect the public from being imposed upon by those whose claims for support and attention were insufficient and to squarely resist any attempt to encourage immature talent on the score of its being American.

At the same time, the public has a right to expect that particularly those writers who have the command of the columns of the journals of large circulation and influence would always use their opportunities in a constructive way, and so, would lend encouragement to such of our young artists and musicians as could show that they not only possessed talent but had made serious and proper studies in the many excellent music schools, and under many notable, conscientious and experienced music teachers that we have had for years.

This would also particularly apply to those Americans who entered the field as composers. . . .

* * * * *

✻ 1917 — PHILIP H. GOEPP, MUSIC CRITIC AND COMPOSER

From "The Rise of the American Symphony," *The Etude* 35/5 (May 1917), 305-06.

Attorney-turned-music critic Philip H. Goepp (1864-1936) considered the prejudices that met the American composer and offered a formula for changing audience perceptions. While Goepp was clearly conservative in his aesthetic tastes, he maintained that nationalism was merely a trend and that those works that will withstand the test of time will be those that are well crafted and beautiful.

In a discussion of America's share in the creation of a modern music we encounter not merely a foreign prejudice, that always exists against a new country in art, but a strange diffidence of our own, a kind of disinclination to believe that we can really produce great music—as if it were an exotic that could not grow on our soil.

One has a way of taking for granted that the countries that were once the home of the classics must continue, *ipso facto*, to be the centers of art, to the exclusion of all others. . . . Various kinds of prejudice are here united. There is the provincial feeling that the familiar figure who lives in your own town cannot possibly produce a great work of art, cannot vie with the wonderful foreign names you see on the programs of symphony concerts. Of course this feeling always existed, and accounts for the tragic struggles of each of the masters in his lifetime. But it is naturally greater in the youngest of nations.

History shows how difficult it is to overcome the presumption against a new country in art. It was true in Italy in the sixteenth century and in Germany in the eighteenth. Perhaps we are a little like the people in [Hans Christian] Andersen's fairy tale of the *Emperor's [New] Clothes*, that only the wise could see. We hear many extravagant, cacophonous novelties of futurist composers, and we applaud for fear of not being "wise," when in reality we see or hear nothing of beauty. But we do not ever give an ear to the noble productions of our own composers. . . .

In reality the whole question of American music, and in particular of American symphonies, is one of attitude. Once it is admitted that they may be considered, the battle is more than half won. Somehow, it seems, American composers, like children, are meant to be seen (though rarely in print) rather than heard.

What is most needed is a bold and frank criticism. In a mad chase for novelty for its own sake we will acclaim much that is merely decadent art, or, still worse, is a reflection of a certain destructive spirit abroad that is in revolt against all human ideals. And at the same time we will ignore the works of American musicians that in sheer reality are more beautiful.

Perhaps one difficulty with American music, as with all American art, is that the wrong kind of thing is expected. The world has always looked for "typical" qualities, with a certain primitive, uncouth, rudeness. It is thus that [Walt] Whitman has been hailed abroad, above poets of a nobler and profounder Muse.

It is time to recognize the truth that nationalism in art is no special gain, is [incidental] at best—a limitation rather than a virtue. It is a strange fact that music today moves in national grooves more than at any other time in its history. It seems a kind of paradox in view of the rapid growth of intercommunication.

In the days of Bach there was a certain common style and standard of music, whether for the stage, the chamber or the church. Music was not merely national, but simply music. Since then folksong has been discovered and greatly overdone. In a way the sharp division of national groups of art was a sinister omen of the present cataclysm. After the World War is ended we may find in the language of tones the ideal of the ancient builders of the Tower of Babel. For music is, in its nature, a single language for the world, as its alphabet rests on ideal elements. It has no national limits, like prose or poetry; its home is the whole world; its idiom the blended song of all nations.

So, if we really wish to find American music, we will discover it in plenty. But we must not look for a new national type or a new tonal dialect. It is in the blending and mixing of various and different national qualities that will lay the strength and distinction of American music. . . .

Before the final close it is important to point to the chief needs of an American reception of an American music. They are, in brief, (1) the production of the best, not the worst or the mediocre American compositions; (2) a spontaneous abandon of responsive feeling and of frank critical judgement, unbiased by fads or prejudice; (3) a repeated performance of the best works. No music can achieve recognition in merely one hearing. If a work seems to please, let the impression be confirmed and heightened in later repetitions.

In conclusion, we cannot resist the prophetic feeling that we are on the eve of an age when the various schools of symphony will merge into a higher phase of the art; when transplanted national tradition will vanish before a broader spirit—the symbol of a new humanity and brotherhood. Here America will lead in the ideal expression of the tonal art, as in the practical realm of statesmanship.

❋ ❋ ❋ ❋ ❋

❋ 1917 — Carl Van Vechten, Writer, Arts Critic, Photographer

From "The Great American Composer," *Interpreters and Interpretations* (New York: Alfred A. Knopf, 1917), 269-84.

Carl Van Vechten (1880-1964), who became the champion of many of the artistic luminaries associated with the Harlem Renaissance, decried the classical composers of the day while also attacking the imposing body of popular sentimental song in America. But in "ragtime," by which Van Vechten means popular music with a close relationship to classic ragtime, he found a fresh, spontaneous, and wholly American voice, a complicated style expressive of the complexities of modern American life.

When some curious critic, a hundred years hence, searches through the available archives in an attempt to discover what was the state of American music at the beginning of the twentieth century do you fancy that he will take the trouble to exhume and dig into the ponderous scores of Henry Hadley, Arthur Foote, Ernest Schelling, George W. Chadwick, Horatio W. Parker, and the rest of the recognizedly "important" composers of the present day? Will he hesitate for ten minutes to peruse the scores of *Mona*, the *Four Seasons Symphony* or *The Pipe of Desire*? A plethora of books and articles on the subject will cause him to wonder why so much bother was made about Edward MacDowell, and he will even shake his head a trifle wearily over the saccharine delights of "The Rosary" and "Narcissus." But if he is lucky enough to run across copies of "Waiting for the Robert E. Lee," "Alexander's Ragtime Band," or "Hello Frisco," which are scarcely mentioned in the literature of our time, his face will light up . . . and he will attempt to find out, probably in vain (until he disinters a copy of this article in some public library) something about the composers, Lewis F. Muir, Irving Berlin, and Louis A. Hirsch, the true grandfathers of the Great American Composer of the year 2001.

There are difficulties in his way. Nothing disappears so soon from the face of the earth as a *very* popular song. . . .

The sentimental song, however, has been largely obliterated in the output of the best new music of the twentieth century, into which a new quality has crept, a quality which may serve to keep it alive, just as the "coon songs" which preceded it in the nineteenth century have been kept alive. . . . But ragtime, as it exists today, had not been invented in the eighteen nineties. The apotheosis of syncopation had not begun. . . .

It is my theory that the American composers of today (I am still speaking of Irving Berlin, Louis Hirsch, Lewis F. Muir, and others of their kind) have brought a new quality into music, a spirit to be found in the best folk dances of Spain, in gypsy, Hungarian, and Russian popular music, and a form entirely new. They have been working for a livelihood, to be sure, but in that respect they have only followed the precedent established by [Jacques] Offenbach, Richard Strauss, and [Giacomo] Puccini. . . .

The most obvious point of superiority of our ragtime composers (overlooking the fact that their music is pleasanter to listen to) over Messrs. Parker, Chadwick, and Hadley, is that they are expressing the very soul of the epoch while their more serious confreres are struggling to pour into the forms of the past, the thoughts of the past, rearranged, to be sure, but without notable expression or inspiration. They have nothing new to say and no particular reason for saying it. . . .

The complicated vigor of American life has expressed itself through the trenchant pens of these new musicians. It is the only music produced in America today which is worth the paper it is written on. It is the only American music which is enjoyed by the nation . . . ; it is the only American music which is heard abroad . . . and it is the only music on which the musicians of our land can build in the future. . . .

If the American composers with (what they consider) more serious aims, instead of writing symphonies or other worn out and exhausted forms which belong to another age of composition, would strive to put into their music the rhythms and tunes that dominate the hearts of the people, a new form would evolve which might prove to be the child of the Great American Composer we have all been waiting for so long and so anxiously. . . .

Americans are inclined to look everywhere but under their noses for art. It never occurs to them that any object which has any relation to their everyday life has anything to do with beauty. . . .

It is impossible to appreciate that which is constantly before our eyes, that which is buzzing in our ears. We are so accustomed to ragtime that we scarcely know that it exists. It would be absurd, you think, to consider it as art, because it is so commonplace. One might as easily consider the Woolworth Building or the Manhattan Bridge works of art and how could anyone possibly do that? Just the same I am inclined to believe that the Woolworth Building, the Manhattan Bridge, and that "roaring, epic ragtime tune," "Waiting for the Robert E. Lee" [1913, music by Lewis F. Muir, lyrics by L. Wolfe Gilbert] are among the first twenty-four beautiful things produced in America. It is no more use to imitate French or German music than it is to imitate French or German architecture. The sooner we realize this the better for all of us.

* * * * *

✻ 1918 — HENRY F. GILBERT, COMPOSER AND FOLK MUSIC ENTHUSIAST

From "Composer Gilbert on American Music," *New York Times* (24 March 1918), 4: 9.

> Clearly writing with a large chip on his shoulder, composer Henry F. Gilbert (1868-1928) attacked the European domination of America's musical culture but acknowledged that America was making gains despite its conformity to traditional compositional procedures inherited from Europe. Proudly independent, he was one of the first Americans to approach the Native American and African-American traditions as materials for the creation of American concert music

Musical America is in the grip of Europe. Europe dictates to us what music we shall hear, tells us the kind we should prefer, and, worst of all, insists upon dictating to our composers what kind they should write. . . .

The serious composers of present America, those who are in earnest in their art, are naturally divided into two classes–those who are satisfied to continue in the practice of their art the sedulous and faithful imitation of European formulae, and those who, having a more independent turn of mind, seek by diverse forms, new rhythms, and piquant and unusual melodic turns, to express something which shall at least be different (whether it be American or not) from the overwhelming European musical culture with which we are now flooded. These two classes are conservatives and nationalists. They are hardly definitely divided, as frequently radical twinges are found in the work of the conservatives, whereas many conservative formulae are in evidence in the compositions of the nationalists. For the sake of this discussion it may be better to divide all music into that which accords with European ideas of musical beauty and that which seeks independence from them.

Now it is almost a commonplace to assert that "publicity" is the best friend of the artist. To the composer it is his daily bread. Without it his very development is arrested, stunted, prohibited. Publicity is to the composer what going out into the world and winning his way is to the ordinary man. And who will dispute the educative, formative, and developing character of this process [?] Composers who have arrived and others complacently remark: "When your work is good enough to be performed it will be given, but symphony orchestras cannot afford to spend valuable time and energy in producing an immature work." A statement of this kind, while it would be true enough in any of the highly civilized countries of Europe, is not true in America, considering that the conditions of our musical life are as they are. A truer statement would be something like the following: "When your work is in accord with European ideas of musical beauty and technique it will be performed, even though it be of slight musical value; whereas, if it shows signs of a variance from these things, no matter how perfectly and artistically that variance is carried out, it shall, as far as our programs are concerned, receive absent treatment." I affirm the truth of this supposititious proposition, having received some of the "absent treatment" in my own person. Concerning the first part of the statement, I refer anyone who cares to investigate it to the programs of our leading symphony orchestras for the last ten years.

The result of such an investigation will show, first, that many immature works have been performed, works which should never have found a place on a symphony program; second, that nearly all the works by American composers which have been performed have been composed in strict accordance with European musical tradition and have slavishly conformed to European canons of taste; and, third, (which is very significant) that many inconsequential works by European composers have been performed apparently for no other reason than that they are European. The net result of these procedures has been considerably to retard the development of a native American music. Let me say at once that music written by American composers in conformity to European models is not American music. It is imitation European music, and frequently a pretty poor imitation. In fact, the better imitation it is the poorer American music it is. Thus is the radical element in American music—the only significant element—denied by conditions the publicity which it must have to develop.

I am not one of those who insist that there is a large quantity of meritorious American music as yet unheard. There is almost no real American music at present in existence. But there are tendencies, somewhat blind and groping as yet, but still earnest and sincere. . . .

* * * * *

Military bands representing the Union and the Confederacy played an important role during the Civil War in providing comfort and inspiration to both the troops and civilians. This portrait (ca. April 1865) of the Band of 10th Veteran Reserve Corps of Washington, D.C., communicates some of the pride of its members and the seriousness of their endeavors.

Courtesy of the Library of Congress Prints and Photographic Division: LC-B817-7879.

❊ 3 — Music of the Civil War Era

1862 – *Dwight's Journal of Music*
From "The Relation of the War to Music"

1865 – Louis Moreau Gottschalk
From *Notes of a Pianist*

1867 – Thomas Wentworth Higginson
From "Negro Spirituals"

1871 – *The New York Times*
Three Reports on an Opera Production

1871 – K. G. S.
From "Negroes' Spirituals"

1876 – John Sullivan Dwight
From "Musica Peripatetica"

1886 – George Washington Cable
From "Creole Slave Songs"

1889 – George Kimball
From "Origin of the John Brown Song"

1891 – George F. Root
From *The Story of a Musical Life*

1898 – William Foster Apthorp
From "Musical Reminiscences of Boston Thirty Years Ago"

1899 – Thomas Ryan
From *Recollections of an Old Musician*

1905 – Theodore Thomas
From *A Musical Autobiography*

1905 – Delavan S. Miller
From *Drum Taps in Dixie: Memories of a Drummer Boy, 1861-1865*

The Civil War and its aftermath saw a number of important and fascinating trends in music. Not the least of these was the increasing propensity of musicians to take to the road: military bandsmen performed widely in the service of battle, while popular musicians like Louis Moreau Gottschalk gave concerts throughout the western territories. Both phenomena contributed to a substantial awareness in the United States of instrumental music, although "peripatetic" musicians were not appreciated by everyone. In addition, popular song became more widely disseminated, in part, because of its essential role in war. Songs sung by Union and Confederate soldiers served to rally the troops to battle and provided a much-needed balm for their emotional pain. Increased contact by Northerners with the atrocities of slavery also created a deep interest in the music of Blacks.

❊ 1862 — *DWIGHT'S JOURNAL OF MUSIC*

From "The Relation of the War to Music," *Dwight's Journal of Music* 21/25 (20 September 1862), 196.

Nationhood and patriotism absorbed much attention during the Civil War years. The first selection presented here was culled from the Boston-based *Journal of Music* presided over by John Sullivan Dwight (1813-1893). The unidentified author proposed sources for the forging of a national song, especially in light of the War and its accompanying drama. This writer also appreciated that the young American nation exhibited a tremendous musical appetite.

It has been said that the great revolution which our land is experiencing will produce changes in our national and individual associations which shall give our American character a new stamp, and mold our institutions and customs anew. What effect this general proposition (if it be true) shall produce in the realm of music, is yet to be considered.

Admitting, then, the truth of the statement, we ask first, what change shall be wrought in the national compositions? Without dwelling a moment upon the various choruses, hymns, and melodies that we call national, we will avoid traveling over ground that has many times been thoroughly explored, and start with the affirmation, that none of our national songs, however excellent in some respects, *meet the demand of the people, and, at the same time* [exhibit] *a proper regard to musical composition.* There are indispensable requisites to a melody becoming *national* and *enduring.* Among them may be named the absence of any pilfering from the musical stock of any other nation. To make it *sui generis* [i.e., unique] must be the author's unyielding purpose, not suggestive of any associations with the songs of other nationalities. . . .

A national song should be written within an easy compass of voice (say, upon the staff) so that it may be attainable by those of average capacity, both as to compass and execution; and presuming it is to be arranged for mixed voices, the harmony must be such as shall be satisfactory to the popular ear, and though rich, free from disagreeable successions or suspensions. Something might be said of the movement or time in which it shall be written; but this depends, of course, upon the subject and spirit of the words with which it may be placed in connection. . . . We observe, however, that words and music awakening a profound sense of reverence, gratitude and earnest devotion to one's country, and one's God, in view of past mercies, deliverance, and future greatness and prosperity, are most likely to impress the common mind with noble emotions, and enduring attachment. Who shall say that the wonderful scenes through which we are now passing, shall not give birth to nobler inspiration of undying love of country, greater sacrifice for its good, calling forth our heart's most ardent praise in poetry and in song?

In other departments of music we may not speak with so much clearness, for America is not renowned for the production of musical works, other than tunebooks, and the lighter forms of musical composition, such as songs, polkas and waltzes. The latter have already received their impress of the spirit of the times, but we do not regard them as exercising any permanent influence on the musical growth and culture of the country. Music making is certainly a mania in this land, and a great deal is published that never should have escaped the prolific brain of its gifted possessors; . . . These light effusions, made to sell, are the natural fruit of existing circumstances; the form which the steady flow of claptrap pieces has assumed, in obedience to the demand of an enthusiastic and capricious public.

But it is of the higher forms of composition we would speak; forms which shall exercise (as they always have) a powerful influence on the cultivated musical taste of the nation. May it not be seriously asked, if there is not in the passing events, that which is ample *material* for *symphonies*, *marches funèbre*, or *triumphales*, and vocal works of the dramatic character? We think we may safely reply in the affirmative, and certainly there is no lack of genius to gather the valuable facts of this pregnant period, and give form and meaning to them, in imperishable productions.

✻ ✻ ✻ ✻ ✻

✻ 1865 — LOUIS MOREAU GOTTSCHALK, COMPOSER AND VIRTUOSO PIANIST

From *Journal* (13 June 1865); reprinted *Notes of a Pianist*, ed. Jeanne Behrend (New York: Alfred A. Knopf, 1964), 311-13.

> The detailed journals of one of America's first homegrown virtuosi, Louis Moreau Gottschalk (1829-1869), offer early descriptions of the legendary itinerant musician's life. His accounts are often humorous, always candid, and here provides a rare glimpse of audience behavior in Nevada.

We arrive at Dutch Flat [Nevada], a pretty little village, concealed at the bottom of a wooded gorge like a nest in the bush. The neat white houses are covered with magnificent rosebushes whose flowers cover the trellises as high as the roofs. They are small frame houses, very neat, very small, etc.

Concert this evening. Almost one hundred seventy persons. Audience very quiet—very quiet because they do not applaud. It is true that they did not otherwise show their discontent. I very much suspect that they regretted [spending] their dollar and a half. "Taken in," said one of them sometime later, and added, to console himself, "It is true that it is only once." It will be the givers of the concerts right after me who will feel their resentment. I still cannot help remarking [on] the propriety of conduct of these audiences who, however wearisome our music must appear to them, submit to it without protest.

It often occurs to me when playing to look at my audience. There are certain passages where I am so accustomed to see their countenances brighten up that in civilized audiences I am wont to consider it an indissoluble thing like cause and effect. For example, the close of "Murmures eoliens" or even "[The] Last Hope," or the end of "Ojos criollos." Here I perceive that it is exactly as if I was speaking Chinese; they hardly understand it, and inquisitively regard me exerting myself with that curious and vacant air which other ignoramuses, for instance, cast upon the hands of a telegraph operator. How many things are there to learn, we often cry out! Come here, and in seeing these audiences, you will see how many things it is possible to be ignorant of.

In order to give you an idea of the artistic ignorance here, it will suffice to copy an account that has appeared today. "Last evening the opera hall was filled to overflowing (there were dances, comedies, etc.). X. was received with thunders of applause, but he is [a] past master of his art. His imitations upon the violin of birds, quadrupeds, are inimitable. His music is what can be felt and understood without any need of being a musician (a blow at me). Everybody understood it." And here is the measure of the tastes of Nevada. O ignorance, when will you cease to be pretentious and insolent!

I have been sick for three days. I cannot recollect in fifteen years of travels and vicissitudes having passed eleven days so sadly as here. I defy your finding in the whole of Europe a village where an artist of reputation would find himself as isolated as I have been here. If in place of playing the piano, of having composed two or three hundred pieces, of having given seven or eight thousand concerts, of having given the poor one hundred or one hundred and fifty thousand dollars, of having been knighted twice, I had sold successfully for ten years quarters of salted hog, or had made a great fortune by selling dear what I had bought for cheap, my poor isolated chamber would have been invaded by adorers and admirers. Decidedly the country of money is not the one of artists. . . .

* * * * *

✻ 1867 — THOMAS WENTWORTH HIGGINSON, HISTORIAN, ESSAYIST, EDITOR, AND SOCIAL REFORMER

From "Negro Spirituals," *Atlantic Monthly* 19 (June 1867), 685-94.

Because of his first-hand acquaintance with the sacred songs of African-

Americans during his Civil War service as a captain in the first black Union regiment, Thomas Wentworth Higginson (1823-1911), a former Unitarian minister, was able to provide insights concerning their oral transmission as well as to offer testimony to the strength of the former slaves' faith.

The war brought to some of us, besides its direct experiences, many a strange fulfillment of dreams of other days. For instance, the present writer has been a faithful student of the Scottish ballads, and had always envied Sir Walter [Scott] the delight of tracing them out amid their own heather, and of writing them down piecemeal from the lips of aged crones. It was a strange enjoyment, therefore, to be suddenly brought into the midst of a kindred world of unwritten songs, as simple and as indigenous as the border minstrelsy, more uniformly plaintive, almost always more quaint, and often as essentially poetic.

The interest was rather increased by the fact that I had for many years heard of this class of songs under the name of "Negro Spirituals," and had even heard some of them sung by friends from South Carolina. I could not gather on their own soil these strange plants, which I had before seen as in museums alone. . . .

Often in the starlit evening I have returned from some lonely ride by the swift river, or on the plover-haunted barrens, and, entering the camp, have silently approached some glimmering fire, round which the dusky figures moved in the rhythmical barbaric dance the Negroes call a "shout," chanting, often harshly, but always in the most perfect time, some monotonous refrain. Writing down in the darkness, as best I could—perhaps with my hand in the safe covert of my pocket—the words of the song, I have afterwards carried it to my tent like some captured bird or insect, and then, after examination, put it by. Or, summoning one of the men at some period of leisure—Corporal Robert Sutton, for instance, whose iron memory held all the details of a song as if it were a ford or a forest—I have completed the new specimen by supplying the absent parts. The music I could only retain by ear, and though the more common strains were repeated often enough to fix their impression, there were others that occurred only once or twice. . . .

As [the Negroes] learned all their songs by ear, they often strayed into wholly new versions, which sometimes became popular, and entirely banished the others. This was amusingly the case, for instance, with one phrase in the popular camp song of "Marching Along," which was entirely new to them until our quartermaster taught it to them, at my request. The words, "Gird on the armor," were to them a stumbling block, and no wonder, until some ingenious ear substituted, "Guide on de army," which was at once accepted, and became universal. . . .

I never overheard in camp a profane or vulgar song. With the trifling exceptions given, all had a religious motive, while the most secular melody could not have been more exciting. A few youths from Savannah [Georgia], who were comparatively men of the world, had learned some of the "Ethiopian Minstrel" ditties, imported from the North. These took no hold upon the mass; and, on the other hand, they sang reluctantly, even on Sunday, the long and short meters of the hymnbooks, always yielding gladly to the more potent excitement of their own "spirituals." By these they could sing themselves, as had their fathers before them, out of the contemplation of their own low estate, into the sublime scenery of the Apocalypse. I remember that this minor-keyed pathos used to seem to me almost too sad to dwell upon, while slavery seemed destined to last for generations; but now that their patience has had its perfect work, history cannot afford to lose this portion of its record. There is no parallel instance of an oppressed race thus sustained by the religious sentiment alone. These songs are but the vocal expression of the simplicity of their faith and the sublimity of their long resignation.

* * * * *

✻ 1871 — *THE NEW YORK TIMES*

From "Italian Opera," *New York Times* (5 January 1871), 4.

> New York City was rapidly becoming famous for its theatrical productions. There was much hope in musical circles that theater's cousin, opera, would take hold. These three brief excerpts from the *New York Times* document the rise and fall of a single production of Verdi's *Il Trovatore* (1851) within the space of two weeks; a few of the problems are described.

So many New York seasons of Italian opera have begun with *Il Trovatore* to come speedily to an untimely end, that there was something ominous in its selection to open a fresh season last night. There is, too, a well-founded suspicion in the public mind that the announcement of operas "easy to do," argues [a] poverty of resources, and suggests doubts about the future that do not help to commence a season with the desirable briskness and *éclat*. To this of course it may be said, and is said, that the opportunities afforded by Verdi's threadbare work for the principal singers, and the ready familiarity of choristers and musicians, afford reasons for setting out with it which are supported by weighty prudential considerations. We can honestly say that last night's performance was its own simple justification. Take it for all in all, we have rarely heard *Il Trovatore* better sung. . . .

The French Theater . . . was bright and gay, much better filled than we expected to see it, and highly appreciative. . . .

From "Collapse of the Opera" *New York Times* (12 January 1871), 4.

Italian opera in New York has again proved a failure. The season begun last week at the theater [on] Fourteenth Street has come to an end with the fourth performance. A sliding scale of disaster seems of late to attend our lyric stage, so that with a couple of trials more we may expect that an Italian opera season will begin and end on the same night. Such an arrangement would be attended with the minimum of loss, and could hardly be more mortifying than the fiascos recently witnessed. . . .

If New York desires this elegant, but costly pleasure, New York must pay for it. We must all admit that it is rather derogatory to so rich and splendid a city that even a small Italian opera house is not sustained here. At the same time, it is only justice to our public to say that these repeated failures simply show that there is no demand for the article dealers have offered to supply. It is not that there is no love of musical art, but that the methods of illustration fail to satisfy the general taste. To put the matter more plainly, opera has been so very badly done here that lovers of opera are disgusted, and, unless for a furtive peep on a first night, they resolutely stay away from the houses where it is announced. . . . No opera is better than bad opera, and until the time has arrived for better things we hope to be spared any further essays of the makeshift order, which reflect credit neither upon the Metropolis nor upon the speculators concerned.

From "Public Amusements," *New York Times* (15 January 1871), 4.

Although deprived of Italian opera, the New York public is by no means left without amusements. It is probable that the dramatic entertainments of the city have never been at once so numerous and so excellent of their kind as at present. . . .

The theatrical world of New York is just now profoundly stirred by several important events. . . .

Even in the absence of opera, New York does not languish for want of amusement; and, in addition to the regular resorts, open daily or nightly, an endless series of musical performances adds to them a much enjoyed variety. . . . The Philharmonic, although somewhat behind the age, affords periodic occasion for fashionable gatherings, and popular concerts at a low rate of admission may be listened to each week at Association Hall. . . . None need lack rational amusement in the Metropolis, then, and that of a high grade; and experienced observers who contrast the public diversions, halls and theaters of New York with those of foreign capitals, must own that, with the one exception of the opera, there is nothing in the comparison to make us ashamed.

* * * * *

✳ 1871 — K. G. S.

From "Negroes' Spirituals," *Lippincott's Magazine* 7/15 (March 1871), 331-34.

> A writer in *Lippincott's Magazine* commented on the musical nature of African Americans based on what appears to be personal familiarity. Although the author voiced demeaning stereotypes about the perceived inability of the former slaves to learn the "science" of music (i.e., reading notes, learning rules of composition, etc.), he did provide insights about oral transmission and the evolution of the repertoire, while also delivering a glimpse at the celebration of a traditional religious ceremony.

Among the things that are passing away and in danger of being forgotten are the "Spirituals," or religious songs, peculiar to the colored people, after having served for generations as lullabies in every nursery of the South, formed the principal part of Negro worship, been echoed as boat songs on the Southern rivers, and wailed at every "setting up" with the dead of the colored race.

This wild, sad music is now almost extinct, having given place to "Tramp, Tramp, Tramp," "Rally Round the Flag, Boys" [better known as "The Battle-Cry of Freedom"], and similar songs. It is now only heard on remote plantations, or occasionally in the tremulous tones of an old "maumer" [mama] (the general term of Southern children for their nurses), whose gray hairs are still covered by the bright turban which always gave such dignity to the appearance of the nursery ruler. . . .

All who know anything of Negroes have remarked [on] their quick, correct ear for music, and wonderful facility for forming vocal harmonies. Many have fine voices—very few have none. The greater number of the many I have known could catch almost immediately not only the air [melody] of a song, but the words, and these sometimes in a foreign language of which they did not understand a word. . . . But I do not think, with all this, that their voices could ever be cultivated very much, or that they could be taught the science of music. What suits them and is delightful is their own music sung by many voices. . . .

Religious negroes will not *dance*, and a violin is an offense to one who has joined the Church; but in place of those wicked indulgences, when they meet together they "shout" to their own singing of a spiritual, which, when once begun, has no end for many hours. Sometimes, after they have assembled, there is some hesitation as to who is to begin: different ones are urged, and a variety of tunes suggested, until finally one of the youngest "sister-members" will take her place in the middle of the floor, and with a jerky, sideways sort of motion go round the floor, clapping her hands softly in time while singing [music excerpt omitted] . . .

As soon as she comes to the chorus, beginning [with the word] "Believer," others join her, or rather follow her, until all who can are moving, and the chorus is thundered out, the leader's voice, however, always keeping a little ahead of the others, and always singing the word "Believer" alone. The members too old to shout sit around the wall and sing, rocking themselves from side to side by way of keeping time, and when specially warmed up [by] clapping hands, always in perfect time. These gatherings wind up with a prayer by one of the elderly men of the plantation when they become exhausted from excitement and exertion. . . .

* * * * *

❋ 1876 — JOHN SULLIVAN DWIGHT, MUSIC CRITIC AND JOURNAL EDITOR

From "Musica Peripatetica," *Dwight's Journal of Music* 36/8 (22 July 1876), 270-71.

John Sullivan Dwight (1813-1893) commented on the phenomenon of traveling orchestras and made note of their detrimental effect on Boston's local musical scene. In an era when transportation and communication were becoming increasingly sophisticated and available, musicians could often earn sizable sums by taking their art to those communities that lacked a cultural presence. Dwight observed that, as musicians fled from Boston, his own opportunities to hear good music were diminished.

We do not propose to treat of dog-day music—of organ grinders and street minstrels, who like mosquitoes haunt the ear the most when days are hottest. That sort of music we have with us always, and doubtless always shall have, and in its way it is all well enough. But our attention is now drawn to the comparatively new aspect of which music, as a matter of performance and of hearing, presents in this country today. Music in its more pretentious forms has grown peripatetic; and the traveling propensity seems more and more to take possession of all competent musicians. . . .

Now there is no denying that there is a great deal of good in all this. Every town and city in the [Theodore] Thomas [Orchestra] circuit is indebted to him for much good music which it would not otherwise have heard, and even for awakening the musical perception, doubtless, in thousands. It has raised the public standard of orchestral playing, and put musicians everywhere upon their mettle. It has enlarged the repertoire—whether for good or evil may be still a question; but at any rate it has gratified curiosity, and allowed many to judge, or get impressions, through their own ears, of new composers, new works, new schools, so much read and talked about. . . .

The worst of it is, that it becomes more and more difficult to keep good musicians in our city [Boston]. If they are not encouraged by all the orchestral employment that can be given them; if these nobler tasks are withdrawn from them; if, instead of twenty Symphony concerts, or even one every week throughout the season or the year, they cease to find support for ten only in a year, what motive have they any longer, either artistic or material, for continuing to reside with us? . . .

But this is not all. If the peripatetic movement weakens or destroys our orchestra, no less is it destructive to our chances for good chamber concerts—the string quartets, quintets, etc., which did count among the choicest musical resources of a community long favored this way. Never before has it been so hard to keep among us first-class violinists, cellists, etc. . . .

What are we musically as a people, a great nation, at this moment celebrating its proud century of progress, if every town and city is to depend for everything orchestral on the periodical or chance visits of a traveling company, however admirable, just as we have always had to depend on speculating impresarios for opera?

Thus there is evil as well as good done by the fine traveling orchestras. Let us hope, as we said, that the evil will be short-lived and the good will survive. . . .

* * * * *

✻ 1886 — GEORGE WASHINGTON CABLE, AUTHOR AND ESSAYIST

From "Creole Slave Songs," *Century Magazine* 31/6 (April 1886), 807-828.

> Writer George Washington Cable (1844-1925) chronicled the culture of Louisiana in both fable and fact. His many stories and reports, widely disseminated in the northeastern part of the United States, brought this strange, colorful, and exotic region to life for many readers. In this excerpt from a long, detailed essay Cable discussed slave love songs, a genre limited in subject matter and, of course, deeply affected by the conditions of slavery.

. . . Among the songs which seem to have been sung for their own sake, and not for the dance, are certain sentimental ones of slow movement, tinged with that faint and gentle melancholy that everyone of Southern experience has noticed in the glance of the African slave's eye; a sentiment ready to be turned, at any instant that may demand the change, into a droll, self-abasing humor. They have thus a special charm that has kept for them a place even in the regard of the Creole of today. How many ten thousands of black or tawny nurse "mammies," with heads wrapped in stiffly starched Madras kerchief turbans, . . . have made the infants' lullabies these gently sad strains of disappointed love or regretted youth, will never be known. Now and then the song would find its way, through some master's growing child of musical ear, into the drawing room; . . .

It is strange to note in all this African-Creole lyric product how rarely its producers seem to have recognized the myriad charms of nature. The landscape, the seasons, the sun, moon, stars, the clouds, the storm, the peace that follows, the forest's solemn depths, the vast prairie, birds, insects, the breeze, the flowers–they are passed in silence. Was it because of the soul-destroying weight of bondage? Did the slave feel so painfully that the beauties of the natural earth were not for him? Was it because the overseer's eye was on him that his was not lifted upon them? It may have been–in part. But another truth goes with these. His songs were not often contemplative. They voiced not outward nature, but the inner emotions and passions of a nearly naked serpent-worshipper, and these looked not to the surrounding scene for sympathy; the surrounding scene belonged to his master. But love was his, and toil, and anger, and superstition, and malady. Sleep was his balm, food his reinforcement, the dance his pleasure, rum his longed-for nepenthe, and death his road back to Africa. These were his themes, and furnished the scant figures of his verse. . . .

✻ ✻ ✻ ✻ ✻

✻ 1889 — GEORGE KIMBALL, SOLDIER IN THE UNION ARMY

From "Origin of the John Brown Song," *New England Magazine* 7/4 (December 1889), 371-76.

> George Kimball provided an essay about the much-disputed origin of the "John Brown Song," better known as "The Battle-Hymn of the Republic." Although Julia Ward Howe's famous text is associated with the song today, Kimball witnessed the creation of the original tune during the Civil War and vehemently rejected alternate theories concerning its birth.

On the 17th of April, 1861, I became a member of the Second Battalion of Infantry ("Tigers"), a Massachusetts militia organization of some local repute, with headquarters at old Boylston Hall, Boston. . . . We were momentarily expecting to be ordered upon active duty by Governor Andrew, and twelve days after I joined the corps it proceeded to Fort Warren, Boston Harbor, that stronghold being without a garrison. . . .

. . . During our long evening in quarters, too, we sang almost constantly.

Religious hymns were as popular with us as secular songs. Among the former none gave greater satisfaction than a hymn, at that time a great favorite in revival meetings, entitled, "Say, brothers, will you meet us?" This seemed to be admirably adapted to our needs. Its music was not difficult, and it had that swinging, easy movement and agreeable rhythm so popular always with the masses. Its chorus, moreover, was round and spirited, and when sung with vigor by large bodies of men, the effect was very striking. This hymn was sung a great deal, and became finally the foundation upon which the famous "John Brown Song" was built, its music being quickened a little to fit it to the requirements of the doggerel rhymes that were from time to time brought forward, but its chorus remaining in the grand old war song substantially the same. . . .

How the music of "Say, brothers, will you meet us?" was made to do duty in the building up of the "John Brown Song" will appear in what follows.

We had a jovial Scotchman in the battalion, named John Brown. He was among the leading spirits, foremost always in fun-making; and as he happened to bear the identical name of the old hero of Harper's Ferry, he became at once the butt of his comrades. A great deal of pleasantry was indulged in at his expense, and he was often guyed unmercifully. . . .

This nonsense was kept up from day to day, and these expressions, particularly the ones referring to the defunct condition of Brown, were so often heard that they became by-words among us, and were repeated at all times and in all places, whether our Scotch friend with the suggestive name was within hearing or not. They were usually followed by exclamations of feigned surprise, such as "Is that so?" Finally ditties composed of the most nonsensical, doggerel rhymes, setting forth the fact that John Brown was dead and that his body was undergoing the process of dissolution, began to be sung to the music of the hymn above given. These ditties underwent various ramifications, until eventually the lines were reached—

"John Brown's body lies a-moldering in the grave,
His soul's marching on."

And—

"He's gone to be a soldier in the army of the Lord,
His soul's marching on."

These lines seemed to give general satisfaction, the idea that Brown's soul was "marching on" receiving recognition at once as having a germ of inspiration in it. They were sung over and over again with a great gusto, the "Glory Hallelujah" chorus being always added. . . .

The song continued to gain in popularity notwithstanding the departure of the "Tigers." The Eleventh and Fourteenth (First Heavy Artillery) Regiments came to the fort, and among the men of these organizations, too, the song immediately gained a firm foothold. It was probably by the men of the First Heavy Artillery that President Lincoln and Mrs. Julia Ward Howe heard it sung several months later, in the fortifications of Washington, when Mrs. Howe, at Mr. Lincoln's suggestion, gave the world her famous "Battle Hymn of the Republic."

. . . Thus successfully launched, the grand old war song sailed forth upon its career with wonderful success and rapidity. It seized upon every blue-coated organization throughout the land with fascinating power, and it is certainly true that no song of the war became more popular. . . . East and west, it was preeminently *the* song of the war. . . .

There has been a good deal of discussion as to the origin of the famous song, some writers even claiming that it was sung previous to the breaking out of the war. But all such speculations are utterly groundless. It originated substantially as I have stated. The music is old—very old; and it is the music, undoubtedly, which those writers have in mind who have attributed its origin to times and places other than Fort Warren in May, 1861. Other ditties may have been sung to the same music, but the grand old war-song of which I write had its birth in the Second Battalion of Infantry, at the time and in the manner which I have stated.

* * * * *

* 1891 — GEORGE F. ROOT, EDUCATOR, COMPOSER OF POPULAR SONGS, AND MUSIC BUSINESSMAN

From *The Story of a Musical Life* (Cincinnati: John Church Company, 1891), 132-34.

> George F. Root (1820-1895) was a native New Englander who decided in his youth to make music his career. An associate of Lowell Mason and an influential music teacher, Root was involved in the early efforts to make music an integral part of the curriculum in Boston's public school system. He later moved to Chicago, where he was a partner in the music publishing firm Root & Cady and where he penned a number of remarkable songs. In his important autobiography Root recorded the circumstances surrounding the first performance of his "Battle Cry of Freedom" (1862), one of the great songs of the Civil War.

In common with my neighbors I felt strongly the gravity of the situation [the Civil War], and while waiting to see what would be done, wrote the first song of the war. It was entitled "The first gun is fired, may God protect the right." Then at every event, and in all circumstances that followed, where I thought a song would be welcome, I wrote one. And here I found my fourteen years of extemporizing melodies on the blackboard, before classes that could be kept in order only by prompt and rapid movements, a great advantage. Such work as I could do at all I could do quickly. There was no waiting for a melody. Such as it was it came at once, as when I stood before the blackboard in the old school days.

I heard of President [Abraham] Lincoln's second call for troops one afternoon while reclining on a lounge in my brother's house. Immediately a song started in my mind, words and music together:

> "Yes, we'll rally round the flag, boys, we'll rally once again,
> Shouting the battle-cry of freedom!"

I thought it out that afternoon, and wrote it the next morning at the store. The ink was hardly dry when the Lumbard brothers—the great singers of the war—came in for something to sing at a war meeting that was to be [held] immediately in the courthouse square just opposite. They went through the new song once, and then hastened to the steps of the courthouse, followed by a crowd that had gathered while the practice was going on. Then Jules's magnificent voice gave out the song, and Frank's trumpet tones led the refrain—

"The Union forever, hurrah, boys, hurrah!"

and at the fourth verse a thousand voices were joining in the chorus. From there the song went into the army, and the testimony in regard to its use in the camp and on the march, and even on the field of battle, from soldiers and officers, up to generals and even to the good President himself, made me thankful that if I could not shoulder a musket in defense of my country I could serve her in this way.

* * * * *

✻ 1898 — WILLIAM FOSTER APTHORP, MUSIC AND DRAMA CRITIC AND WRITER ON MUSIC

From "Musical Reminiscences of Boston Thirty Years Ago," *By the Way* (Boston: Copeland and Day, 1898), 48-82.

William Foster Apthorp (1848-1913), a one-time student of John Knowles Paine at Harvard, a prominent Boston critic, and the program annotator for the Boston Symphony Orchestra, remembered in his memoirs two of the city's most venerable musical institutions: the Handel & Haydn Society and the Harvard Musical Association. Recalling the halting effect that traveling organizations had on the musical evolution of Boston, he echoes Dwight.

One of the great events of the period about which I am now writing—1860-1870 in round numbers—was the demi-centennial festival of the Handel & Haydn Society in 1865. What I especially remember about this particular festival was the orchestra. The orchestral resources of Boston had never been conspicuous, either for quality or numbers; since the beginning of the war, the orchestra of the Orchestral Union and those which made us yearly visits with opera companies had been miserably small. I doubt if any of my generation, certainly of those whose experience did not extend to New York or the other side of the Atlantic, had ever heard a well-balanced orchestra. Our notions of orchestral effect were derived from what we heard. I remember distinctly how impossible it was for me, at the time I speak of, to understand what older musicians meant by calling the strings the "main power" in an orchestra. In all orchestras I had heard, the woodwinds—let alone the brass and percussion—[were] more powerful dynamically than the often ridiculously small mass of strings; especially as the then wind-players seldom cultivated the art of playing *piano* [softly]. But, for this demi-centennial of the Handel & Haydn, our local orchestra was increased to nearly a hundred by the addition of players engaged from New York and elsewhere. I shall never forget the overwhelming effect of the third and fourth measures of the symphony to Mendelssohn's *Hymn of Praise* [Symphony No. 2, op. 52, *Lobgesang*]—where the unison trombone phrase of the first two measures is answered *fortissimo* [very loudly] in full harmony by the orchestra. Nothing I have heard since, in Berlioz's or Wagner's most resounding instrumentation, has sounded so positively tremendous to me as this first onslaught of an orchestra with a large mass of strings! This was the beginning, not of large, but of what might be called normal orchestras in Boston. . . .

The Handel & Haydn demi-centennial came and went in the spring of 1865; before the year was out, the Harvard Musical Association began its symphony concerts—or did these concerts begin after New Year? I forget; at any rate, they began either in December, 1865, or January, 1866. . . .

The symphony concerts of the Harvard Musical Association began flourishingly, and their success went on increasing for some years. Crowded houses were the rule. This success did not, however, continue far into the seventies; the audiences began to drop off, subscriptions to decrease, and little by little the stigmata of unpopularity began to show themselves on the institution. There were several reasons for this, most, if not all, of which may be summed up in one fact that the H. M. A. concerts were the connecting link between the old and the new musical Boston. They represented our transition period.

The Association started out on pretty severe classical and conservative principles; and, when the time came for going with the general current of musical thought and feeling, they continued to be strongly conservative and even reactionary. The head-center—if not the heart and soul—of the Association was the late John S. Dwight; and his musical principles are still too well known to need dilating upon here. Many influential members of the association were eager to have it join hands with what was then generally called the party of progress; but Dwight was inexorable, and would not yield an inch. No committee man could, in the end, make headway against his triumphant "system of inertia"; the spirit of the concerts remained conservative to the end.

Another reason for the growing unpopularity of the concerts was still less in the Association's power to overcome. In 1869, Theodore Thomas began making [to] our city flying [i.e., quick] visits with his New York orchestra, then unquestionably one of the finest in the world; and his concerts gave us Bostonians some rather humiliating lessons in the matter of orchestral technique. The H. M. A. was naturally slow in taking these lessons to heart; indeed it only did take them to heart when it was already too late to profit by them, after the yearly income from the concerts had so dwindled away that it was well-nigh hopeless to think of affording the needful money for engaging better orchestral material and having more rehearsals. In fact the only practical influence I can remember the Thomas concerts having upon the H. M. A. was that, for some years, both conductor and a large part of the orchestra seemed bitten with the extreme-*pianissimo* [very softly] mania; we had a series of the most astounding half-audible *pianissimo* string-effects, even in Beethoven symphonies. That silly little muted-string transcription of Schumann's *Traumerei*, which Thomas played again and again, had turned all heads! Still the public could not but draw its own comparisons between the playing of the Thomas Orchestra and that of our own; and such comparisons only added to the already serious unpopularity of the H. M. A. "Dull as a symphony concert" almost passed into a proverb.

* * * * *

✻ 1899 — THOMAS RYAN, VIOLIST AND CHAMBER MUSICIAN

From *Recollections of an Old Musician* (New York: E. P. Dutton, 1899), 162-71.

Another side to the tales of traveling musicians may be learned in the essays of Thomas Ryan (1827-1903). An Irish immigrant with skill on both the viola and the clarinet, he founded the influential Mendelssohn Quintette Club of Boston in 1849. The Club comprised five members to make a string quartet, but two of its members also played wind instruments. While the ensemble performed a fair amount of the standard string quartet literature, its members often produced special arrangements adapted for the unique instrumentation. In this memoir Ryan, who performed as a member of the Club for fifty years, described his travels in the western United States and boasted that his tours spawned numerous imitators.

. . . To return to my narrative, after that trial trip I decided that it was a safe thing to undertake a traveling concert season, and that we did not need "stars" to attract audiences. Individual star singers and players had been heard everywhere in the west; *ensemble* playing was the novelty. We prepared for the long season's travel, and engaged one of our charming home singers to accompany us, Miss Addie S. Ryan (not a daughter of mine, as many imagine). She had a rich and very sympathetic voice, was a good all-round singer, and very "taking" in ballads. She became a great favorite wherever heard.

The financial result of the long season of travel was good, and for many years we made similar trips, and (which will surprise many persons) without the help of any advance agent. All details and arrangements for our appearance in towns and cities were made by correspondence. To be sure, it kept me busy, but the west of that period was not the west of today. To a certain degree we had the entire western country to ourselves. There were no other musical people traveling. There were very many minstrel companies (which did not injure us), and a few dramatic troupes. We were in demand everywhere; the main trouble was to get dates. Money was plentiful—everyone was "flush" after the war.

Before long we began to have imitators—either in '63 or '64. The first musical organization to follow in our wake was the "Redpath Parlor Opera Company," organized in Boston. It was a quartet of good home-singers. . . . They began first as a concert company, and afterwards wisely turned into a parlor opera company, doing acts of either [Flotow's] *Martha* or [Donizetti's] *Don Pasquale*. They were very successful and in a little while they in turn had imitators.

Little by little companies enlarged their personnel till the full-fledged affair appeared and captured the country with [Gilbert and Sullivan's *H.M.S.*] *Pinafore*. I gladly turn over to future historians this line of the divine art of music, knowing that they will have a "nice little job" to keep track of the numberless big and little opera companies who are now actively competing with each other in the struggle for existence.

* * * * *

✻ 1905 — THEODORE THOMAS, ORCHESTRA AND OPERA CONDUCTOR

From A *Musical Autobiography*, 2 vols. (Chicago: A. C. McClurg, 1905), I, 50-58.

The German-born conductor Theodore Thomas (1835-1905) described the travels of the famous orchestra that carried his name, and the successes that eventually led the ensemble to settle in New York City. From there it still traveled throughout the country and influenced musicianship in America for generations. Although Thomas was clearly the foremost practitioner of an activity that both Dwight and Apthorp had railed against, his ensemble became widely regarded as America's finest orchestra, one fully on a par with the best in Europe.

In 1862 I concluded to devote my energies to the cultivation of the public taste for instrumental music. Our chamber concerts had created a spasmodic interest, our programs were reprinted as models of their kind, even in Europe, and our performances had reached a high standard. As a concert violinist, I was at that time popular, and played much. But what this country needed most of all to make it musical was a good orchestra, and plenty of concerts within reach of the people. The [New York] Philharmonic Society, with a body of about sixty players, and five yearly subscription concerts, was the only organized orchestra which represented orchestral literature in this country.

It is true that the public was admitted to a number of its rehearsals, in addition to its concerts, but their influence was not salutary. The orchestra was often incomplete. If a member had an engagement, he would go to it instead of the rehearsal. When one of the wind choir was thus absent, his place would be filled for the occasion as best it could. A clarinet or oboe part would be played on a violin, or a bassoon part on the cello, etc. The conductor therefore could not rehearse as he ought, and the audience talked at pleasure. Under these circumstances justice could not be done to the standard, much less to the modern and contemporary works. Such conditions debarred all progress.

I had been prominent before the public in chamber concerts, and as concertmaster (leader of the violins), of the opera since 1855, and during later years, also, as conductor of concerts and opera, and I thought the time had come to form an orchestra for concert purposes. I therefore called a meeting of the foremost orchestra musicians in New York, told them of my plans to popularize instrumental music, and asked their cooperation. I began by giving some concerts at Irving Hall, and conducted some Brooklyn Philharmonic concerts, alternating with Theodore Eisfeld, and in 1864 I gave my first series of Symphony Soirees, with an orchestra of about sixty men. These concerts were at once successful artistically but only moderately so financially. During the summer of 1865 a series of concerts was given in the afternoon at Belvedere Lion Park, One Hundred and Tenth Street, with an orchestra of thirty players.

During the winter of 1865-66 more concerts were given, and in the summer of 1866 a series of one hundred Summer Night Concerts was inaugurated at Terrace Garden, with enough success to give promise for the future. An audience had been collected and educated to enjoy that form of entertainment, and I had succeeded in finding a respectable occupation during the summer months for a small orchestra. During the season of 1866-67 several concerts were given, the number of which was increased by the opening of Steinway Hall. There were concerts with many soloists and an occasional symphony, under the management of L. F. Harrison, and a series under the management of Bateman, in which Madame [Euphrosyne] Parepa was the chief attraction, as well as many others in both New York and Brooklyn. In this year also I was elected conductor of the Brooklyn Philharmonic Society for the season, which added to the income of my orchestra, an engagement of twenty performances—fifteen rehearsals and five concerts.

The music season in New York closed with a festival under the management of Mr. Harrison, in which I did not take part, having gone to Europe to learn what orchestras were doing there. It lasted a week, and the programs are worth transcribing as typical of the times.

In 1867 a second season of Summer Night Concerts was given at Terrace Garden, which opened June 10, and continued until September 15. During my absence in Europe they were conducted by F. J. Eben and George Matzka. I returned July 1, in time to conduct, bringing many novelties with me. These concerts were very successful, and the programs had improved and advanced. It was in this season that some business men offered to build a hall for me, which would be suitable for summer concerts. The Terrace Garden concerts had always been given in the open air, the orchestra playing in an enclosure, while the audience was seated under the trees. When it rained there was a scramble for a hall in the adjacent building. . . .

The season of 1867-68 was a repetition of the previous year, but on May 25 the new hall, Central Park Garden, was opened with the first concert of the Summer Night series, which continued nightly through the entire summer and even into November. The occupation of the orchestra during the summer season seemed now assured. During the winter months there were the Symphony Soirees, the Brooklyn Philharmonic concerts and public rehearsals, and numerous miscellaneous concerts besides. The thought of a permanent orchestra was natural and inevitable. The support of the public was growing, the orchestra was progressing in every way, and it had gained in size and quality of tone. For the Symphony Soirees, even as early as 1867, we had already increased the number of the orchestra to eighty men.

In the season of 1868-69, I began to travel with the orchestra. I found, however, that although New York and Brooklyn did not provide engagements enough to fill the necessary time of an orchestra, they nevertheless offered too many to permit us to go far from home. After the summer of 1869, therefore, I thought the orchestra was sufficiently well known over the whole country, and I decided, as the only means whereby I could keep my organization together, to devote our entire time to traveling. Accordingly I organized my orchestra on a permanent basis, and for the first time (1869), went to Boston. Our success there was instantaneous, and the people of that city were loyal to me as long as I traveled. I gave a large number of concerts there every winter until I went to live in Cincinnati.

After Boston I went west as far as Chicago, touching every city on our route, and returning by way of St. Louis, Cincinnati, Pittsburg, and intermediate cities, to New York. In the latter city, however, I had abandoned my Symphony Soirees and all regular series of concerts in winter. We traveled over the whole country, giving concerts daily, and on May 9, the Central Park Garden Summer Night Concerts began again, continuing until September 24, a series of one hundred and thirty-four consecutive concerts. The season was very successful, and the size of the orchestra was now enlarged. After this traveling was resumed, and in 1870, which was the centennial anniversary of the birth of Beethoven, I gave a Beethoven program, including a symphony, all over the country.

The next year brought again the regular Summer Night Concerts at Central Park Garden, and in the fall we traveled again. The orchestra had now become a first-rank organization, numbering sixty permanent members. Leading solo artists were sitting at all the first desks, and a high standard began to appear–higher, in fact, than had ever been reached before in America, both in programs and in execution. The public began to be interested, and the future looked bright. . . .

*****

✻ 1905 — DELAVAN S. MILLER, DRUMMER BOY IN THE UNION ARMY

From *Drum Taps in Dixie: Memories of a Drummer Boy, 1861-1865* (Watertown, N.Y.: Hungerford-Holbrook, 1905), 18-23, 70-71, 165.

> The moving memoir of a drummer in a Union regiment during the Civil War by Delavan Miller (1849-1912) documents events from his early youth and first days in the military through his numerous experiences with music and with enemy rebel forces. Of particular interest are Miller's remarks on the expected standards for drummers and how, by the time Miller wrote his book in 1905, these standards had declined. While most of the excerpts here consider music, Miller's book also gives a striking account of the fear and violence that accompanied the daily lives of soldiers on both sides of the conflict.

. . . The Second New York had been organized as a light artillery regiment and was then known as the "Morgan Flying Artillery," so called in honor of Gov. Morgan, but only one company got their guns and horses when it was decided that no more light batteries were wanted. So the balance of the regiment was turned into heavy artillery (heavy infantry.)

A DRUMMER BOY

The change called for fifers and drummers instead of buglers, and the Jefferson county boy [i.e., Miller himself] was the first drummer the regiment had, his drum being a present from the officers at Fort Worth.

A full regimental drum corps was soon organized, and right here it may be proper to say that an old army drum corps in the sixties could make music. A boy would not "pass muster" in those days unless he could do the double and single drag with variations, execute the "long roll," imitate the rattle of musketry, besides various other accomplishments with the sticks. . . .

THE FIRST DRUM

It is with feelings of real tenderness that I write of my first drum. It was none of the common sort such as [that] furnished by Uncle Sam, but was the best that money could buy. . . . How well I remember the day when I accompanied Capt. Joslin to Washington, and he, taking me to a large music store on Pennsylvania Avenue, ordered the clerk to let me have the best drum in the store.

How anxious I was to get back to our camp in Virginia so I could test it, and how my heart went pit-a-pat, as, alone, I marched with my new drum down the line at dress parade the next day. Several months later my precious drum was put out of action by a piece of a rebel shell at

Bull Run and was among the trophies gathered up by the Confederates in the stampede that followed. . . .

DRUMMERS' DUTIES

It is hardly to be wondered at that the drummer boys of the '60s got to be very proficient in the handling of the sticks, for when in camp they were having practice from early morn until late at night, and many a time they had to get out in the night and beat the "long roll" for ten or fifteen minutes.

They were the early risers of the camps, too, for at daybreak the fifers and the drummers of a regiment would assemble and sound the reveille, which was several minutes of exercise of the most vigorous kind. . . .

Martial music seems to have gone out of fashion in these up-to-date days, and what little there is, is but a poor apology, with the bugle blasts interjected between the rub-a-dub-dubs of the drummers who hardly know their ABC's about snare drumming. . . .

THE OLD WAR SONGS

How many of our readers remember the old songs and melodies that were so popular in the sixties? People sang them in their homes and the soldiers in the camps and on the march, and they furnished inspiration for many a tired regiment to go into battle.

As I write there comes to my mind snatches of many of the old favorites such as "We'll Rally Round the Flag Boys," [and] "Tramp, Tramp, Tramp, the Boys are Marching."

A story is told of a regiment who went into battle nearly one thousand strong and came out with less than half the number, but the survivors with their blood-stained banners and smoke-begrimed faces marched to another position in the line singing:

"We'll rally round the flags, boys
We'll rally once again, shouting the battle cry of freedom."

"When Johnnie Comes Marching Home Again" was always a favorite in the ranks, but in the quiet of camp the songs were a little more sentimental and suggestive of home and the loved ones. . . .

DIXIE TO THE LAST

Among the prisoners captured . . . was a rebel brass band, and they were allowed to retain their instruments. As the column of Confederates was marched along the roadside, which was lined up on either side by the Union forces, they were headed by the band, playing their national air of "Dixie."

The scene was an impressive one. They were prisoners of war, bleeding from wounds, faint and famished, ragged and nearly barefoot and their last hope gone, but as the familiar strains of the music floated back over the line their faces brightened, their steps quickened and they marched as they had marched many a time behind their beloved leader, General [Robert E.] Lee.

Our men had too much respect for these brave men to jeer at them. . . .

Music and music education provided early opportunities for integrating blacks into mainstream American society as seen in this photograph (ca. 1900) of an African-American man giving a piano lesson.

Courtesy of the Daniel Murray Collection, Prints and Photographs Division, Library of Congress: LC-USZ62-63575.

❊ 4 — Educating Americans in Music

1869 – *Harper's Bazaar*
From "Piano-Forte Instruction"

1871 – *Church's Musical Visitor*
From "Music in America"

1873 – *Church's Musical Visitor*
From "The Necessity of the Hour"

1874 – *Church's Musical Visitor*
From "Music in Current School Education"

1874 – Constance F. Woolson
From "Euterpe in America"

1880 – F. D.
From "Conservatory Life in Boston"

1881 – Theodore Thomas
From "Musical Possibilities in America"

1890 – Frederic Louis Ritter
From "Survey of the Present State of Musical Activity,"
Music in America

1896 – Louis C. Elson
From *European Reminiscences*

1898 – Edward MacDowell
From "Suggestion in Music"

1900 – Waldo S. Pratt
From "New Ideals in Music Education"

1903 – George W. Chadwick
From "Musical Atmosphere and Student Life"

1903 – Mabel W. Daniels
From *An American Girl in Munich*

1911 – *The Outlook*
From "Music and City Children"

1916 – Thomas Whitney Surette
From "Public-School Music"

The challenges associated with educating a large, diverse population occupied the minds of many essayists and musicians. At the onset of the Civil War, music was primarily an activity pursued in the home. But over time, as Americans sought to improve themselves, music-making was transformed into a public activity, one intended to bring its "civilizing effects" to children and adults alike through activities in the public schools and other institutions, such as colleges and conservatories. This chapter addresses important aspects of music education; many themes sounded here still resonate today.

❋ 1869 — *HARPER'S BAZAAR*

From "Piano-Forte Instruction," *Harper's Bazaar* 2/18 (1 May 1869), 282.

A writer for *Harper's Bazaar* noted that the rise of piano playing had displaced group vocal music in an increasingly secular society. As the modern world approached, fewer busy individuals were inclined to take time to participate in group rehearsals at their churches or with local choral clubs.

By all means let every girl begin by learning the piano. Such a chance of gaining a sympathetic companion for life should never be thrown away. Even to the unmusical girl it is valuable as a training, but to the musical girl its value is beyond price. If a woman's life is often a life of feeling rather than of action, and if society, while it limits her sphere of action, frequently calls upon her to repress her feelings, we should not deny her the high, the recreative, the healthy outlet for emotion which music supplies. Joy flows naturally into ringing harmonies, while music has the subtle power to soften melancholy by presenting it with its fine emotional counterpart. A good play on the piano has not infrequently taken the place of a good cry upstairs, and a cloud of ill-temper has often been dispersed by a timely practice. . . .

But if any person is not musical, pianoforte instruction after a certain point is only a waste of time. It may be said, "Suppose there is latent talent[?]" To this we reply that, as a general rule, musical talent develops early or not at all. It sometimes, though very seldom, happens that a musical organization exists with a naturally imperfect ear. In this case it may be worthwhile to cultivate the ear. But when the ear is bad, and there is no natural taste for music, we may conclude that the soil is sterile, and will not repay cultivation.

❋ ❋ ❋ ❋ ❋

❋ 1871 — *CHURCH'S MUSICAL VISITOR*

From "Music in America," *Church's Musical Visitor* 1/3 (December 1871), 6.

> The periodical *Church's Musical Visitor* was a powerful proponent of music education. The anonymous author of the following article noted difficulties faced by students who sought a musical education in America and admitted that children—boys and girls alike—had not developed a genuine love of the art.

The road to musical proficiency in America is rendered entirely too rugged and toilsome by the interposition of innumerable and needless difficulties. Many of the plainest and simplest rudiments of musical education have been enveloped in an air of mystery quite uncalled for; the great principles and leading rules of the art, though in themselves easily explained, and as easily understood, have been buried beneath a mass of useless and perplexing technicalities. . . . There is no royal road to proficiency in music, any more than there is to the science of mathematics. All that any work of instruction, or any teacher of the art can do, is to divest it of all unnecessary obscurity, and present its principles in the simplest and most comprehensive manner. The remainder of the work must be left to the intelligence and patient application of the student. . . . In the aristocratic mansion, the young Miss takes lessons in music because it is fashionable, very seldom for the love of the art itself. Boys are seldom allowed to study music at all, the parents, in most instances, looking upon music as a sort of butterfly accomplishment, fit only for girls. All this will have to be changed before America can claim the proud distinction of being considered a musical nation. It is altogether different in Germany. . . . In Germany, more than in any other nation, may be seen what a peculiar charm music bestows upon the existence of children, and what animation and vivacity it gives to the adult, and how much upon the whole it contributes to the happiness and welfare of the nation at large.

❋ ❋ ❋ ❋ ❋

❋ 1873 — *CHURCH'S MUSICAL VISITOR*

From "Necessity of the Hour," *Church's Musical Visitor* 2/12 (September 1873), 6.

> In the early days of public school education it was recognized that more was at stake in these institutions than mere learning. Public education facilitated the socialization of children and gave the nation an opportunity to mold its future citizens. This editorial plea advocated making music integral to the school curriculum, thereby ensuring future musical success throughout American society.

Music is essentially republican in its every essence: and as the groundwork of all true republicanism lies in the education of the masses, so must the cornerstone of our musical republic be laid deep and strong—cemented by the might of popular [i.e., public] education.

Much has been said, and still more written, upon this point; but it cannot be too much agitated —too often brought home to the popular heart. Educate the young, and to their care, thus educated, we may safely entrust the future.

Let us see to it, then, that the foundation stone is laid in the common schools: let the study of the fundamental principles of musical science be made one of the standard branches of the common school education; and to the more advanced aid of the conservatory, musical institute, and convention, we may safely rely for the fitting, successful culmination of our hopes. Thus shall we not only retain our present well-earned laurels, but we shall achieve, in the future, still nobler, still grander triumphs.

* * * * *

✻ 1874 — *CHURCH'S MUSICAL VISITOR*

From "Music in Current School Education," *Church's Musical Visitor* (February 1874), 5.

> The following essayist considered music education as it was practiced in three different areas of the nation: New York City, Boston, and the Midwest. The tremendous impact of the German population is noteworthy, as are "the more advanced stages of the science," which were being taught in Boston.

The influence of music in human culture has been a subject of frequent allusion among poets, essayists, and orators, since the old Greeks fabled Orpheus to have drawn the rocks and the trees after him by the sweet sounds of the lyre. . . . The art [of music] is recognized as a branch of study among our higher collegiate institutions, and most of the minor colleges are following the example of Yale and Harvard in endowing professorships of music. But this alone does not touch the main question at issue. It is not with music and musical knowledge, regarded as an ornament or one of the graces of education, but as an essential, that this brief discussion has to do. In other words, we would inquire how far the study of music might be carried with advantage to our schools? . . .

The idea of musical study as a feature of the public school system has already been agitated more or less in our different cities, but it needs to be more thoroughly and exhaustively discussed. The experiment has been also made to some extent, but in so imperfect and indifferent a manner that it is not fair to judge of the possible results by the present status of the system. New York City may be taken as an example. Music is part of the daily school drill, but the impression made on the visitor, it must be confessed, rather tends to make the matter ridiculous. The pupils are taught to sing a certain number of tunes in a mechanical fashion, as if it were a disagreeable part of the school routine, to be hurried through as fast as possible.

What little instruction in the principles of the science of music is given, is so crude and halting, so entirely without uniformity in the different schools, that it is no matter of wonder that the scholars [i.e., students] should feel but little interest in a branch of knowledge so bunglingly taught. In the western cities, Chicago, Cincinnati, and St. Louis, musical instruction in the schools is far more intelligent and systematic. This department has a regular superintendent, thoroughly competent for his work, and the methods of tuition are carefully prescribed. But there is a vast field for improvement even there, and it is an encouraging fact that the increasing numbers and importance of the German population will be likely to enforce a steady improvement in the modes and processes used in the public schools. Boston has been making by far the most ambitious experiment in the direction indicated among American cities. Not only is singing taught in her schools, but there is an attempt to give careful tuition in the principles of harmony and musical composition. In other words, at least a glance is had at the more advanced stages of the science. . . . The value of a general musical education for the people being admitted, there is no reason why adequate methods cannot be adopted for our public schools, at least in the large cities throughout the land. Twenty years of a well-devised and careful method of teaching would tell a marvelous result for the musical growth of the nation.

* * * * *

* 1874 — CONSTANCE F. WOOLSON, AUTHOR OF SHORT STORIES AND TRAVEL SKETCHES

From "Euterpe in America," *Lippincott's Magazine* 14/40 (November 1874), 627-33.

> Constance Woolson (1848-1894) provided information on the general course of music education for women in America. While perhaps essential for girls, music education was considered inappropriate—or at least undesirable—for boys for many years.

A limited knowledge of music is now considered an essential part of a young girl's education, and the daughters of our land study music as inevitably as they study French. Go into any boarding school and the sounds of conflicting pianos and voices will greet your ear. Go into any house where there are daughters, and you will find piles of sheet music covering the piano, the stand and the table, while as a side remark it may be noted that the pages are generally in hopeless confusion–a ballad under the cover of a cavatina, quadrilles interleaved with oratorios, and heavy sonatas frigidly uncomfortable in the company of frothy waltzes from the latest *opéra bouffe*. In some seminaries the favorite music teacher is a German, and forthwith all the scholars [i.e., students] are introduced to the classical composers and come forth well-drilled in Beethoven and Mendelssohn, Bach and Schumann; . . . if they live in the country, they look forward to the annual tours of Theodore Thomas and the Mendelssohn Quintette Club–if they live in New York, they attend the Philharmonics. . . .

* * * * *

* 1880 — F. D.

From "Conservatory Life in Boston," *Lippincott's Magazine* 26/32 (October 1880), 511-14.

With verbiage such as "divine" and "exalted" to convey an almost religious zeal, this author's dramatization of "Cecilia" in Boston reflected a number of important aspects of musical life in the United States. One of these is the vital role women played in spreading the gospel of music; another is the laying of the groundwork for the much hoped-for American musical Messiah.

Our aspiring young friend [Cecilia] from the rural districts who comes to Boston, the great musical center, for the art training she cannot enjoy at home, is full of enthusiasm as she crosses the threshold of that teeming hive, the New England Conservatory of Music. The conflicting din of organs, pianos and violins, of ballad, scale and operetta, though discordant to the actual ear, have a harmony which is not lost to her spiritual sense. . . .

But this is not all. There are exercises at the Conservatory apart from her special lessons which are too valuable to a broad musical education to be neglected—the instruction in harmony, sight reading, the art of teaching, analyses of compositions, as well as lectures and concerts. . . .

At the expiration of her first term Cecilia realizes that her condition is one of constant growth: quickening influences are in the air. She came to Boston to learn music: she is also learning life. She perceives, moreover, that in her musical progress the aesthetic part of her nature has not been permitted to keep in advance of technique. Heretofore she was ever gratifying herself and her friends by undertaking new and more elaborate pieces, not one of which ever became other than a mere superficial possession. Now her taste is inexorably commanded to wait for her muscles: the discipline has been useful to her. After a few more such winters she will return to Woodville a teacher, herself become a quickening influence to others. Musical thought will be truer, will find a more adequate expression, in her vicinity. She will act as a reflector, sending forth rays of light into dark corners farther than she can follow them.

And this is the motive, the mission, of the conservatory system in this country, inasmuch as organized is more potent than individual effort to elevate our national taste, to prepare the way for the future artist, that he may be born under the right conditions, his divine gift fostered and directed to become worthy of its exalted destiny. Already centuries old in Europe, the conservatory is a young thing of comparatively limited experience on our soil. . . .

✻ ✻ ✻ ✻ ✻

✻ 1881 — THEODORE THOMAS, ORCHESTRA AND OPERA CONDUCTOR

From "Musical Possibilities in America," *Scribner's Monthly Magazine* 21/5 (March 1881), 777-80.

Theodore Thomas (1835-1905) railed against the "movable do" system and the limitations it places on the advancement of the art; he was one of the few artists of the period to be frankly critical of music education efforts in the United States. Thomas's outlook was highly forward-looking, as he always hoped to build musicians and audiences of the future.

When we consider that music is taught in the public schools throughout the country, we might expect some evidence or result of this teaching among the people. Much money is spent in our schools for instruction in this branch, and what does it amount to? Many of the children learn like parrots, and soon forget the little which they have learned. Those who retain this knowledge find it a drawback when wishing to go on in the study of music. The fault is not in them, but in the system taught. So faulty is that system that it would be better to abolish singing entirely from the schools than to retain it under the present method. It does more harm than good. I consider the system at present followed in this elementary instruction, called the "movable *do* system," fundamentally wrong, and experience has confirmed me in this opinion. It is a makeshift, invented by amateurs. Pupils should learn something about [the] absolute pitch of tones, instead of merely their relative pitch. The "movable *do* system" shuts the door against this knowledge. The first tone of the scale in every key is *do*, and that term *do* never suggests to one who has studied music any fixed, absolute conception of pitch; for example, *do* is sometimes C and sometimes D, while to the musician C and D are as distinct sounds as the vowel a and e. The system will enable a student to sing a simple hymn tune which has no accidental sharps or flats, but it is wrong thus to limit pupils to so restricted a capacity. In my experience, those who have learned to read music according to this method never free themselves altogether from it. It should be considered as necessary to be thorough in the study of music as in that of mathematics. I do not say that it should be carried to the same extent, but that, so far as it is carried, it should be taught understandingly and well—taught so as to pave the way for future study, when desirable, and not so as to block it up. I attach a great deal of importance to this matter of correct musical instruction. If we start right in the schools, the public taste will soon advance to a higher standard. It is from the young that the church choirs and singing societies must be recruited, and if a correct foundation is laid when the rudiments are learned, the progress to a more advanced position is natural and easy.

While singing under proper direction is a healthy exercise, great injury can be done to the throat and vocal organs by allowing the children to sing, or rather scream, at the top of their voices. Most of the school singing which I have heard in this country is screaming, not singing, while in England and Germany I heard nothing of the kind. On the principle that no person can teach another what he cannot do himself (a principle which I believe in to a great extent), I hold to the opinion that the teachers of singing should themselves be singers, with a good method. Singing ought also to be taught without the aid of an instrument, unless it be occasionally to support the pitch.

At present, the musical standard of the American public, taken as a whole, must be pronounced a low one. If we should judge of what has been done in music by the programs of concerts given in the larger cities, we might rightly claim for this country a high rank in cultivation. Those concerts, however, appeal not to the general public, but to one class only, and that a limited one, as any one who observes the audiences can easily see. This class is growing in numbers as well as in cultivation, but it is still far too small to support more than a limited number of concerts, as at present those of the New York and Brooklyn Philharmonic societies. The general public does not advance in music, partly from want of opportunity, partly from the habits of the people. The average American is so entirely absorbed in his work that when he goes out in the evening he looks for relaxation in some kind of amusement which makes little or no demand upon his intellect, and he has no difficulty in finding it.

* * * * *

❊ 1890 — FREDERIC LOUIS RITTER, MUSIC HISTORIAN, COMPOSER, AND EDUCATOR

From Frederic Louis Ritter, "Survey of the Present State of Musical Activity," *Music in America* (New York: Charles Scribner's Sons, 1890), 475-506.

Frederic Louis Ritter (1826-1891), who served as the Director of the School of Music of Vassar College, wrote of the important role of women in building the foundation for music in America and their pervasiveness in the musical community, which stood in stark contrast to the limited contributions of men.

Who studies Music. – The above remarks naturally lead us to the consideration of another important question bearing on the ultimate results of vocal instruction as given in the public schools, and the class of children enabled to profit by it. Any casual observer must have perceived, that, as a rule, the American woman is the *musician of the land.* She not [only] receives private instruction in singing or on the pianoforte, whenever her parents can afford to engage a music teacher, but she also enjoys the privilege of being able to attend school for a longer period of time, and has consequently greater opportunity to profit by vocal instruction, as taught in school, than her brother. The American boy generally leaves the public schools at the age of about fourteen years, to enter as apprentice to some business; a comparatively small number of boys stay at school until they are able to go through the high school. The girl is in the majority at the high school; she sings solos at the high school exhibitions. But this not alone holds good as regards the girl's opportunity to become musically a good sight reader during her stay at the public schools—at least, one has a right to expect her to become so; peruse the lists of pupils that frequent the numerous music schools of all styles to be found in the cities throughout the land, and you will perceive an infinitesimal fraction of boy pupils. The great colleges for young women, the young ladies' seminaries, boarding schools, etc., all offer ample opportunity for the study of music in some form or other.

Musical *matinees* of all sorts, as given in large and small cities, are almost exclusively patronized by women; whenever and wherever a musical society is formed, women, able to read music well, are in the majority over men. Since young American gentlemen are, in imitation of German [men's] societies, establishing male glee clubs, the ladies, being better musicians, have naturally established in their turn ladies' singing clubs. The woman goes to musical lectures, and has earnestly taken up the study of musical history, harmony, and composition.

The American boy, when out of school, very seldom receives any sort of musical instruction; he generally also soon forgets the degree of knowledge of reading music, which he may have gained while at school. The boarding schools for boys, the military schools, the seminaries, do not provide—as far as I can gather—instruction in elementary vocal music. To be sure, here and there we find a few boys, taking lessons on the flute, cornet, banjo, or the drum, seldom on the pianoforte or the violin. Among the great colleges for young men, Harvard and the University of Pennsylvania alone have chairs for a musical professorship; the professor at

Yale College simply fills the position of an organist. Young men's college glee and banjo clubs are private affairs for temporary amusement.

* * * * *

✻ 1896 — LOUIS C. ELSON, MUSIC HISTORIAN, MUSIC EDITOR, AND MUSIC CRITIC

From *European Reminiscences* (Philadelphia: T. Presser, 1896), 248-70.

The essays of Louis C. Elson (1848-1920), who was affiliated with several Boston area journals as well as New England Conservatory, testify to the growing availability in the United States of a "musical atmosphere" similar to that which existed in Europe. He was an early admirer of the French school of composition and among the first to discern that a fine musical education could be obtained in Paris.

I am often asked by young musical students, "Where ought I to go to study in Europe?" The question is so vast and demands such detail in its answer that I have determined to leave, for a while, the paths of travel, and speak of musical Europe in its relations to the student. America at present offers as thorough a curriculum, to the musician, as Europe. There are, in the conservatories of our own land at present, many musicians who have been members of the faculties of foreign conservatories, and it is not to be imagined that their teaching is inferior in America, to what it was in transatlantic countries. The fault is to be sought elsewhere; many a musical student, when studying in his native land, takes matters altogether too easily; the same party, when placed in a foreign land, separated from friends and kindred, studies as if life itself depended on his efforts. It is not an extravagant statement to say, that if musical students would give the same ardor to their work in America that they do in Europe, they would achieve the same results.

"But," says the apologetic student, "there is a musical atmosphere in Europe, which is not attainable in America!" This idea is so firmly rooted in the American mind, that it seems almost impossible to tear it out; yet I can truthfully say that I have heard music in Munich that would have been hissed in New York, and some operas given in La Scala do not begin to compare with the same works as presented in the Metropolitan Opera House in New York. . . .

Europe must stand to America, in the domain of music, exactly as foreign countries do to France in the matter of its advanced musical students. When, for example, a student has won the great prize for composition, the Prix de Rome, at the Paris Conservatoire, he is sent into other countries for a while, to study other schools, in order that his work may not be one-sided. In exactly the same manner, after the student has attained the best that our country can afford him, he should go to other countries for the finishing touches, that he may not become wedded exclusively to the style of his teachers. When a student, male or female, has become a master of his art in his own country, then let him seek Europe with a firm conviction that it will broaden his views and help his work. . . .

But about musical study in Paris; there are few Americans who pursue the French course of musical study, because most of our countrymen believe that the Germans have a first mortgage on music, and no other nation has anything to do with tuition. This is a mistake; while giving every homage to the excellence of Teutonic pedagogy, I must say that the course at the Paris Conservatoire is remarkably thorough and effective. . . .

And this leads to a very important statement; no young lady should ever dare to study in France or Italy without a parent, or a brother, as protector or advisor. Americans often think those who raise this cry prudish, but the cold, calm truth had better be insisted on; it is not safe! In more phlegmatic Germany the unprotected musical female may sometimes venture, in the more fiery Latin furnace, never. . . .

In the matter of piano playing and composition, the American student generally turns to Germany, and wisely, for although the French course in composition is very thorough, Munich or Leipzig present no such temptations to turn aside from work to pleasure and dissipation as Paris does. The models, too, are somewhat higher in Germany, for Mozart is generally made the foundation and Bach the apex there. Counterpoint can be studied in either Munich or Leipzig to advantage, for [Josef] Rheinberger in the former city, is one of the greatest of modern contrapuntists, and [Salomon] Jadassohn in the latter, is one of the most fluent writers in canon and other intricate forms, that the world possesses today, and he has besides the faculty of making his pupils enthusiastic in their work. . . .

✻ ✻ ✻ ✻ ✻

✻ 1898 — EDWARD MACDOWELL, COMPOSER AND MUSIC EDUCATOR

From "Suggestion in Music," *Critical and Historical Essays* (Boston: Arthur P. Schmidt, 1912), 261-73. [Based on lectures delivered between 1896 and 1898]

> Composer Edward MacDowell (1860-1908) upheld the idea of music as a high art and yearned to get closer to his audience. To him music was more than a simple entertainment. His view that music can affect both the body and the mind, especially in a physiological way, is a theme that was seldom heard during this era.

In speaking of the power of suggestion in music I wish at the outset to make certain reservations. In the first place I speak for myself, and what I have to present is merely an expression of my personal opinion; if in any way these should incite to further investigation or discussion, my object will in part have been attained.

In the second place, in speaking of this art, one is seriously hampered by a certain difficulty in making oneself understood. To hear and to enjoy music seems sufficient to many persons, and an investigation as to the causes of this enjoyment seems to them superfluous. And yet, unless the public comes into closer touch with the tone poet than that objective state which accepts with the ears what is intended for the spirit, which hears the sounds and is deaf to their import, unless the public can separate the physical pleasure of music from its ideal significance, our art, in my opinion, cannot stand on a sound basis.

The first step toward an appreciation of music should be taken in our preparatory schools. Were young people taught to distinguish between tones as between colors, to recognize rhythmic values, and were they taught so to use their voices as to temper the nasal tones of speech, in afterlife [i.e., adulthood] they would be better able to appreciate and cherish an art of which mere pleasure-giving sounds are but a very small part.

Much of the lack of independence of opinion about music arises from want of familiarity with its material. Thus, after dinner, our forefathers were accustomed to sing catches which were entirely destitute of anything approaching music.

Music contains certain elements which affect the nerves of the mind and body, and thus possesses the power of direct appeal to the public—a power to a great extent denied to the other arts. This sensuous influence over the hearer is often mistaken for the aim and end all of music. With this in mind, one may forgive the rather puzzling remarks so often met with; for instance, those of a certain English bishop that "Music did not affect him either intellectually or emotionally, only pleasurably," adding, "Every art should keep within its own realm; and that of music was concerned with pleasing combinations of sound." In declaring that the sensation of hearing music was pleasant to him, and that to produce that sensation was the entire mission of music, the bishop placed our art on a level with good things to eat and drink. Many colleges and universities of this land consider music as a kind of *boutonniere* [decoration].

This estimate of music is, I believe, unfortunately a very general one, and yet, low as it is, there is a possibility of building on such a foundation. . . .

* * * * *

✻ 1900 — WALDO S. PRATT, MUSIC HISTORIAN AND MUSIC EDUCATOR

From "New Ideals in Music Education," *Atlantic Monthly* 86/518 (December 1900), 826-32.

> Although largely self-taught in music, Waldo S. Pratt (1857-1939) proposed several possibilities for new avenues of delivering music education in America. Excerpted here are his thoughts regarding the possible inclusion of "scholastic" musical studies in college music programs. This represents an early recommendation that musicology and theory serve as significant parts of the music curriculum.

Musicians are apt to say that a music student should devote himself to making music, either as performer or as composer, and that all scholastic study about music and scientific prying into music are useless simply because they are not music. . . .

The most serious obstacle to scholarly musical work is that of providing the student with materials of study, with laboratory or museum facilities. The trained musician secures these by personal reproduction of examples, by playing or singing through such works as are to be known and studied, or by hearing recitals, concerts, operas, church services, and the like. But music, like the drama, is an art of progressive action that cannot be photographed or diagrammatized [*sic*]; [music is] an art of tones not reproducible in words, usually not representable by anything except itself. Consequently, its study requires altogether unique museum provisions. . . .

There is an immense opportunity for rational and systematic classroom work in music, if only teachers would see it. . . . Such work takes time and thought, is liable to abuse, and is not well systematized as yet. But with its advent comes the awakening of many a groping mind to musical realities, and a sudden intuition of their vital relation to other worlds of thought.

The essentials in a teacher working for higher musical education along these lines are three. First, he must be analytic in method, with the mastery of definition and classification that follows. Second, he must have a broad historic sense, since nothing in musical progress is luminous or correct in perspective except in its historic relations. Third, he must have a sure hold on the bearing of all the fine arts, music included, upon the fundamental features of human life. Each of these assertions would bear indefinite expansion and justification. The bare mention of these as "essentials" may be sufficiently startling. Yet surely a college department under a teacher defective in all three must be educationally a farce. . . .

* * * * *

* 1903 — GEORGE WHITEFIELD CHADWICK, COMPOSER AND MUSIC EDUCATOR

From "Musical Atmosphere and Student Life," *New England Conservatory Magazine* 9/4 (May 1903), 138-41. [Reprinted by permission of New England Conservatory]

> Composer George Whitefield Chadwick (1854-1931) believed that the best course for American students was to learn the basics of the craft of composition in the United States and then travel to Europe for study in an effort to broaden their musical palette. A major theme in his essay is the importance of camaraderie among artists, especially those friendships made during formative years. He spoke from experience: early in his training, he befriended the likes of painter Frank Duveneck, conductor Theodore Thomas, and fellow composer Horatio Parker; the latter became one of Chadwick's closest friends. Also noteworthy are his remarks regarding the study of instrumentation and his commentary on German teaching methods and on the impatience the average American had with them.

Twenty-five years ago or so it was considered necessary for the music student who wished to be thoroughly equipped to go to Europe to study. There were plenty of teachers in America for the pianoforte, organ, and violin, as well as of singing and harmony, but Europe was supposed to be the only place where there existed such a musical environment that it was possible for one to envelop himself in a musical atmosphere.

I suppose that it may have been necessary at that time, since although there were good teachers with us then, yet there were not many of great authority or reputation. Many of the best were Europeans who had settled in this country after careers as virtuosi, and who naturally brought with them the methods, and possibly the prejudices as well, of their own upbringing.

We were not devoid of a musical atmosphere, however, for we had some good concerts, and there was certainly a great deal of interest in music making in the family. There was decided enthusiasm for chorus singing, and choral clubs and choruses were in a very flourishing condition; moreover, there was a good deal of amateur instrumental music. Still, the low standard of education for the professional musician which existed throughout America up to such a recent time was an unfavorable feature of our musical life.

Stephen Emery was once asked how one should go about the study of instrumentation. He said, "I suppose that Mr. [John Knowles] Paine will teach instrumentation, but I think no one else in the country can do so." As a matter of fact, Mr. Paine was probably at that time the only man in this country who really knew much about the subject. Contrast this with the fact that in Europe every Kapellmeister [music director] could teach it.

Of course, in this period such a thing as American composition was unknown, and it was not until certain American composers had achieved some success in Europe that they gained a hearing on this side of the water. So far as I know, the first piece of American music by an American composer to be performed at the Harvard Symphony Concerts, which were then our only orchestral performances, was the Overture to *Don Munio*, by Dudley Buck; shortly after came John K. Paines's First Symphony, performed by the [Theodore] Thomas Orchestra, and not long afterwards Mr. J. C. D. Parker's beautiful *Redemption Hymn*, written for a festival of the Handel & Haydn Society. The production of these works was a great stimulus and encouragement to the young musicians of that time.

In considering the question as to whether the German conservatories of twenty years ago were as efficient as the best American type of today, I can only speak from experience of the Leipzig and Munich schools. There were two serious faults in the methods of these schools: first, a lack of severe discipline, and, second, a fondness for certain old-fashioned and pedantic methods, which to the American student seemed like a stupid waste of time. The students in the Leipzig Conservatory of those days were given a schedule of classes which they were supposed to attend; but very little fault was found with them if they did not do so, and the result was that they did very nearly as they pleased.

As illustrating the pedantry of the instruction of that time, mention may be made of a new pupil who came to our piano class in Leipzig and was asked what he had studied. He replied that he had played ten or twelve studies by Cramer. The teacher said, "Very well, take number *thirteen*"; but did not ask him to play anything. A student in the organ class was asked to play the scale of A major on the pedals. He did so with entire accuracy, but by putting his right toe on the G-sharp and his right heel on A. The teacher remarked, "My son, that is incorrect. All pedal scales should be played with alternate feet," which he proceeded to illustrate in the most painful and clumsy manner.

Another illustration: a certain class in instrumentation was required to spend almost the whole forenoon copying a table of impossible trills for the flute, after which they were informed that all trills for the flute were now possible, according to the Boehm system, but that it was useful for them to know the trills on the flute *as it used to be*.

It is such methods as these that make the average American student impatient with the grinding-out process to which he is usually subjected in the German school.

But that there is an atmosphere of art and serious study is not to be denied. Moreover, I believe that this atmosphere now exists in this country, and in this city of Boston, if the student is really earnest and serious enough to take advantage of it. Take the experience of any one of a hundred music students who may be seen on a Friday afternoon at Symphony Hall. We will suppose that a young man is here for the purpose of studying composition–incidentally, perhaps–also the organ or pianoforte. On Monday he goes to his lesson, during which he is referred to a half-dozen books or scores, which he may consult in the Allen Brown Library [at Boston Public Library], and from which he may make notes for his studies. Perhaps he may spend the rest of the day in this employment. He may be so fortunate as to secure through a friend a ticket to the concert of the Kneisel Quartet in the evening; if not, he may attend the meeting of a musical fraternity, whose members are all working for the same object that he is. The next day he may hear a students' orchestra rehearsed all the afternoon. On Wednesday he has more lessons, ending with a general sight-singing class, and may perhaps attend a lecture on organ construction or church music. On Thursday he tries to find a little time to study scores, or possibly to play [with] four hands the music for the week's Symphony Concert, spending an hour after luncheon in hearing a lecture on musical instruments or musical history, or some other subject connected with music. Possibly, too, he may be fortunate enough to hear a rehearsal of the Cecilia [Society] chorus in the evening. On Friday at 11:30 a.m. he is merrily stamping his feet on the steps of Symphony Hall, with a sandwich in one pocket and a score in the other, and here he finds himself surrounded by good company. Not much to be done after 4:30 on *that* day except to hunt up the boys and talk the concert over. On Saturday he may attend a pupil's recital, and later in the day may hear a good choir rehearsed and trained. On Sunday he goes to hear his teacher or some other good organist, and possibly gets into the rehearsal of the Handel & Haydn [Society] chorus in the evening. That is, unless he has other occupations for his time, for it often happens that such a student is able to assist himself materially by playing the organ or singing in a choir, or playing in a small orchestra, or giving a few lessons; all of which is in the direct line of his training. If this does not constitute a musical atmosphere it would be difficult to define one.

The average type of American music student who has perhaps passed most of his life away from a large musical center does well to become thoroughly grounded in his technical education in this country before going abroad to study. In Europe the American temperament is often misunderstood, and the alacrity of the American mind underappreciated.

There is nothing more important to the student than the formation of early friendships and acquaintanceships with those of his own profession. Such friendships often have a very decided influence on one's after life and occasionally shape one's entire career; especially is the association with experienced artists, of whatever branch [of the arts], to be highly valued by the young student. It is almost a liberal education in itself to associate with a fine artist and such opportunities can be found only in places where the artists are valued and appreciated. The principals of musical art are so comprehensive that pianists, organists and composers can learn very much from the experience of singers, violinists and conductors. The reverse of this is also true. It is only by such associations that a broad and catholic taste may be acquired.

* * * * *

❋ 1903 — MABEL W. DANIELS, COMPOSER AND MUSIC EDUCATOR

From *An American Girl in Munich* (Boston: Little, Brown, 1912), 226-28. [Excerpt from a letter written in April 1903].

Composer Mabel Daniels (1878-1971), writing as a conservatory student in Europe, told the story of her own performance experiences and described the throngs of American women trying to make their mark in opera there. It is widely known that European instrumentalists traveled in high numbers to America and that American composers routinely sought their educations abroad. The tale of American singers seeking success in opera in Europe—because opportunities were extremely scarce in the United States—remains largely untold.

Just a line before I go to sleep to tell you that everything went off beautifully at the concert tonight. . . . You cannot imagine anything more terrifying than to stand on the platform and look down on this human barricade [of professors] which shuts one off, as it were, from all that is friendly and encouraging. . . . There was a certain horrible fascination about it all, for try as I would to look over into the audience or up at the balcony, I found my glance always nervously returning to some dignified head posed at a critical angle, or some pair of hands with finger tips pressed together in judicial attitude.

The moment after I made my very quaint, very German [curtsy]–a ceremony insisted on by the Frau Professor–I suddenly became terribly conscious of the fact that I was an American, that all these people before me were German, and that I was about to sing to them in Italian. If I had dared, I should have smiled. It was as if Italian were a language of commerce, by means of which I was to make a communication to the audience. But, dear me! I forgot all about that and everything–yes, even the depressing effect of the front row–when once I got to singing. And when it was over I could have hugged the fellow who cried "*Bravo! Amerika! Amerika!*" What mattered it that it was only an unpretentious pupils' concert? . . .

When one studies singing merely for the love of it, it is all very well, but it would make your heart sick to see the number of American girls over here who are half-starving themselves in order to study for the grand opera stage. One sadly wonders how many of them will "arrive," but when an argument is raised or a doubt expressed as to their ultimate success, they immediately cite the case of Geraldine Farrar, the American who is at present singing leading roles at the Berlin opera house. The brilliancy of her success blinds their eyes to hundreds of utter failures, to countless half-way successes and to the untold drudgery which lies along the road.

❋ ❋ ❋ ❋ ❋

❋ 1911 — *THE OUTLOOK*

From "Music and City Children," *The Outlook* 97/4 (4 March 1911), 483-84.

By the time this article was printed, New York City's efforts in music education had improved dramatically. Here is provided a fine overview of several of the many activities that engaged children throughout the city and a convincing closing argument that supported the teaching of music in public and private schools.

One of the surprises of the Child Welfare Exhibit has been the discovery of an unexpected amount of good teaching of instrumental and vocal music in the public and private institutions in the City of New York. The singing by children in the public schools . . . was of especial beauty. On the opening evening a choir of one thousand children and on two other evenings choirs of five hundred children were heard; and on still other evenings boys' or girls' glee clubs from different high schools. A choir of thirty little Italian boys came from the Mission of our Lady of Loretto; a chorus from the Colored Orphan Asylum, at Riverdale on the Hudson; an orchestra of one hundred and thirty players from the Music School Settlement (an institution which is doing very remarkable work in character-building among the children of the tenements), whose playing suggested the precision and tone of mature artists. Public School No. 21 sent a band of Italian boys whose instruments and instruction had been paid for by a public-spirited citizen; the Brooklyn Disciplinary Training School sent a band of thirty pieces; the Hebrew Orphan Asylum, a band of twenty-five pieces. The Three Arts School sent an orchestra of fifty well-trained players; the Morris High School of the Bronx sent an orchestra to accompany the singing of five hundred children from the Bronx public schools. Public School No. 62, Manhattan, from the Russian-Jewish quarter, sent both a choir of singers and an orchestra. . . . An interesting feature was a military drill by boys from the New York Institution for the Instruction of the Deaf and Dumb, who brought with them a brass band, which played with precision and skill. . . . The question may be asked, What is the use of all this teaching of music? and one practical answer is that those children who have special musical ability are given a start, from which they can, if they choose, develop themselves as professional musicians, and so earn a better living than they might otherwise earn. If, however, this were the only answer, it probably would be said that the number who are likely to develop special musical ability is comparatively small, certainly not enough to justify all the musical training. The real answer lies in the fact that it is quite as important to provide amusements for people of every age and condition as it is to provide food, clothing, and shelter. If the children of the ignorant and destitute poor are not taught how to provide proper and reasonable amusements for themselves, they are likely to indulge in improper and vicious amusements. It should, therefore, be a part of all educational and charitable work to teach the children of the city how to provide for themselves sane and uplifting forms of pleasure. The development of the mental, spiritual, and imaginative side of life is of the first importance, and the results of these musical entertainments at the Child Welfare Exhibit have shown how through music the children of the people may have a quick, easy, and permanently effective means to such development.

* * * * *

⁕ 1916 — THOMAS WHITNEY SURETTE, MUSIC EDUCATOR

From "Public School Music," *Atlantic Monthly* 118/6 (December 1916), 812-23.

By 1916 Thomas Whitney Surette (1861-1941), an important early innovator in music education and music appreciation, voiced ideas that sound positively contemporary, especially with regard to the public school as a laboratory for "the testing of theories." Surette disdained sight singing (and we may infer that he also disdained sight reading by instrumentalists) as unnecessary except under unusual circumstances. This is all the more fascinating because sight reading and sight singing are skills still widely emphasized today. Surette stressed the importance of good teaching and the. necessity of providing students with a well-rounded education.

It is characteristic of our complaisance in matters educational that of late years we have seen subject after subject added to the curricula of our public schools, and have cheerfully voted money for them, without having much conception of their value or of the results obtained by introducing them. Education is our shibboleth, our formula. The school diploma and the college degree constitute our new baptism of conformity. We do not question their authority or their efficacy. They absolve us. Our public schools have become experimental stations for the testing of theories, until the demand for more and more specialization has resulted in an overcrowding of the curricula and a consequent superficiality in the teaching. . . .

I believe in keeping the music lesson as a bond of sympathy between the grade teacher and the children. Singing is an entirely natural art for any human being who begins it in childhood and pursues it through youth. I look forward to the day when we all shall sing. I object to the displacement of the grade teacher in the one function of school life which is intimate, free, and beautiful, in which facts, numbers, places, events, names are forgotten, and in which the spirit of each child issues forth *under the discipline of beauty*. (I place these words in italics because I am constantly being told that the great thing in the education of children is to give them self-expression; to which I reply that self-expression except under discipline–using the word in its larger sense–has never helped either the individual or the [human] race.) . . .

But the real failure in the administration of school music is due to a false ideal. And it is in this mistaken ideal or purpose that the crux of the whole matter lies. Nearly the whole stress of teaching is laid on expert sight-reading of music. Go into a schoolroom with a supervisor to hear his class sing, and he will almost invariably exhibit to you with pride the capacity of the children to sing at sight. He will ask you to put something impromptu on the blackboard as a test of their proficiency. He will exhibit to you classes of very young children who have already learned to read notes and who can sing all sorts of simple exercises from the staff.

What is meant by the term "sight-singing"? It means, if it means anything, that a person shall be able to sing correctly at the first trial his part in any piece of vocal music which he has never seen or heard before. And this, which we spend our money for, is an entirely artificial attainment, since in real life we are almost never required to do it. "Sight-singing" has become a shibboleth. What we want is a reasonable capacity to read music, for that is all we are ever called upon to do in actual life. . . .

One of the encouraging signs of our advancement is in orchestral playing. School orchestras have become important features of school life, and the excellence of some of the orchestral playing is remarkable. It often outshines the singing, and it is frequently self-contained, being under the direction, not of the music teachers, but of the headmaster or one of his assistants. In this department of music teaching, as in the singing lessons, much depends on the attitude and the qualifications of the headmaster. In our Boston schools there are notable examples of fine music fostered and sustained by enthusiastic and capable headmasters, who lay great stress on that as contrasted with mere technical expertness. . . .

Singing by ear spontaneously and without technical instruction, but rather for the joy of doing it, and for the formation of the taste on good models, is the proper beginning of all musical education. Such experience, coupled with proper rhythmic exercises, constitutes a real basis, not only for reading music but for performance on any instrument. No child should be admitted for possible credit in pianoforte playing or be allowed to enter violin classes until so prepared in singing and in rhythm. . . .

* * * * *

Patrick S. Gilmore, pictured here circa 1885, was considered the greatest bandmaster of his time. After the Civil War he organized mammoth musical extravaganzas in Boston—the Peace Jubilees.

Courtesy of the George Grantham Bain Collection, Prints and Photographs Division, Library of Congress: LC-USZ62-123529.

⁂ 5 — "A Cherished Monstrosity": Gilmore's Peace Jubilees

The National Peace Jubilee, 1869

1871 – Patrick S. Gilmore
From *History of the National Peace Jubilee*

1901 – William Dean Howells
From "Jubilee Days," *Suburban Sketches*

World's Peace Jubilee and International Musical Festival, 1872

1872 – Murillo
From "Boston," *Church's Musical Visitor*

1872 – *The New York Times*
From "Musical Quackery"
From "Summary of Amusements"

1872 – John Sullivan Dwight
From "The Second Gilmore Jubilee"

1872 – Murillo
From "Boston," *Church's Musical Visitor*
From "Music," *Atlantic Monthly*

1899 – Thomas Ryan
From *Recollections of an Old Musician*

The "Revivified" Jubilee, 1889

1889 – Louis C. Elson
From "Music in Boston"

Patrick Sarsfield Gilmore's legendary National Peace Jubilee of 1869 and the subsequent World's Peace Jubilee and International Musical Festival of 1872, both held in Boston, were powerful events in American cultural history. Not only were they significant in bringing fine music to Americans in substantial quantities, but they were massive concert spectacles produced on a scale unheard of before their time.

THE NATIONAL PEACE JUBILEE, 1869

* 1871 — PATRICK S. GILMORE, BANDMASTER, IMPRESARIO, AND COMPOSER

From *History of the National Peace Jubilee* (Boston: Lee & Shepard, 1871), 1-17.

The most important and comprehensive history of the 1869 event was written by Gilmore (1829-1892) himself. Writing in the third person, the bandmaster portrayed his initiative in positively Biblical terms and gave every indication that his vision of the event sprang, fully formed, from his head in an instant. An Irish immigrant, Gilmore was a dedicated musician, an accomplished cornetist, and the undisputed leader of America's robust band movement.

In June of 1867 Mr. P. S. Gilmore was passing a few days in the city of New York, and it was at this time that the first thought of a national Jubilee, to commemorate the restoration of Peace throughout the land, flashed upon his mind. The carrying out of the idea he well knew would afford an opportunity for the grandest Musical Festival the world had ever known.

The scenes with which he was then surrounded immediately lost their interest, and he became absorbed by the grandeur of his conception. The general plan of the scheme, as afterwards adopted, seemed at once to unfold itself. Indeed, had the scenes of Broadway been instantly changed by the wand of a magician, they could not have been transformed into a series of more enchanting dissolving views than were vividly portrayed to him like a panorama of the coming event. A vast structure rose up before him, filled with the loyal of the land, through whose lofty arches a chorus of ten thousand voices and the harmony of a thousand instruments rolled their sea of sound, accompanied by the chiming of the bells and the booming of the cannon—all pouring forth their praise and gratulation in loud hosannas with all the majesty and grandeur of which music seemed capable. As his imagination reveled in the scenes his thought pictured, every nerve quivered with the intensity of his delight, and he was impressed with all the fervor of religious belief that it was his especial mission to carry out the sublime conception. . . .

He anticipated that such questions as these would be raised—"How could he possibly expect to organize a chorus of ten thousand voices?" "Where were the singers to be found?" "The largest musical organizations in the land had never numbered a thousand members in their grandest festivals."

But he knew that chorus singing was extensively practiced among the people, particularly in New England, and that he would be able to convince any one of ordinary intelligence that a chorus of ten thousand voices *could* be procured. *Massachusetts alone could furnish the entire number*! Admitting that the voices might be obtained, the questions then arose—"Could they be made to sing together?" "Would the laws of sound admit of such a vast body being so united and controlled as to produce a clear and pure harmony?"

No entirely satisfactory reply could be made to these questions, as the employment of such great numbers in chorus had never been attempted, and the effect could only be proved to the satisfaction of doubters and croakers by actual experiment. But Mr. Gilmore had no doubt of the effect himself. He imagined, in the rendering of such choruses as "The Heavens are telling," from Haydn's *Creation*; the "Hallelujah Chorus," from Handel's *Messiah*; "Thanks be to God," from Mendelssohn's *Elijah*; and compositions of a similar character, he could hear the mighty waves of sound rushing and rolling down, now from the *sopranos*, then from the *altos*, here from the *tenors*, there from the *basses*—all coming together occasionally, meeting and mingling, not in confusion, but in stately and majestic grandeur, lifting and carrying the soul and senses into the most exalted realms of harmony and musical bliss.

All this he could imagine; but the actual performance of such music, rendered in the form he had in view, he felt would produce results of the greatest benefit to art in America, and he believed that his energies could not be devoted to the accomplishment of a higher or nobler purpose. It was to him the mission of his life, and it must be fulfilled.

* * * * *

* 1901 — WILLIAM DEAN HOWELLS, NOVELIST, ESSAYIST, AND EDITOR

From "Jubilee Days," *Suburban Sketches* (Boston: Houghton, Mifflin, 1901), 195-219.

> The well-known novelist and essayist William Dean Howells (1837-1920) attended the 1869 event. Although self-admittedly not a musical person, Howells possessed the novelist's eye for detail and brought the grandiosity of the festival to life with remarks about its atmosphere and spectacle. Importantly, his article stands as one of the few not written by a music critic: Howells's account is marked by the frank outlook and opinions of the non-musical observer.

I do not know if I shall be able to give an idea of the immensity of this scene; but if such a reader as has the dimensions of the [Boston] Coliseum accurately fixed in his mind will, in imagination, densely hide all that interminable array of benching in the parquet and the galleries and the slopes at either end of the edifice with human heads, showing here crowns, there occiputs, and yonder faces, he will perhaps have some notion of the spectacle as we beheld it from the northern hillside. Some thousands of heads nearest were recognizable as attached by the usual neck to the customary human body, but for the rest, we seemed to have entered a world of cherubim. Especially did the multitudinous singers seated far opposite encourage this illusion. . . .

It was as difficult to distribute the various facts of the whole effect, as to identify one's self. I had only a public and general consciousness of the delight given by the harmony of hues in the parquet below; and concerning the orchestra I had at first no distinct impression save of the three hundred and thirty violin bows held erect like standing wheat at one motion of the director's wand, and then falling as if with the next one he swept them down. Afterwards files of men with horns, and other files of men with drums and cymbals, discovered themselves; while far above all, certain laborious figures pumped or ground with incessant obeisance at the apparatus supplying the organ with wind.

What helped, more than anything else, to restore you your dispersed and wandering individuality was the singing of [Euphrosyne] Parepa-Rosa, as she triumphed over the harmonious rivalry of the orchestra. There was something in the generous amplitude and robust cheerfulness of this great artist that accorded well with the ideal of the occasion; she was in herself a great music festival; and one felt, as she floated down the stage with her far-spreading white draperies, and swept the audience a colossal courtesy [i.e., curtsy], that here was the embodied genius of the Jubilee. I do not trust myself to speak particularly of her singing, for I have the natural modesty of people who know nothing about music, and I have not at command the phraseology of those who pretend to understand it; but I say that her voice filled the whole edifice with delicious melody, that it soothed and composed and utterly enchanted, that, though two hundred violins accompanied her, the greater sweetness of her note prevailed over all, like a mighty will commanding many. What a sublime ovation for her when a hundred thousand hands thundered their acclaim. . . .

When Parepa (or Prepper, as I have heard her name popularly pronounced) had sung, the revived consciousness of an individual life rose in rebellion against the oppression of that dominant vastness. In fact, human nature can stand only so much of any one thing. To a certain degree you accept and conceive of facts truthfully, but beyond this a mere fantasticality rules; and having got enough of grandeur, the senses played themselves false. That array of fluttering and tuning people on the southern slope began to look minute, like the myriad heads assembled in the infinitesimal photograph which you view through one of those little half-inch lorgnettes [i.e., opera glasses]; and you had the satisfaction of knowing that to any lovely infinitesimality yonder you showed no bigger than a carpet-tack. The whole performance now seemed to be worked by those tireless figures pumping at the organ, in obedience to signals from a very alert figure on the platform below. The choral and orchestral thousands sang and piped and played; at a given point in the *scena* from Verdi, a hundred fairies in red shirts marched down through the somber mass of puppets and beat upon as many invisible anvils.

This was the stroke of anti-climax; and the droll sound of those anvils, so far above all the voices and instruments in its pitch, thoroughly disillusioned you and restored you finally to your proper entity and proportions. It was the great error of the Jubilee, and where almost everything else was noble and impressive—where the direction was faultless, and the singing and instrumentation as perfectly controlled as if they were the result of one volition—this anvil-beating was alone ignoble and discordant—trivial and huge merely. . . .

In the performance I recall nothing disagreeable, nothing that to my ignorance seemed imperfect, though I leave it to the wise in music to say how far the great concert was a success. I saw a flourish of the director's wand, and I heard the voices or the instruments, or both, respond, and I knew by my program that I was enjoying an unprecedented quantity of Haydn or

Handel or Meyerbeer or Rossini or Mozart, afforded with an unquestionable precision and promptness; but I own that I liked better to stroll about the three-acre house, and that for me the music was, at best, only one of the joys of that festival. . . .

❋ ❋ ❋ ❋ ❋

THE WORLD'S PEACE JUBILEE AND INTERNATIONAL MUSICAL FESTIVAL, 1872

❋ 1872 — MURILLO, MUSIC CRITIC

From "Boston," *Church's Musical Visitor* 1/10 (July 1872), 4.

> Writing for *Church's Musical Visitor*, "Murillo" is roundly enthusiastic about the 1872 jubilee but is forced in a later article to report on its dismal financial showing (see page 72).

[Dateline June 18] – We are in the midst of a hurricane of musical sounds. . . . The building was well filled with people from all parts of the United States and the world. Our streets are thronged with spectators and business is almost entirely suspended. Undivided attention is paid to this monster festival, everything else being dropped out of mind. . . .

The grand and massive chorale, "Old Hundredth," which began the musical performances, was given in a broad and stately manner, and the effect produced by the full fortissimo that marked the second verse was inexpressively awe-striking. The tremendous blare of the brass . . . sent a visible thrill through the audience, and taken in connection with the impressive and noble nature of the psalm, the vast numbers engaged in its performance, the solemn and striking simplicity that distinguishes it and seems to peculiarly fit it for the worship of the Most High, created so profound an impression upon the audience that at its conclusion there was an instant or two of profound silence before it broke into an expression of admiration that was almost delirious in the enthusiasm that accompanied it. . . .

It is now fully demonstrated that Mr. Gilmore's "experiment," even though considered one of the most chimerical of the age, and laughed at accordingly by European scoffers and unbelievers, is a success beyond the possibility of a failure, and America has the credit of being the scene of a musical festival on a grander scale than has ever before been dreamed of.

❋ ❋ ❋ ❋ ❋

❋ 1872 — *THE NEW YORK TIMES*

From "Musical Quackery," *New York Times* (20 June 1872), 4.

> Two anonymous *New York Times* reporters disdainfully articulated the musical challenges of providing nuance and delicacy at so large an artistic event, difficulties that purportedly prevented enjoyment by "serious lovers of art."

The Boston Jubilee has been in noisy activity for three days, and has afforded a fair sample of what the rest of its boisterous session will be. From what has already taken place in and about the [Boston] Coliseum, the following conclusions may be drawn.

The affair was not so successful pecuniarily as there was reason to suppose that it would be. . . . The managers naturally expected that every New Englander who could pay his fare to Boston, and had the price of an admission ticket still at his command, would come to the Jubilee. Unfortunately, they forgot that a chorus of twenty thousand, and an orchestra of two thousand, would produce a volume of sound that the wooden walls of the Coliseum could not monopolize. The result has shown that the choral and orchestral music can be heard outside the Coliseum quite as well as inside. The astute New Englander has profited by this fact . . . .

While the singing of Mme. [Minna] Peschka-Leutner . . . has proved an unexpected success, the rest of the soloists have disappointed public expectation. Both chorus and orchestra appear to have acquitted themselves better than could have been expected by those who were aware of the singular deficiency of proper rehearsals with which the Jubilee opened. . . .

As to the character of the program, it has been well adapted to draw a promiscuous [i.e., diverse] audience. . . .

The Jubilee certainly does credit to the energy and perseverance of Mr. Gilmore. It is not, however, a musical event in which the intelligent lover of music can altogether delight. . . .

From "Summary of Amusements," *New York Times* (23 June 1872), 3.

Mr. Gilmore's cherished monstrosity has had quite as much attention as it deserves. While there are features about it of undeniable interest and importance, the general effect is that of a huge, showy sham. The unskillful may laugh or go into fits of enthusiasm over the Peace Jubilee–wherest the initiated and cynical may laugh in their sleeves–but the judicious, the true lovers of art, must surely grieve. . . .

✻ ✻ ✻ ✻ ✻

✻ 1872 — JOHN SULLIVAN DWIGHT, MUSIC CRITIC AND JOURNAL EDITOR

From "The Second Gilmore Jubilee," *Dwight's Journal of Music* 32/8 (13 July 1872), 270-71.

By 1872 Dwight had had enough of the "monster concert" phenomenon in general and Gilmore's incarnation of it in particular. No fan of the first festival, he was irritated to no end by the second one. But while his criticisms of the 1869 event had focused on music and spectacle, his attacks on the World Jubilee were often levied against Gilmore himself and those who helped him organize and pay for it. Dwight clung to a view of aesthetic purity that could not abide "infecting" the art with the "disease of popularity," and the substantial gains made by American publicity and advertising were to him abhorrent. Boston had received international attention for the first jubilee, and the second promised to deliver the same results. In terms of

> marketing and the business of music, Boston was well ahead of its time. Only in recent years have cities begun to realize the economic boom that accompanies a healthy arts environment.

The great, usurping, tyrannizing, noisy and pretentious thing is over, and there is a general feeling of relief, as if a heavy, brooding nightmare had been lifted from us all. Verily the Gilmore dog-star *has* raged, as we anticipated, through a "heated term" of three long, weary, crowded, confused mid-summer weeks, during which one saw nothing, heard nothing, read nothing, ate and drank and breathed nothing but jubilee, jubilee, and everybody suffered from an oppressive sense of *over-much-ness* in the very atmosphere, while all newspaperdom kept up such a multitudinous ringing chorus in praise of our dear old Athens [i.e., Boston], that no one would be surprised to hear her name pronounced hereafter, *Boast-Town*. God forbid! A little modest dignity and self-possession, neighbors, a little less of childish sensitiveness to New York criticism and whether playful or malicious satire, a little less ambition for the display of enterprise on an unprecedented scale, will win the world's respect in the long run more than a thousand "jubilees."

We wish to do all justice to this strange and mammoth enterprise; we would estimate it at its true worth, if possible, and show in what sense and in what degree it has or has not been successful; for *nothing* is distinctly said in that cheap, vague, convenient catchword of the newspapers: the Jubilee is a "success," Gilmore is a "success," etc. But at the outset a puzzling difficulty presents itself in the strangely ambiguous aspect of the whole thing. If it had only been more uniform or more consistent in its professions of its own intention! What did the Jubilee purport to be? One thing today, another thing tomorrow; all things apparently, to all men. If you measured it by its high-Art pretensions, the jubilee advocate would answer: "O you must not judge it from an artistic standpoint; it is not for artists and for refined tastes, it is for the *People*, a people's holiday affair, etc., a magnified, protracted, glorified Fourth of July enthusiasm." But turning to the official advertisement, you found it proclaimed as the greatest musical event in all history. . . .

If to some the Jubilee project wore the face of Music, to others that of Peace or Patriotism, it had still another face for the more numerous and more enterprising class on whom it most relied for solid guaranty and vigorous organizing, advertising energy. It flattered the business pride of our ambitious city in this period of remarkable material expansion. It was to be a great advertisement of Boston, a signal demonstration to the world of Boston business enterprise and means, of Boston organization and good order. It was to crowd hotels and railroad cars, and all our streets for weeks, so that business might increase, and the newspapers have a topic whereon to expatiate without stint, and plain businessmen of enterprise might rise into importance in what seemed to be a patriotic work of culture, and the name of Boston [would] be no more provincial—hard to find upon the globe. This was the point of view in which it was most vigorously pushed; this argument was most used in the appeal for guaranty subscriptions; . . .

In short, the Press being the great medium of advertising, and advertising being the main lever and machine of modern trade, the Press instinctively put all its shoulders to the wheel, and virtually became as much a part of the Peace Jubilee as Gilmore and his Band. The man has always had a knack of managing the Press; he is a rare virtuoso on the paper trumpet, whatever he may be on the brass. . . .

Whatever else it was, it was a thing of most magnificent pretensions. Recall the first official trumpet blast; read that "Prospectus" which the Projector [i.e., Gilmore] circulated through the length and breadth of all the land, likewise in Europe, to impress the general imagination and to "fire the people's heart." What startling promises! A chorus of 20,000 voices, an orchestra of 2,000 instruments, military bands from "every nation," delegations even "from classic Greece and the Holy Land, from Turkey, China, and Japan," etc., etc., unprecedented glory for "God Save the Queen," a Coliseum that "will seat a Hundred Thousand people!" And then, when it came to shaping programs, "the greatest series of concerts ever given in the world," the "greatest chorus ever organized, in *Oratorio selections every day*;" the "orchestra of 1000 skilled musicians in *classical* and popular *Overtures*, *Symphonies*, etc., *each day*;" the "Bouquet of Artists;" "Anvil chorus" with 100 anvils, cannons, all the city bells, *each day*; marvelous pianists on a colossal, marvelous pianoforte, the "greatest living Soprano," other great Sopranos, "the great [Johan] Strauss" (who sets the waltzes whirling), the "great composer [Franz] Abt" (hero of German sentimental part-song clubs)—all this array of talent to "interpret the noblest compositions ever written" to the largest crowd that ever listened! Of course it excited a vast deal of innocent enthusiasm, and of strange, half feverish expectation. . . .

* * * * *

✻ 1872 — MURILLO, MUSIC CRITIC

From "Boston," *Church's Musical Visitor* 1/11 (August 1872), 6.

> Murillo, continuing his chronicle of the festival for *Church's Musical Visitor*, sounded positively dismayed about the event and the legacy it left behind.

[Dateline July 17] – Once more, and probably for the last time, I am to refer somewhat at length to the Jubilee. The great storm of music has passed, and the humdrum of everyday life has returned. . . . Financially the Great International Peace Jubilee and Musical Festival of 1872 may be recorded as a failure, the loss aggregating something like a hundred thousand dollars. . . .

This unfortunate termination of the Jubilee will be everywhere regretted, but it confirms the belief that the enthusiastic Gilmore attempted too much. Certainly he did, so far as musical effect is concerned; for notwithstanding the assurance of the Boston papers that the Jubilee has been "the greatest musical achievement of the age," it will scarcely pass for so much into the pages of history.

* * * * *

✻ 1872 — *THE ATLANTIC MONTHLY*

From "Music," *Atlantic Monthly* 30/179 (September 1872), 376-79.

One of the more balanced assessments of the 1872 festival was delivered by an unidentified writer for *Atlantic Monthly* who noted the financial problems and the generally low standard of musical culture that accompanied this event. He also acknowledged that it filled a void by exposing many people—especially the participating choristers—to fine music. In an interesting twist of logic the writer asserted that, because the 1869 festival increased the general appreciation and knowledge of music among New Englanders, attendance suffered at the later festival because of the generally low standard of the offerings.

At last the Jubilee is over. The monster whose coming was heralded some months ago by such portentous rumblings in and about the Hub [Boston], and whose fitful career was anxiously followed by the eyes and ears of so many thousands, has in its turn become a thing of the past. Its career at times has been a brilliant, at times a sluggish, at all times an almost oppressive one. But if the monster came in like a lion, it certainly went out like the mildest of lambs; and even in its leonine days of vigorous youth, its roar was neither so terrible nor so lion-like as those who like roaring might have desired. . . .

We think the Jubilee, on the whole, a failure, as whatever results were attained were vastly disproportionate to the means employed. We have hinted that this failure was owing to the want of any unity of purpose in the whole scheme. The thing tried to be too many things at once. It tried to combine a music festival with a sort of all-the-world's Fourth of July; even the musical part of it was with too indefinite an artistic purpose. The programs were from the first rather generally conciliatory than guided by any artistic principle, either good or bad; there was a want of backbone about the musical arrangement of the whole. . . .

The most interesting as well as the most successful part of the Jubilee was the appearance of the French, English, and German bands. Apart from the musical excellence of their various performances, the evident friendly feeling between them and the audience was in itself something worth witnessing. This was particularly noticeable in the reception of the English band. The whole audience seemed to welcome them as brothers and kinsmen; and when at last they responded to the continued applause with the "Star-Spangled Banner," which was in turn answered by "Auld Lang Syne," a feeling came over all present deeper than that to be roused even by the noblest music. Considered musically, the French band was the most artistic. . . . The Germans played with great fire and precision, but in loud passages they greatly overblew their instruments, especially their low brass. . . . Another interesting point in the Jubilee was Johann Strauss's conducting. There was a demoniac, electric *je ne sais quoi* about the man that was peculiarly fascinating. His command over the orchestra was simply wonderful; they were like an instrument with him, and he played upon the men under his *baton* just as much as he played upon the violin in his hands. Hearing his waltzes led by himself, after having heard them played by [Theodore] Thomas's orchestra, was like hearing our old friend of the ballroom, Mr. J. S. Knight, play them, after the matter-of-fact strumming of some school girl. . . .

And now a word as to the advisability of jubilees of this sort from a purely musical and educational point of view. First, as to the good they do. It may be safely said that fully half of the members of the chorus would never have become acquainted with much of the better class of choral music but for these festivals. The months spent in careful rehearsal of even one of these

Bach chorales, and a few Handel, Haydn, and Mendelssohn choruses, cannot fail to be of great benefit to a large class of music lovers who would otherwise in all probability never have studied anything better than common choir psalmody or poor street ballads. The performances of the foreign bands were no doubt of benefit, and we hope to see some consequent improvement in our own bands in the future. So far, good. But, on the other hand, great harm is done by creating in the general public an unnatural and perverted appetite for what is merely big, rather than for what is great and good, a craving after quantity rather than an appreciation of quality. Even though a large mass of the public probably heard fine specimens of classic music for the first time on coming to the Jubilee, the performance of the music was, from the nature of things, so vaguely imperfect and ineffective that little if any real good can be hoped from their making its acquaintance in such a manner. Enterprises like the Jubilee are only pardonable on the supposition of a very low degree of general musical culture in this country, and we think the small success of the last one, as compared with the Festival of 1869, shows that our people have already made a great advance in musical culture. We are not prepared to deny that the first Jubilee may have been an important agent in educating them up to this point. If it was, it certainly did a good work, and Mr. Gilmore should now be content to repose on his fairly earned laurels. But for the future it must be borne in mind that the people have been educated up to the appreciation of something better.

* * * * *

✻ 1899 — Thomas Ryan, Violist and Chamber Musician

From *Recollections of an Old Musician* (New York: E. P. Dutton, 1899), 198-203.

> Thomas Ryan (1827-1903), reflecting on the second jubilee nearly thirty years after its passing, commented on its importance to America's vigorous band movement and on its impact on Gilmore's posthumous reputation. Unlike many other commentators who were largely detractors, Ryan's appreciation of Gilmore's efforts was genuine.

The second Jubilee was held in 1872, and, like all repetitions of a similar nature, it was found to be impossible to get up a popular excitement equal to that which attended the first one. It was therefore not a financial success. The new building designed for it, and everything else, was on a larger scale, and not so easily handled. There were some notably fine features, but the whole was less of a strictly home affair.

Gilmore's plans again showed his genius. They were bold, well conceived, but very costly. He went to Europe, and "talked the crown heads" (that was the popular phrase) "into letting their crack" military bands come over to play in the Jubilee. He obtained the band of the Grenadier Guards from London, about forty-five strong, under Dan Godfrey; a German infantry band, about thirty-five men, under [Heinrich J.] Saro; and that of the Garde Republicaine, from Paris, of about forty-five men. It was said that this latter was reinforced by fine artists from the opera, and was not therefore a fair sample of French bands. There was also a little insignificant band, the Royal Constabulary, from Ireland.

These bands had an English day, and German, French, and Irish days. The English band was good, the German, too brassy, the French, magnificent. . . . Their performance of the *William Tell* Overture was superb.

It is to be remembered that, in 1872, the political antagonism between the French and Germans was great. The Franco-Prussian War had left rankling hatred between the two peoples. The sight of a German to a Frenchman was like shaking a red rag in the face of a bull; consequently, on the day the French band of La Garde Republicaine marched down the broad aisle in full uniform, surrounded (in their imagination) by their enemies, the German musicians, it was certainly an anxious moment for the Frenchmen. It seemed to me—perhaps it was the effect of the sympathetic current created by the situation—that they were pale with anxiety. It was to be their battlefield; they were to be judged by prejudiced listeners, and they were on their mettle.

The performance of the band was musically so perfect that all prejudice was annihilated. Metaphorically the Germans embraced the Frenchmen; we were all of one brotherhood—politics and race differences had vanished—the music had disarmed all evil spirits. We were simply musicians, ready to award praise to merit. When the band ended the overture, the players all about them were as wild in their applause as the general public. And I am sure I saw some of the Frenchmen wipe away tears of joy at their well-won victory. Mr. Gilmore had cap-tured several rare lions and lionesses for his musical menagerie, chief among whom was the royal lion, Johann Strauss—the famous waltz composer from Vienna—and Madame [Minna] Peschhka-Leutner, a coloratura singer of extraordinary ability. This lady captivated her audiences with her clear, telling, high, and powerful soprano voice, her almost matchless execution, style, and other rare vocal gifts. She was a genuine success.

Then there was a Madame [Hermine] Rudersdorf, a splendid singer, of broad, classic, oratorio style. She was of great value to the city of Boston, for she settled there and became a teacher of teachers.

Strauss, violin in hand, conducted the orchestra daily, in one of his most popular waltzes, and also in some little knick-knacks, such as the *Pizzicato Polka*, which became at once a great favorite. His manner of conducting was very animating. He led off with the violin bow to give the *tempo*, but when the right swing was obtained and the melody was singing out from the orchestra, he joined in with his fiddle as if he *must* take part in the intoxication of the waltz. While playing or conducting he commonly kept his body in motion, rising and falling on his toes in a really graceful manner. . . .

This second Jubilee had a "coda," or tail, in the shape of a financial deficit, but the noble army of martyr guarantors "faced the music" like men.

Mr. Gilmore reached the apogee of his greatness at the period of the festivals. To conceive and carry out such plans showed much forethought and executive ability. First, to get those large military bands over from Europe—foreseeing that it would set the European world to talking of Gilmore and his band—was a pretty big thing; then to follow it up (after he moved to New York City) by actually taking his New York band over to Great Britain, France, Germany, and (I think) Italy, was certainly not only bearding the lion in his den, or carrying coals to Newcastle, but it was undertaking a financial venture of the most uncertain kind—and yet Mr. Gilmore, with clear vision of success in his eyes, boldly carried out the project, and returned from Europe with all his colors flying.

I think it can be seen that the brave, loyal bandmaster, Patrick Sarsfield Gilmore, filled a good page in the musical and social history of our country. We hopefully believe he now rests in peace.

* * * * *

THE "REVIVIFIED" JUBILEE, 1889

* 1889 — LOUIS C. ELSON, MUSIC HISTORIAN, MUSIC EDITOR, AND MUSIC CRITIC

From "Music in Boston," *Musical Visitor* (July 1889), 178.

> In 1889 Gilmore and his band appeared again in Boston for a series of concerts that Elson (1848-1920), writing under the pseudonym "Proteus," dubbed the "revivified Jubilee." That he referred to the original event a full twenty years after it occurred gives an idea of the lasting impact of Gilmore's Jubilee on Americans of the day, especially those hailing from Boston.

"Gilmore the great and his wonderful band," said the glaring posters on the walls of Boston last week, and the tawdry style of the announcement quite accurately heralded the tawdry style of the revivified Jubilee. Gilmore's band is an excellent organization so far as its brasses are concerned, but its woodwind is very frequently out of tune, and one E-flat clarinet seemed to be playing a solo all the time. Besides, one does not care to hear Wagner and Weber overtures, which demand the delicacy of [an] orchestra, given by a brass band at a constant fortissimo. The climax of this species of absurdity was reached when two movements of Beethoven's [piano] sonata [Op. 13] "Pathétique" were given. Fancy this work arranged for brass band. . . . The concerts (nine in number) were all well patronized, and proved beyond doubt that there is a very large public in Boston, as elsewhere, who do not rise to the symphonic level, and whose want can be catered to in a more noisy manner. Well, I shall quarrel with no one's taste, and surely enjoyment of a good brass band is better than not enjoying music at all; only I could wish Gilmore "the great" to let the classical works rest in peace.

* * * * *

Swedish violinist Ole Bull was renowned for both his virtuosity and his onstage theatrics. Like many stars of the day, Bull toured throughout the United States. He is pictured here circa 1865.

Courtesy of the Brady-Handy Photograph Collection, Prints and Photographs Division, Library of Congress: LC-DIG-cwpbh-01994.

⁂ 6 — Performers and Personalities

1862 – John Sullivan Dwight
From "Gottschalk in Boston–Then and Now"
From "Gottschalk's Concerts"

1864 – Louis Moreau Gottschalk
From *Notes of a Pianist*

1872 – *Scribner's Monthly*
From "Culture and Progress: Music"

1886 – *Century Magazine*
From "The American Opera Company"

1894 – William Foster Apthorp
From "John Sullivan Dwight,"
Musicians and Music-lovers and Other Essays

1896 – Albert L. Parkes
From "Great Singers of This Century"

1898 – William Foster Apthorp
From "Some Not Wholly Random Speculations about Paganini,"
By the Way

1901 – William Mason
From "Thomas as Conductor,"
Memories of a Musical Life

1903 – *The New York Times*
From "Opera Season Opens with Great Éclat"

1913 – Amy Fay
From Letter to Madeline Smith

1917 – Richard Aldrich
From "The Passing of the Kneisel Quartet"

A great deal of America's musical culture has been shaped not by American composers, but by performers, conductors, and critics whose impact often reached far beyond that of a typical composer. While large and important centers of music such as New York City, Boston, Chicago, St. Louis, and San Francisco engaged much of our attention because they were home to major institutions, legions of soloists and chamber musicians toured zealously throughout the American hinterland. There were several contributors to the popularity of art music in this age. The widespread emphasis by Americans on their own self-improvement encouraged concert attendance, and a rapidly developing transportation system enabled musicians to take their talents to many smaller cities, towns, and villages. Likewise, the proliferation of music periodicals and the rapid growth of the postal service just after the Civil War gave critics—and artists' managers who were eager to publicize their musicians—a larger audience than they had previously enjoyed.

✻ 1862 — JOHN SULLIVAN DWIGHT, MUSIC CRITIC AND JOURNAL EDITOR

From "Gottschalk in Boston–Then and Now," *Dwight's Journal of Music* 32/2 (11 October 1862), 222-23.

The following three excerpts offer a glimpse into one of the more compelling feuds in American music history, that between composer / pianist Louis Moreau Gottschalk (1829-1869) and critic John Sullivan Dwight (1813-1893). At issue was Dwight's insistence on the performance of recognized "classics" of piano literature and his appreciation of thoughtful restraint and the civilizing effects of music, which contrasted sharply with Gottschalk's flamboyant, theatrical playing and his body of original compositions that drew on many sources including African and Caribbean. In truth, Dwight admired Gottschalk's piano playing but reviled his popularity and thought that the pianist's efforts to remain popular (by performing widely and composing affable music) inhibited what was obviously an enormous talent. For his part, Gottschalk seems to have cared but little. He continued to compose music—several of his best-known works date from the mid-1860s—and he toured widely in both the United States and South America.

Mr. Gottschalk, the great pianist, and great theme of controversy, is again announced in Boston. It is nine years since his first and last appearance here before, when he gave only two concerts, under not perhaps the most favorable circumstances, and with so much less than his accustomed brilliancy of outward success, that it appears to have soured his temper with regard to Boston ever since, and to have put this naughty "Athens" [Boston] under ban, dooming it to the terrible "punishment" of being passed by on the other side by the indignant artist, while other cities, even the "rural districts" right about us, have been refreshed by the Olympian rain.

with which Christine Nilsson closes her cycle of one hundred appearances in opera on this side of the ocean. It would be labor wasted to aim at new statements or more profound appreciation of the great singer, and her potent charm over our feelings or our imagination. Out of the mass of conflicting opinion and statement which her visit here has called forth two facts stand out in unmistakable distinctness. That she is, on the whole, a noble executant, seems admitted even by those who except and carp at what they allege as special points of technical shortcoming. Her great merit, in this respect, is indisputably the value of *vocal emission*. Whatever her merits or demerits in other regards, in purity of tone formation, in the admirable way in which she *gets her voice out of her*, Christine Nilsson has exceptional power. And when we consider how strong is the sway of this silvery purity of tone—this *spiritual spontaneity* of musical utterance —over the feelings and imagination of susceptible people, it is not strange that we should exercise upon her auditors a fascination which passes from the artistic to the personal, and blends the warmer tones of individual sentiment with the calmer aesthetic judgment.

This personal spell is only deepened by her dramatic skill. She has little of the effusive passion of the conventional Italian school, but, instead, a calm and thoughtful depth of conception, which appeals to the cultivated taste far more powerfully than the spasmodic and superficial intensity of [Verdian] sentiment. Miss Nilsson's peculiar power is quite as much temperamental and individual as artistic in the narrower sense. She represents the force of a clear brain and strong, healthy, magnetic nature, quite as much as that of a merely perfected technique. . . .

* * * * *

✻ 1886 — *CENTURY MAGAZINE*

From "The American Opera Company," *Century Magazine* 32/1 (May 1886), 162-63.

> German-born musician Theodore Thomas (1835-1905) began his career as a violinist and became one the first great American orchestral conductors. He was widely regarded as an expert opera conductor as well, but this aspect of his career is seldom considered today. The two seasons he led the American Opera Company, an important English language-only organization, were of watershed importance in American opera history. Two entries included here chronicle this operatic side of Thomas's genius (see also page 88).

After one of the early rehearsals of [Hermann Goetz's] *The Taming of the Shrew*, by the American Opera Company, a member of the orchestra said, "That's splendid music; *it's too good for opera*." The remark shows what opera is often supposed to be—an exhibition of a few stars against an insignificant background. The interest of the performance is monopolized by three or four artists; the orchestra is only an accessory; the chorus only [a] bridge over intervals, and [intended to] help things along. For this kind of opera the elaborate instrumental music of *The Taming of the Shrew* would perhaps have been too good. But our contemptuous fiddler found out presently that opera would not be given by an American company on the easy old plan. The representations under Theodore Thomas's direction were distinguished for the careful manner in which all the agencies of musical and dramatic expression were fitted together in an organized work of art. Parts which are commonly neglected as subordinate were raised to their proper rank as factors in the general result. . . .

This close knitting together of all the parts—something much more than we usually mean when we speak of the *ensemble*—was the characteristic note of the representations which Thomas began at the New York Academy of Music last January. He plays opera as he would play a symphony. To him it is a symphony of voices and instruments. The incomparable orchestra, the fresh young chorus, always correct, sure, and in tune, the whole assembly of stars and satellites, respond to his command, and respond together, exactly as the well-trained band answers him, as if by one impulse, in Beethoven's [Symphony No. 3] *Eroica*. Thus it is not only in the singing of soprano or tenor that we feel the glow of passion, but the whole mass is burning with magnetic fervor. . . . This symphonic method of playing an opera cannot be taught by written directions on the musical page; it depends upon the conductor's musical insight, sympathy, and poetical temperament, together with an exceptional power of control over his subordinates. Many intelligent conductors who have the requisite delicacy of feeling never acquire the art of communicating their intentions to the performers, and so they fail.

There was a remarkable example of Thomas's control of the whole stage in the "Invocation" of the first act of [Wagner's] *Lohengrin*. With slight gestures he restrained one part, enlivened and accented another, disentangled the theme from the crowded score, heaped effect upon effect until the swelling orchestra quivered with sensibility; then, lifting his hand towards the scene, he loosed little by little the growing tide of voices, and at last hurled all the impatient forces together in an outburst that thrilled the house. Of course the remarkable crescendo is indicated in the score; but just think how many years we had to wait before a conductor brought out its full splendor. . . .

There we saw great conducting! There we had also an earnest [introduction to] the high artistic purpose with which the new enterprise seems to have taken up its work. An American Opera Company which begins its career with such an achievement takes rank at once as a very important institution.

* * * * *

✻ 1894 — WILLIAM FOSTER APTHORP, MUSIC AND DRAMA CRITIC AND WRITER ON MUSIC

From "John Sullivan Dwight," *Musicians and Music-lovers and Other Essays* (New York: C. Scribner's Sons, 1894), 277-86.

The Boston writer John Sullivan Dwight (1813-1893) was a leading music critic of his day. Today he is often ridiculed for his "conservative" outlook and his amateur status, but among musicians the reviews he published in his outstanding *Journal of Music* over the twenty-nine years of its existence were largely considered authoritative. It was widely recognized that a good review by Dwight put the stamp of approval on a composition or a perform-

ance for a majority of his readership. The present essay by a fellow leading music critic in Boston tells the seldom-told story of Dwight the optimist.

The remarkable man who just passed away was one of the most unique figures Boston has ever claimed as her own. Men of naturally fine and sensitive artistic nature, yet without productive promptings, are not very uncommon; neither is it very seldom that we find a man of this sort who has been content to develop his aesthetic bent in a wholly general way, without giving much heed to the minutiae of special, quasi-technical cultivation in any particular direction. But it is exceedingly seldom that one finds such a man pass a long life in intimate, almost daily, communion with literature and the fine arts, and preserve intact all the native spontaneity and naiveté of his feelings, so that he remains quite free from any taint of self-conscious dilettantism, and wholly uninfluenced by merely artificial standards.

What most made Dwight remarkable was his inveterate instinct for culture—as distinguished from mere learning. Perhaps it may have been in large measure a certain unconquerable mental indolence that prompted him always to take the royal road in everything, to skip lightly over the dry rudiments of every study—or what to men otherwise disposed would have been study—and abort immediately what he could of its final essence. Mentally indolent he certainly was to a high degree; he abominated work; the necessity for work seemed to him, upon the whole, a sad mistake in the scheme of the universe. And, though he did a good deal of it, first and last, in the course of his life, it was never otherwise than irksome to him; he worked, as it were, under protest. . . .

Dwight's artistic gift was of a very general sort. His choice of music from among the fine arts as his daily companion through life was undoubtedly less owing to any special aptitude than to the extraordinary vividness and intensity with which musical impressions affect almost all artistic natures. Music was the art which could be enjoyed most intensely, immediately, and with the least effort; so he took to music. What Carlyle called that "kind of inarticulate, unfathomable speech, which leads us to the edge of the infinite, and lets us for moments gaze into that," was just the art of all others to appeal most irresistibly to a dreamy, sybaritic, intellectually luxurious nature like Dwight's. His life-long communion with it was, as it were, predestined. . .

He never developed anything that could fairly be called a musical facility; he never handled musical notation with the ease of a craftsman, and always found some difficulty in following performances from the score, especially when things went at a rapid tempo. His naturally musical ear never developed to more than an average pitch of delicacy; technical slips seldom disturbed him, and "rough performances" fully satisfied him, if only the right spirit was there.

Yet, with and in spite of all this, his musical instincts and perceptions were, in a certain high respect, of the finest. He was irresistibly drawn toward what is pure, noble, and beautiful, and felt these things with infinite keenness; he had an inborn and unconquerable horror of the merely grandiose, of what is big without being great, of the factitiously intense, of the trivial and the vulgar. He was an optimist, through and through, and wished all art to be as optimistic as himself; what was morbid had little attraction for him, and the divinities he most worshipped were the "healthy, eupeptic" composers: Bach, Handel, Haydn, Mozart, Gluck, Beethoven, Schubert, Weber, and Mendelssohn. Of the more morbidly sensitive and analytically introspective composers he could sympathize only with those in whom he found morbid sensibility constantly cured and atoned for by immaculate beauty and perfect clarity of expression, such as

Schumann and Chopin. His utter distaste for music of the more modern schools, for Berlioz, Liszt, Wagner, and even Raff and Brahms, has too often been ascribed to sheer prejudice. No doubt prejudice did play some part in the matter; these modern men came upon Dwight somewhat late in life, when, although he retained all his naiveté and enthusiasm, his musical receptivity had become to a certain extent anchylosed into immobility, and he found it difficult to throw off old habits and adopt new points of view. But there was nevertheless a deeper and more solid ground for his abhorrence of these composers: the whole essentially modern spirit which pervades their work, with all of its high-strung nervous energy, restless striving, and lack of serenity and repose, the way their music reflects the characteristic strenuousness and turmoil of modern life, were totally antipathetic to his nature. He was essentially a Hellene and an idealist; any too drastic and realistic presentation of the morbid side of life shocked his finer sensibilities and seemed to him unworthy of the sacredness of Art.

* * * * *

✻ 1896 — ALBERT L. PARKES, THEATRICAL MANAGER AND WRITER

From "Great Singers of This Century," *Godey's Magazine* 133/794 (August 1896), 177-83.

> Italian operatic tenor Italo Campanini (1845-1896) was revered in the second half of the nineteenth century. While not the first opera star to create excitement in the United States, he was a clear favorite among the cognoscenti in New York's burgeoning opera circles. A deft artist with charm and international performance credentials, Campanini gave local premieres of numerous works, including an Italian version of Wagner's *Lohengrin*.

In these days of massive operatic compositions, with their wearing demands upon delicately sensitive and highly cultivated vocal organs, many old opera habitués recall pleasant recollections of that bygone, melodic half of this century when orchestra brasses and drums were subordinated to such harmonic requirements as aided and embellished the singer's work. At that period ear-stunning orchestral effects were sparsely and judiciously utilized for contrast and variety, while the main aim of opera composers and producers was to create lyric vehicles to demonstrate the marvelous possibilities of the human voice. . . .

Operatic impresarii, taught by experience, invariably pin their financial faith to the magnetism exercised upon the public ear and eye by young, pretty and talented women, yet there are exceptional years when a tenor's good looks and captivating voice prove to be a source of joyful profit to ticket speculators within and without the customary "choice" reserved-seat combinations. In this category, Signor Italo Campanini ruled New York's fashionable roost for several seasons, despite his having been a married man, with a loving and watchful wife, whose constant companionship evidently conduced to their mutual happiness. This makes it clear that Signor Campanini's great popularity here resulted from his commanding talents as a lyric artist of the first class and to his alert keenness as a business man. . . .

[Gounod's] *Faust* and [Wagner's] *Lohengrin* were the mediums chosen for Campanini's initial appearances [in New York in 1874], and the warmth of his reception fully attested the effect wrought upon the expectant hearers by his sympathetic voice, manly bearing and artistic phrasing. He bounded into general favor and at one leap mounted the pedestal of fashionable interest, heretofore so long occupied by Signor [Pasquale] Brignoli. . . .

Signor Campanini's emotional singing of "Salve dimore" [from *Faust*] and the ardency of his love-making in the garden scene carried the audience by storm. Later on, as Rhadames in Verdi's *Aida*, Campanini's soldierly bearing, his passionate declamation and artistic singing conquered criticism and caused him to become fashionable town talk.

Tenors, especially when much petted, are only mortal, and the Academy [of Music] green-room gossipers began to intimate that the new favorite had fallen prey to enlargement of the cranium. This, to a limited extent, was pardonable because the descendants of Brignoli's admirers hungered for a change of tenor diet, and Campanini supplied this in appetizing abundance. . . .

❊ ❊ ❊ ❊ ❊

❊ 1898 — William Foster Apthorp, Music and Drama Critic and Writer on Music

From "Some Not Wholly Random Speculations about Paganini," *By the Way* (Boston: Copeland and Day, 1898), 11-23.

> The legendary Norwegian violinist Ole Bull (1810-1880) was known equally for his incredible, if unconventional, technique and for a famously flamboyant personality. Bull toured the United States tirelessly. In 1843 he toured for two years and gave over 200 concerts. He maintained a similarly rigorous schedule through four more well-attended tours until 1880. Bull's fiery violin playing, dashing good looks, and theatrical stage gestures contributed to make him one of America's earliest "matinee idols."

The last remnant of this sort of violin playing in our day was probably to be found in Ole Bull. He was, to be sure, an eccentric, unquestionably great as his technical virtuosity was; ask any musician who ever heard him, and he will tell you that Ole Bull's style was, to say the least, excessive. But he had a very distinct and appealing personality, and used to make people cry by the bucketful; no man drew larger audiences, nor drove them to wilder raptures. He, too, would play a phrase as if its extent and significance were boundless; in him you still found the old grand violin style, though pushed to singular extremes. . . .

Ole Bull has sometimes been described as "[Niccolò] Paganini, *only more so*;" but I have my grave doubts as to the extent of the *more so*. Look carefully at the anecdotic history of the two men, and you will find quite surprising points of resemblance. The peculiar, magical influence they exerted upon the general musical public was very similar; it was, in a certain sense, diabolic and partaking of the nature of witchcraft. Both were purely solo players; Paganini, to be sure, had, at one time, a fondness for playing the first violin part in Beethoven quartets: but the result is reported to have been a tragicomic failure; none of the three other players could keep time with him, when he played as he wished to—and when he played fairly and squarely, he had no effect. I think that anyone who ever heard Ole Bull would guess that his quartet-playing must have amounted to pretty much the same thing. Again, let any musician who never heard either Paganini or Ole Bull play look through the music each one of them wrote for himself; he will stand aghast at such music's ever having moved great crowds to enthusiasm and the verge of hysteria. Paganini's has more to say for itself than Ole Bull's; but the so much lauded magic is now discoverable in neither. This magic unquestionably resided in the overpowering personality of the two players; also, to a great extent, in their peculiar styles of playing. And what I suspect is that their styles were in many—perhaps in most—respects very similar. . . .

* * * * *

✻ 1901 — WILLIAM MASON, PIANIST, COMPOSER, AND PEDAGOGUE

From "Thomas as Conductor," *Memories of a Musical Life* (New York: The Century Company, 1901), 197-202.

> Theodore Thomas (1835-1905) has long been heralded as one of the most —if not the most—important figures in nineteenth-century American art music. Although famous for his interpretations of classic symphonic works, especially the Beethoven symphonies, less is generally known about his skills as an instrumentalist and as a conductor of opera. These brief insights by William Mason (1829-1908), who played chamber music with Thomas in the 1850s and 1860s, offer a glimpse of Thomas's musicianship and personality that is rarely considered.

Thomas's fame as a conductor has entirely overshadowed his earlier reputation as a violinist. He had a large tone, the tone of a player of the highest rank. He lacked the perfect finish of a great violinist, but he played in a large, quiet, and reposeful manner. This seemed to pass from his violin playing to his conducting, in which there was the same sense of largeness and dignity, coupled, however, with the artistic finish which he lacked as a violinist. He is a very great conductor, the greatest we have ever had here, not only in the Beethoven symphonies and other classical music, but in Liszt, Wagner, and the extreme moderns. Why should he not conduct Wagner as well as anybody else, or better? Everything is large about Wagner, and everything is large about Thomas. His rates of tempo are in accord with those of the most celebrated conductors whom I heard fifty years ago. In modern times the tendency has been toward an increased rate of speed, and this detracts in large measure from the impressiveness of the works, especially those of Mozart, Beethoven, von Weber, and others. . . .

That Thomas had entire confidence in himself was shown in the outset of his career. One evening, as he came home tired out from his work, and after dinner had settled himself in a comfortable place for a good rest, a message came to him from the Academy of Music, about two blocks from his house [on] East Twelfth Street. An opera season was in progress there, and, what was not unusual, the management was in financial difficulties. [Karl] Anschutz, who was the conductor of the orchestra, had refused to take the desk unless paid what was due him. The orchestra was in its place, the audience was seated, but there was no conductor. Would Thomas come to the rescue? He had never conducted opera, and the work of the evening's performance was an opera with which he was unfamiliar [Donizetti's *La favorite*]. Here was a life's opportunity, and Thomas was equal to the occasion. He thought for a moment, then said, "I will." He rose quickly, got himself into his dress-suit, hurried to the Academy of Music, and conducted the opera as if it were a common experience. He was not a man to say, "Give me time until next week." He was always ready for every opportunity.

* * * * *

* 1903 — *THE NEW YORK TIMES*

From "Opera Season Opens with Great Éclat," *New York Times* (24 November 1903), 1.

> Neapolitan tenor Enrico Caruso (1873-1921) is widely regarded among the greatest singers of the twentieth century. He made his debut at New York's Metropolitan Opera in a 1903 production of Verdi's *Rigoletto*. This review of the opening night not only provided commentary about Caruso's legendary voice and his promise for the future, but the reviewer also hinted at the elaborate social trappings that accompanied the event.

Resplendent in new decorations, under a new manager, with every promise of public support such as has never before been given to opera in New York, the Metropolitan Opera House was reopened last evening in a blaze of glory, so far as glory could inhere in a performance of *Rigoletto*. The occasion was an auspicious one, brilliant in every way that wealth and love of luxury and of the outward glitter of artistic things can create brilliancy.

So far as the eye could see or the ear could hear, there was promise of success for the operatic season that was ushered in by last evening's performance of *Rigoletto*. What questions the inward voice of experience and of prophecy may have suggested were drowned in the universal acclaim. The house was filled with an enormous audience, lovers of music and devotees of fashion, not only seats but standing places being entirely filled.

Old *habitués* of the house admired the new decorations that have transformed the interior and that make it a place of festal and dignified appearance. The dull gold and its touches of deep red and the red of the boxes make it a glowing setting for the audience, and the proscenium arch, with a design that shows the brain and skill of an artist, instead of the fretted and meaningless filigree that has adorned it in recent years, afford a frame for the picture on the stage that increases and harmonizes with its brilliancy. . . .

Whether or not there is any significance to be put upon the opening of the season with a work that has been so far outgrown by the public taste as *Rigoletto* is not now to be determined. The opera did not greatly matter. Its performance was in every way superb. It signalized the first performance of one of the most important of Mr. [Heinrich] Conried's new artists, one upon whom much will depend during the coming season—Enrico Caruso, who took the part of the Duke. He made a highly favorable impression, and he went far to substantiate the reputaion that had preceded him to this country. He is an Italian in all his fiber, and his singing and acting are characteristic of what Italy now affords in those arts. His voice is purely a tenor in its quality, of a high range, and of large power, but inclined to take on the "white" quality in its upper ranges when he lets it forth. In mezzo voce [half voice] it has expressiveness and flexibility, and when so used its beauty is most apparent. Mr. Caruso appeared last evening capable of intelligence and of passion in both his singing and his acting, and gave reason to believe in his value as an acquisition to the company.

* * * * *

✻ 1913 — AMY FAY, PIANIST AND LECTURER

From Letter to Madeline Smith (27 November 1913), *More Letters of Amy Fay: The American Years, 1879-1916*, ed. S. Margaret William McCarthy (Detroit: Information Coordinators, 1986), 141-45.

> Over the course of a long career Polish pianist and composer Ignaz Paderewski (1860-1941) gave hundreds of concerts in nearly every major city in the United States and many small ones. Like Ole Bull, Paderewski was an enormously popular figure who maintained a grueling recital schedule that quickly made him rich. He was also admired as a philanthropist who gave generously to artistic and humanitarian causes. One of these was the highly sought-after "Paderewski Prize" in composition, offered to composers of American birth. Amy Fay, an American pianist who had studied with Franz Liszt for a summer, is the author of a celebrated American book on music, *Music-Study in Germany* (1880).

I have been to three recitals of Paderewski, and that idol still remains on his throne, unapproachably great! The beautiful red gold has gone out of his hair, utterly, and left it somewhat grizzled, although still plentiful. It is such a pity, as it takes all the brightness out of his stage appearance. He cuts his hair shorter, and the golden locks do not fly back, as he walks. Still, he is a commanding artistic personality and the public goes mad over him greater than ever! . . .

Paddy's third recital took place on Saturday afternoon, and he was in his very best form, and at the top notch of his powers. The program was perfect, and his vast audience was entranced with delight! . . . The hall was just one roaring mob shouting bravos, and Steinway's men had to come and roll away the grand piano, while the lights were turned out on the stage, after Paderewski had played five encores! He was in a most joyous mood and entirely satisfied with himself! This is his last appearance prior to his departure for the west today, going first to St. Louis then Detroit, Cleveland, Chicago, etc.! . . . Paderewski played two sonatas at his last concert, Beethoven's in D minor, op. 31, no. 2 [*Tempest*], and Schumann's enormously difficult and colossal one in F sharp minor [Op. 11, No. 1]. This work he gave a wonderful interpretation of, and it is considered the touchstone of achievement by the great virtuosi. For one of his closing encore pieces he played the familiar Prelude in A Flat [Op. posth.] by Chopin, with the bell tone in the bass, expressly for me (he said afterwards) as he had heard me say that I liked it. . . .

* * * * *

✻ 1917 — RICHARD ALDRICH, MUSIC CRITIC

From "The Passing of the Kneisel Quartet," *New York Herald* (1 April 1917); reprinted *Concert Life in New York, 1902-1923* (New York: G. P. Putnam's Sons, 1941), 536-40.

> Violinist Franz Kneisel (1865-1926) was enticed to the United States in 1885 by the offer of the position of concertmaster of the Boston Symphony Orchestra. The following year he founded the Kneisel String Quartet, which performed widely until 1917. The quartet became famous for its impeccable readings of standard quartet literature, but Kneisel was also a champion of the American composer. The quartet gave many native composers a first chance to hear their works. A student of John Knowles Paine at Harvard and an associate of Henry Edward Krehbiel, Richard Aldrich (1863-1937) enjoyed prominence as the music critic for *The New York Times* during the early decades of the twentieth century.

Next Tuesday will see the passing of the Kneisel Quartet, so far as its public concerts are concerned. With the close of its career will be ended an important chapter of musical history in this country. This will be a great sorrow and a great loss to many music lovers in New York and many other places in the United States, where the influence of the Quartet has made itself felt. The time never seems ripe for the ending of a career that has meant much in musical education, enjoyment and the unceasing maintenance of the highest standard. . . .

Mr. Kneisel came to Boston in 1885, a boy of 20, to succeed Bernhard Listemann as the concertmaster of the Boston Symphony Orchestra, then entering its fifth year. Young as he was, he had already had a similar experience as the concertmaster of [Benjamin] Bilse's famous orchestra in Berlin, and still earlier of the orchestra of the Hofburg Theater in Vienna. . . .

Henry L. Higginson may properly be credited with the foundation of the Kneisel Quartet, as of the Boston Symphony Orchestra. A quartet of the first rank was a part of his scheme, as well as an orchestra of the first rank. For several years he was the financial backer of the Quartet, as well as of the orchestra. . . .

The career of the Kneisel Quartet in its earliest years in New York was by no means an easy one. The taste for chamber music had not been so developed in this city as to assure sufficient support for its concerts, and after a time it was on the point of giving up its venture here. The persuasion of a few ardent music lovers induced another trial; the turning point arrived and the public, finally educated to the appreciation of what was offered it in these concerts, came to give a firm and unwavering support to Mr. Kneisel and his associates that has endured without interruption to the present time. In this New York repeated the experience of many other cities and towns in this country. Like them it owes a debt to this organization that is hard to compute.

The interest in chamber music, the appreciation of the highest possibilities of its performance, the knowledge of many of the greatest compositions in this form of art were cultivated to the highest point by the Kneisel Quartet. There were earlier workers in the field, pioneers to whom honor and credit are due, and who shall not be forgotten. But the Kneisel Quartet reached a higher level than was attained by any of them, and has exercised a correspondingly greater influence. It has been one of the greatest forces for good in the musical history of this country.

* * * * *

Oil magnate and philanthropist John D. Rockefeller was not known to be especially interested in music, but like all wealthy and educated people of the era, he and his family were expected to cultivate the finer things. This photograph (ca. 1909) shows the music room—complete with a built-in organ—at his New York estate, Kykuit. During later renovations the organ was removed.

Courtesy of the Library of Congress Prints and Photographs Division: LC USZ62-90324.

❊ 7 — Music, Government, and Private Enterprise

Copyright

1867 – James Parton
From "International Copyright"

1884 –George Parsons Lathrop
From "The Present State of the Copyright Movement"

1885 – B. M. [Brander Mathews]
From "Another Side of the Copyright Question"

1887 – Horatio Parker
From "International Copyright of Music–
Opinions of American Musicians"

1887 – George Whitefield Chadwick
From "International Copyright of Music–
Opinions of American Musicians"

1889 – *American Art Journal*
From "Music Publishing and American Composers"

1890 – Henry Cabot Lodge
From "International Copyright"

1906 – John Philip Sousa
From "The Menace of Mechanical Music"

Philanthropy, Government Subvention, and a National Conservatory

1881 – Theodore Thomas
From "Musical Possibilities in America"

1890 – *The Washington Post*
From "Music for the Nation: Mrs. Thurber's Plan for Maintaining Her Conservatory"

1890 – *Harper's Weekly*
From "The National Conservatory of Music of America"

1892 – Charles C. Converse
From "American Music's Future"

1900 – Henry I. Kowalski
From *National Conservatory: Educate Americans in America and Establish a Standard of Art*

1901 – *The Dial*
From "Ten Years of Music"

1902 – David Bispham
From "Music as a Factor in National Life"

1906 – Frank Damrosch
From "The American Conservatory, Its Aims and Possibilities"

1913 – Oscar G. Sonneck
From "A Survey of American Music"

1914 – Henry Lee Higginson
From Address to Members of the Boston Symphony Orchestra

1915 – Daniel Gregory Mason
From "Music Patronage as an Art"

The United States government's role in the musical life of the nation, or, more correctly, its unwillingness to accept a role, was for many a source of enormous irritation. Unlike governments in Europe, which had long histories of leadership in the arts primarily through the patronage of royalty, the American government left art to fend for itself. In a nation where business was king and social needs were pervasive, art was felt by many to be an expensive extravagance. The excerpts in this chapter give voice mostly to those who sought more active participation in the arts by the government and appreciated the importance of civic patronage in America.

THE COPYRIGHT ISSUE

✻ 1867 — JAMES PARTON, BIOGRAPHER

From "International Copyright," *Atlantic Monthly* 20/117 (July 1867), 430-51.

> Musicians, especially composers, were deeply concerned about the nation's plodding journey toward the resolution of the decades-old copyright controversy. Although the issue was spearheaded by authors, composers were affected and started issuing their opinions in the 1880s. The crux of the matter was that literary and musical works produced outside the United States could be reprinted in the States without compensation to the author or composer and without fear of legal retaliation. But the failure to pay foreign artists was only one aspect of the issue. Of greater concern was that publishers could reproduce works by foreign creators cheaply and then had little need or reason to commission or support American works. That, the argument goes, inhibited the creation of American artistic products and slowed the appreciation of them by American consumers. Opponents of an international copyright agreement—led by publishers—correctly believed that all printed works would become more expensive if authors and composers were paid and that their consumption by readers and musicians would be negligible. America's burgeoning literary and musical culture, they argued, would be stifled because of the resulting high prices. Publishers feared that the American consumer would suffer; they were not particularly worried about the impact on American art itself. Naturally, the creators of books and music disagreed. Authors and composers argued that, in addition to the moral outrage of pirate publications, American art could never flourish in a culture that featured only the pilfered works of other nations. The net effect of this controversy on American artists, in terms of encouragement and remuneration, was devastating although many issues were resolved by the Copyright Act of 1909. James Parton (1822-1891), who achieved celebrity as the most famous biographer of his day, argued eloquently for the rights of creative individuals.

It was the intention of the founders of this Republic to give complete protection to intellectual property, and this intention is clearly expressed in the Constitution. Justified by the authority given in that instrument, Congress has passed patent laws which have called into exercise an amount of triumphant ingenuity that is one of the great wonders of the modern world; but under the copyright laws, enacted with the same good intentions, our infant literature pines and dwindles. The reason is plain. For a labor-saving invention, the United States, which abounds in everything but labor, is field enough, and the inventor is rewarded; while a great book cannot be remunerative unless it enjoys the market of the whole civilized world. The readers of excellent books are few in every country on earth. The readers of any one excellent book are usually very few indeed; and the purchasers are still fewer. In a world that is supposed to contain a thousand millions of people, it is spoken of as a marvel that two millions of them bought the most popular book ever published—one purchaser to every five hundred inhabitants.

We say, then, to those members of Congress who go to Washington to do something besides make Presidents, that time has developed a new necessity, not indeed contemplated by the framers of the Constitution, yet covered by the Constitution; and it now devolves upon them to carry out the evident intention of their just and wise predecessors, which was, to secure to genius, learning, and talent the certain ownership of their productions. We want an international system which shall protect a kind of property which cannot be brought to market without exposing it to plunder—property in a book being simply the right to multiply copies of it. We want this property secured, for a sufficient period, to the creator of the value, so that no property in a book can be acquired anywhere on earth unless by the gift or consent of the author thereof. There are men in Congress who feel all the magnitude and sacredness of the debt which they owe, and which their country owes, to the authors and artists of the time. We believe such members [of Congress] are more numerous now than they ever were before—much more numerous. It is they who must take a leading part in bringing about this great measure of justice and good policy; and, as usual in such cases, some one man must adopt it as his special vocation, and never rest till he has conferred on mankind this immeasurable boon.

* * * * *

* 1884 — GEORGE PARSONS LATHROP, LIBRETTIST AND SECRETARY OF THE AMERICAN COPYRIGHT LEAGUE

From "The Present State of the Copyright Movement," *Century Magazine* 29/2 (December 1884), 314-16.

> Philadelphia had long been a center of publishing in the United States, and much of the dissension regarding the passage of a copyright law emanated from that city. Here writer and librettist George Parsons Lathrop (1851-1898), who served as secretary to the American Copyright League, described a difficult point of negotiation revolving around the manufacture of artistic products. American publishing houses were insistent that foreign works should not be imported as ready-made products, but that they should be set, printed, and bound here. Artistic works imported into America were already heavily taxed, but an additional fear of American authors and musicians was reciprocity—that is, any laws unfavorable to foreign writers would surely be enacted abroad to the detriment of American creators.

The American Copyright League was formed in 1883, with the object of obtaining a reform in copyright law which should secure to foreign authors the right of property in their works in this country.

Early in the last session of Congress, Representative William Dorsheimer, of New York, introduced a bill intended to attain that object [The Dorsheimer bill was not heard]. . . .

Now let us count the opposition. Out of all the publishers addressed by the "Publishers' Weekly," only fifteen insisted that, if a foreign book is to have copyright here, it must be manufactured in this country. *Of those fifteen, seven were situated in Philadelphia.* The organized hostility came from that source; and it was based on the theory that American industry would be hurt unless every foreign author were compelled to have his book set up, stereotyped, printed, and bound in this country.

This organized hostility on the part of a small Philadelphia minority of publishers proceeded to work upon the fears of typographers and paper makers by telling them that they would lose their occupation if copyright were given to aliens. . . . The first answer to this is, that any book made abroad is subject to a duty of 20% when imported. Next, it must be kept in mind that our compositors would still have a great deal to do in bringing out new editions of foreign works published before the enactment of an international copyright law. Thirdly, the production of books by American authors would be greatly stimulated, thus adding to the market of compositors and paper makers. Fourthly, the enterprise of our publishers, some of whom are now on good terms with English authors, would enable them to secure books from those authors for manufacture here. . . . But a "scare" was created by the men who said that, unless the inhabitants of this republic can buy most foreign books for, say, from ten to forty cents, and unless foreign books are wholly remade here, the country will be ruined as to its paper and printing interests, and plunged into ignorance.

As if this appalling argument were not enough, they contended that an author, anyhow, has no right to put a price upon the work in which he has invested his time, labor, money, brains, and manual labor—all his capital, in short—and that he ought to be grateful if we give him anything for his production after it is published. . . . It has been supposed that American citizens, even if their occupation be only that of paving streets or writing books, are entitled to have from Congress a fair consideration of their rights, if not redress for their wrongs. I venture to ask all friends of the copyright movement, whether of the literary profession or not, to press upon the members of Congress for their respective districts, immediately, the propriety and importance of at least giving the Dorsheimer Bill a prompt and fair hearing.

* * * * *

✻ 1885 — B. M. [BRANDER MATHEWS], PROFESSOR OF DRAMATIC ART AND ORGANIZER OF THE AMERICAN COPYRIGHT LEAGUE

From "Another Side of the Copyright Question," *Century Magazine* 30/3 (July 1885), 488-90.

Copyright was long considered a moral issue, not merely a financial one. The esteemed teacher and essayist Brander Mathews (1852-1929) noted that many problems must be faced before reaching a satisfactory resolution, but he saw progress in support of American creators. Again, reciprocity remained a concern.

The struggle to secure the protection of our laws for literary property produced by citizens of foreign countries has been long and wearisome. To some it may seem fruitless. An ocean of ink has been spilt and a myriad of speeches have been made; and as yet there are no positive results set down in black and white in the Revised Statutes of the United States. But the best cure for pessimism is to look back along the past, and to take exact account of the progress already made. This examination reveals solid grounds for encouragement in the future. The labor spent, although often misdirected, has not been in vain. Something has been gained. Public opinion is slowly crystallizing. . . .

The argument most generally used in favor of this great moral reform is that it will put an end to an atrocious and systematic robbery of foreign authors. That this is a strong argument no one can deny. As the law stands now we are willing to avail ourselves of the literary labors of the great English writers on science and on history, but we do not think the laborer worthy of his hire; we are willing to get pleasure and to take refreshment from the great English novelists and poets, without money and without price. . . .

A stronger argument, however, than that drawn from our robbing the foreigner is to be taken from our ill-treatment of our own authors. So long as we prey on the authors of other countries, just so long may we expect other countries to prey on our authors. While the writers of Great Britain are without protection in the United States, the writers of the United States will be without protection in Great Britain. In the present state of the case a double wrong is inflicted on the American author: (1) at home he is forced to an unfair competition with stolen goods, and (2) abroad he has no redress when his goods are stolen. . . .

* * * * *

✻ 1887 — HORATIO PARKER, COMPOSER, MUSIC EDUCATOR, AND MUSIC ADMINISTRATOR

From "International Copyright of Music–Opinions of American Musicians," *Century Magazine* 33/6 (April 1887), 969-73.

> New England composers Horatio Parker (1863-1919) and George Whitefield Chadwick (1854-1931) were among musicians nationwide who were invited by *Century Magazine* to submit views on the subject of copyright. Parker, always thoughtful and diplomatic, expressed opinions that were widely held, as did Chadwick, whose points were rather more fiery and direct. Both men addressed the financial and moral aspects of copyright protection.

All the arguments advanced in the controversy regarding an International Copyright Law for the protection of authors are equally applicable in the case of composers. Speaking from the standpoint of an American composer, the musical market is flooded with cheap reprints of the most popular and profitable modern European works, to the great detriment of American compositions of merit. These cannot of course compete with works of foreigners in price, since the publishers not only may, but do, take without remuneration and use with impunity what ought to be the property of foreigners. For no long argument is needed to convince any right-thinking man that the result of brain-labor is as much the maker's own property as the work of his hands. Moreover it is a melancholy fact that there is in this country at present a prejudice against American music. Given two piano pieces of equal merit, one by an American, the other by a foreigner, probably not one teacher in ten would give preference to the former for constant use. The passing of this law would give to American composition an impetus and encouragement which it greatly needs, by tending to place the American composer, at least at home, on the same footing as the foreigner.

The whole question seems naturally to resolve itself into one of simple morality: Has a man the right to the product of his work? It is unreasonable and selfish to expect a composer, after he has labored for years and spent both time and money to acquire his ability, to use that ability merely to enrich the man who buys the paper and has it printed; while he himself who has created something to print is forced to subsist by other means, although by appropriate legislation there could be secured to him a just proportion of the fruits of his toil.

* * * * *

* 1887 — GEORGE WHITEFIELD CHADWICK, COMPOSER, TEACHER, AND MUSIC ADMINISTRATOR

From "International Copyright of Music–Opinions of American Musicians," *Century Magazine* 33/6 (April 1887), 969-73.

The artistic injustice to which composers are subjected for want of an adequate copyright law can scarcely be appreciated by the general public.

The recent litigation in regard to the original orchestration of [Charles] Gounod's "Redemption," and of the Gilbert and Sullivan operas, developed the fact that it is the common practice to rescore, rearrange, reharmonize, republish, and otherwise maltreat, *ad lib.*, the works of any foreign composer that may be found profitable for trade purposes. So shameless has this practice become that the defendants in one of these lawsuits actually made a point of the fact that they had altered all the chords of the seventh in the original composition to common chords in their "edition" (!) and made claim to copyright on that account.

It is a notorious fact that American composers have suffered in the same way in England. The genuine creator in music may be content to wait for recognition, and may even be reconciled to having someone else reap the benefit of his artistic labor; but that any one should have the right to distort and misrepresent his works, which happens every day to *tone* artists, is a shame which no one can endure with equanimity. Common justice demands that the artist shall have the right to the fruit of his labor. *Artistic* justice demands that his creation shall be protected from disfigurement and vandalism, and *common law* [i.e., U. S. law] as well as international law ought to afford such protection.

* * * * *

✻ 1889 — *AMERICAN ART JOURNAL*

From "Music Publishing and American Composers," *American Art Journal* 52/4 (9 February 1889), 49-50.

Chadwick's complaint of artistic disfigurement was addressed even more specifically in the following essay, in which several varieties are mentioned. In a particularly American-sounding appeal, this author called for help from private philanthropists to solve the problem.

Many music publishers are unfavorably regarded by composers, and not altogether without reason. The former may plead that they regard their business from a purely commercial standpoint, and therefore supply the public with what they require, be it good, bad, or indifferent; but it cannot be denied . . . that many stimulate the demand for worthless trash by every conceivable device.

The methods by which unscrupulous publishers pander to depraved musical taste are many and various.

Every passing event, from prize fights to Presidential elections, is signalized by songs, marches and dance music—generally a reproduction of some old stock matters, embellished with an attractive, inartistic pictorial title page.

It is also customary with some large publishing houses to retain on the premises a musical "man of all work," whose business it is to "fix up" adaptations of reputable works in a form attractive to the uneducated public. It is needless to say that reverence or even ordinary respect for a composer is conspicuous by its absence in these cases. Classical songs and piano works of great composers are maltreated, and commonplace accompaniments of the most vulgar type, often, too, abounding in incorrect progressions, etc., are unblushingly substituted for the original; difficult passages are ruthlessly omitted, and these shameless libels are put forth as "special copyright editions" without one word of apology. Songs also are frequently arranged as quartets, trios or duos, or vice versa, curtailed or lengthened to suit the market, and issued as the bona fide productions of the composers who have been subjected to this outrageous treatment.

The absence of an international copyright act has tended very much to aggravate this special evil, for, unlike literary publishers, the music publisher is not content even to allow alien composers to appear in their own garb.

The young American composer of merit has special cause to lament the present state of things, for it is often very difficult to find a publisher for his works if they are of [a] superior type. . . .

If a stringent law were passed prohibiting the sale of improper music as well as improper literature, the musical taste of the public would speedily be purified.

In these days of musical philanthropy it may be suggested that here is a field in which a wealthy art patron can do good work. The establishment of a publishing house for the exclusive benefit of American composers of merit; the [manuscript], submitted to be [refereed] to reliable judges of acknowledged standing, and only those compositions worthy of the art to be accepted. The authors of selected works should be paid a fair sum for copyright and allowed to participate in future profits. Such an institution would soon become self-supporting, and besides effecting a much needed reform would afford a healthful encouragement to our young composers, who are compelled to go abroad to win the recognition denied them at home.

* * * * *

✻ 1890 — HENRY CABOT LODGE, POLITICIAN AND HISTORIAN

From "International Copyright," *Atlantic Monthly* 66/344 (August 1890), 264-70.

> Henry Cabot Lodge (1850-1924), who would later serve as the Republican senator from Massachusetts from 1893 until his death, waged the war in favor of an international copyright law. He did not believe that the results would necessarily make the price of literature and music rise, and he had a good point, given that taxes on imports were quite high. In typical fashion, his arguments are clear and direct.

The opponent declares that international copyright ought not to be permitted because it will make literature dear [i.e., expensive], and thus injure the American people at a most important point; and this is all he says, although he says it at great length and with many rhetorical decorations. The attack can be answered as briefly as it is made. The statement that international copyright would make literature dear is a mere assertion, with no fact to warrant it. . . .

Now for the second part of that which the foes of international copyright call their argument, but which in reality is a mere appeal to prejudice. It is said by them that the measure is in the interests of the publishers, so that they may form a trust [i.e., a monopoly], and raise the price of literature for their own benefit, and incidentally for the benefit of a few American authors and of foreign authors generally. Like most appeals to prejudice, this allegation is absolutely untrue. . . .

For the sake of the American author who is now robbed, for the sake of the foreign author who is now plundered, for the sake of that vast body of people who read books in the United States, and upon whom we now force all the worst and cheapest stuff that the presses of the world pour forth, a bill for international copyright ought to be passed. Most of all, it ought to be passed for the sake of the country's honor and good name. . . .

* * * * *

✻ 1906 — JOHN PHILIP SOUSA, BANDMASTER AND COMPOSER

From "The Menace of Mechanical Music," *Appleton's Magazine* 8/3 (September 1906), 278-84.

> As recording technology developed, the lack of a comprehensive copyright law negatively affected those composers whose recorded music was in demand on disc or cylinder. John Philip Sousa (1854-1932), a vocal proponent of copyright protection and a formidable foe to those who disagreed with

him, was among the first to bring the issue—and its relationship to recorded sound—to the nation's attention.

And now a word on a detail of personal interest which has a right to be heard because it voices a claim for fair play, far reaching in its effects beyond the personal profit of one or many individuals. I venture to say that it will come as an entire surprise to almost every reader to learn that composers of the music now produced so widely by the mechanical players of every sort draw no profit from it whatever. Composers are entirely unprotected by the copyright laws of the United States as at present written on the statute books and interpreted by the courts. The composer of the most popular waltz or march of the year must see it seized, reproduced at will on wax cylinder, brass disk, or strip of perforated paper, multiplied indefinitely, and sold at large profit all over the country, without a penny of remuneration to himself for the use of this original product of his brain. . . .

Is a copyright simply represented by a sheet of music? Is there no more to it than the silent notation? The little black spots on the five lines and spaces, the measured bars, are merely the record of birth and existence of a musical thought. These marks are something beyond the mere shape, the color, the length of pages. They are only one form of recording the coming into the world of a newly fashioned work, which, by the right of authorship, inherent and constitutional, belongs to him who conceived it. They are no more the living theme which they record than the description of a beautiful woman is the woman herself.

Should the day come that the courts will give me the absolute power of controlling my compositions, which I feel is now mine under the Constitution, then I am not so sure that my name will appear as often as at present in the catalogues of the talking and playing machines. . . .

But let the ambiguities in the text of the law be what they may; let there be of legal quips and quirks as many as you please, for the life of me I am puzzled to know why the powerful corporations controlling these playing and talking machines are so totally blind to the moral and ethical questions involved. Could anything be more blamable, as a matter of principle, than to take an artist's composition, reproduce it a thousandfold on their machines, and deny him all participation in the large financial returns, by hiding back of the diaphanous pretense that in the guise of a disk or roll, his composition is not his property?

Do they not realize that if the accredited composers, who have come into vogue by reason of merit and labor, are refused a just reward for their efforts, a condition is almost sure to arise where all incentive to further creative work is lacking, and compositions will no longer flow from their pens; or where they will be compelled to refrain from publishing their compositions at all, and control them in manuscript? What, then, of the playing and talking machines?

* * * * *

PHILANTHROPY, GOVERNMENT SUBVENTION, AND A NATIONAL CONSERVATORY

✻ 1881 — THEODORE THOMAS, ORCHESTRA AND OPERA CONDUCTOR

From "Musical Possibilities in America," *Scribner's Monthly Magazine* 21/5 (March 1881), 777-80.

Conductor Thomas (1835-1905) vigorously advocated building a national conservatory. The issue had been a dear one for some time, and many believed that the establishment of a national conservatory was the only way to ensure the development of "home-grown" talent; it was long understood (or at least assumed) that those musicians who left for training in Europe came back with a European musical outlook.

We want home education and thorough home education, of a kind suited to the needs and demands of our people, and calculated to promote the new life which we hope is opening before us. We want an end of amateurism in teachers and other professionals. Those who present themselves to guide the people must have thoroughly studied music, not dabbled in it. We need some provision for the talent which is developing every day—we need institutions, well endowed, which will not be obliged to adopt a mere commercial standard for want of the means of support. We need them, not only to give instruction to pupils, but to keep up a high standard of excellence. We need them for our numerous earnest teachers to come to from time to time, to rub off the rust of teaching, and refresh themselves by contact with those who live in a musical atmosphere. The greatest enemy to fight is mediocrity, and an institution of standing is the only sure defense against it. Such an institution would afford an opportunity for public or semi-public performances, by which ability would be tested and experience gained. It would also give us—what we have not now—a suitable place for the performance of the works of young composers. A concert of a society like the [New York] Philharmonic is not the proper place for experimental music. . . .

* * * * *

✻ 1890 — *THE WASHINGTON POST*

From "Music for the Nation: Mrs. Thurber's Plan for Maintaining Her Conservatory," *Washington Post* (20 April 1890), 10. [Reprinted courtesy of the publisher]

Mrs. Jeanette M. Thurber (1850-1946) founded the National Conservatory of Music in New York City, where she footed the bills for years. But as this *Washington Post* article shows, by the 1890s she was willing to accept help in ways that at the time were cutting-edge models of philanthropy. Thurber and her board were early builders of endowment funds (called here "permanence" and "maintenance" funds) and advocates of subscription and membership programs.

The very delightful musicale which attracted over three hundred people to the Shoreham [Hotel] last Wednesday night, as the guests of Mrs. Jeannette M. Thurber, was something more than a successful social event. . . . There was a serious purpose underlying it all, a purpose so broad, so noble, and so pregnant with good for art, that it deserves more than the passing mention it has received. It is so characteristic of Mrs. Thurber to be persistent, enthusiastic, and generous. Ever since 1882, when she founded the National Conservatory, which was the concrete expression of many years of previous service in the cause of music, she has devoted her time, her talents, and her money to the development of this institution. An unbounded faith in the certainty of ultimate success has buoyed her up through innumerable storms. She had set before her an ideal and towards this she has steadily progressed.

Everything she has done for art has been cleverly conceived and carried out, and the motive in gathering together her friends at the musicale last Wednesday, while laudable in every way, has had the effect of calling attention to the remarkable characteristics of the National Conservatory of Music, whose instructors Mrs. Thurber invited to furnish the entertainment. In this way for many years she has endeavored to secure recognition for one of the most potent factors in musical art in this country. This factor is the National Conservatory of Music.

A more thoroughly unselfish project cannot be found. Open to all who possess musical talent, the benefits of the institution have been appreciated throughout the United States. Students have journeyed thousands of miles to profit by the advantages offered, and every part of the country is represented in the applications received. . . .

It is a question whether this immense drain should always be made on Mrs. Thurber. An institution which is so thoroughly national as the conservatory, which banishes narrowness, sectionalism, and prejudice from its charter, and which should appeal to the patriotic, ought certainly not be sustained by one woman, no matter how devoted she may be to her art. For this reason Mrs. Thurber was advised to come to Washington, the capital of the country, to try and interest those representing every portion of it in her work. Her first step was to organize a permanent national committee, whose object is to provide ways and means for extending the conservatory work.

The following resolutions were adopted at recent meeting of the board of trustees of the conservatory:

Whereas it is desirable in order to extend the usefulness of the National Conservatory of Music of [A]merica that a permanent fund be established, the income only of which can be used for the purposes of said institution.

Resolved. That this board favors the establishment of such a fund; that all sums donated to such fund shall primarily be deposited in the Central Trust Company of New York, and invested by the trustees of the conservatory for the benefit of said corporation in bonds secured by mortgage upon improved real estate worth double the amount so loaned; or in bonds of cities having at least 200,000 inhabitants; [or] in first mortgage railroad bonds; and provided that should said institution cease to exist or suspend its functions for two years, the principal of all sums donated to said fund shall revert to the donors, their heirs or assigns.

Any person donating $5,000 to said fund shall be designated a fellow and founder, and be entitled to the privilege of nominating one person to a free scholarship, who, upon passing the requisite examination, shall receive all the benefits of said institution free of charge.

Resolved. It is the sense of the board that the donors of the permanent fund shall be represented upon the board of trustees of the corporation, and upon the committee having charge of the investment of said fund.

Be it further resolved. That until in the judgement of the trustees the income from said permanent fund shall be sufficient to maintain said institution, there shall be a maintenance fund, composed of annual subscriptions, and that any gentleman or lady contributing $100 annually to said fund shall be a patron of said institution. . . .

The plan proposed is a very feasible one. Here in Washington the first contributions have been to this maintenance fund, although each State will be asked to give in proportion to the number of pupils at the conservatory. Already the subscription lists here are beginning to be covered over by signatures, and the encouraging beginning shows that the seed which Mrs. Thurber has been so industriously sowing is about to bring forth good fruit. . . .

* * * * *

* 1890 — *HARPER'S WEEKLY*

From "The National Conservatory of Music of America," *Harper's Weekly* 34/1773 (15 December 1890), 969-70.

> The unidentified author here addressed the "quackery" involved in many "conservatories" of the day, where this or that "professor" taught with highly questionable methods. But the writer of this article also brought to the forefront several intriguing aspects that accompanied enrollment at New York's National Conservatory, namely the payments and repayments of tuition and the policy of admitting talented artists regardless of race.

Foreigners and native observers have often laughed at an American trait which induces every haircutter and bootblack to call himself an "artist," and every teacher to assume the title of "professor." This kind of humbug flourishes especially in the musical world. Charlatans who have not brains enough to earn an honest living learn to sing or play a few pieces, and by a combination of insinuating ways and brazen effrontery succeed in persuading non-musical parents that they can teach their children the divine art. Second and third rate piano manufacturers advertise in large type that their instruments are unequaled in tone and action, and are preferred by all artists, whereby ignorant purchasers are constantly duped, and reputable makers lose their dues. One of the most lamentable illustrations of this trait is afforded by the way in which music teachers who have secured a dozen pupils immediately hire a room or two, and put out a large sign-board with "Cosmic Conservatory" or "Mammoth Conservatory," or some other big-sounding name on it. That the public likes to be duped is shown by the flourishing condition of some of these schools; but among the educated classes these sham "conservatories" have done a good deal to bring the word "conservatory," like the terms "professor" or "artist," into just contempt, or at least under suspicion; and it is time that a warning voice should be raised against institutions whose "directors" and "professors" in most cases would be unable to pass examination in any of the branches of musical education, and which in some instances even have the impudence to claim the right of conferring the degree of Doctor of Music, though they are nothing but private music schools, organized for the sole purpose of making money.

Among the few music schools in this country which merit the name of conservatory, the National Conservatory of Music of America in New York deserves special attention, because it was not organized as a money-making institution, but as a sort of musical high school, where pupils could prepare themselves for the career of concert, church, or opera singers, of solo or orchestral players, or of teachers, for a merely nominal sum, or, if talented, without any charge for tuition. This institution was founded in 1885 by Mrs. Jeannette M. Thurber, whose name has become a household word in connection with the development of music in the United States, and who is always the first to help along a meritorious musical enterprise. Passionately fond of music, and a critical student of the art, she has for years devoted her means to helping talented struggling musicians to help themselves; and when the demands outgrew her individual ability, she conceived the idea of establishing a National Conservatory of Music in the United States similar to those of European countries, where instruction of the highest class might be obtained at moderate cost, or free, if need be, where exceptional talent was found to exist without the means necessary for its cultivation. Like the most famous music schools in Europe, the National Conservatory was originally started with one branch (voice)—training young singers for the operatic stage. . . .

It would be impossible in the space at our command to describe in detail all these [various musical] departments and the methods employed in them, but there are some interesting things to be said about certain important features which the National Conservatory alone, of all American music schools, has adopted. One of the most valuable of these is to be found in Signor Sapio's opera class. Signor [Romualdo] Sapio, the principal of the vocal class, is an Italian of the modern school—that is, an Italian who recognizes the weak as well as the strong side of Italian operatic music, and who tries, in a cosmopolitan way, to unite what is best in modern French and German methods with what is best in Italians methods. . . . In Signor Sapio's operatic class pupils are taught not only to phrase correctly (he himself accompanying on the piano), but special attention is paid to the proper attitude in singing, to dramatic expression, and to distinct enunciation of the words. This last point, as everybody knows, is shamefully neglected by most vocal teachers, the consequences being that audiences hearing concert, church, or opera singers are often left in doubt for several minutes whether they are listening to a song in Italian, English, French or German. . . .

To many young women and men who intend to devote themselves to music the question of expenses is of prime importance. To this class the National Conservatory offers special advantages, inasmuch as a certain number who show special talent receive all instruction free, on the condition that, having completed their education, they shall aid others, as they were themselves assisted, by a contribution to the general fund, for the first five years, of one-quarter of the emoluments they receive over and above one thousand dollars a year.

To those who are able to pay, a *moderate* charge is made, with a view to defraying the expenses of the institution and more fully furthering its work. Specially gifted pupils may in the later years of their course of study be able to defray their expenses or obligations by being engaged as repetiteurs, or assistant teachers. The Conservatory is open to those of every race, creed, and color upon the one condition that they give proof of sufficient natural talent to justify the examiners in admitting them. . . .

In a republic, [positive] interference in artistic matters is not easy to secure; but wealthy individuals can assist by means of endowments in building up legitimate art schools as a bulwark against tramp teachers. Millions have been bequeathed to colleges, where young men chiefly are benefited. Why should not some of our millionaires bethink themselves of the music schools, which are chiefly resorted to by young girls engaged in the fierce struggle for existence? In a country proverbial for its gallantry such a state of affairs is certainly anomalous. With the assistance of a few generous endowments, the National Conservatory could be built up into an institution equal to any in Europe. . . .

A word more as to the advisability of studying in a conservatory instead of taking private lessons. At least half a dozen reasons can be given why the former is preferable. In the first place, parents who are unable to judge of the ability of teachers will find a reputable conservatory a protection against charlatans. Secondly, were not conservatories considered the best place to learn music, we would not find that all large cities have one or more schools of this kind with which the most eminent local musicians are habitually connected. Thirdly, as a rule, great artists and composers could not find time and do not care to take on any private pupils; but in a conservatory, where a whole class can benefit by their remarks, they are more willing to give up part of their time. . . . Fourthly, it is very much cheaper to study in a school than to take private lessons. Again, most pupils are benefited by an *esprit de corps* and a feeling of rivalry that can be developed only in a school; and finally, private pupils do not have the opportunity for choral or orchestral practice as they do in a regular institution like the National Conservatory of Music of America. . . .

* * * * *

* 1892 — CHARLES C. CONVERSE, ATTORNEY AND COMPOSER OF SACRED MUSIC

From "American Music's Future," *American Art Journal* 59/5 (14 May 1892), 140-41.

> While contemplating America's future musical prospects, composer Charles C. Converse (1832-1918) pleaded for patience as well as resolve concerning the establishment of an American conservatory. Interestingly, Converse apparently did not view Thurber's National Conservatory as the solution to a national problem. Converse also urged America's wealthiest families to support promising and established musicians.

. . . Give American music time. Wait until the American musical pilgrimage to the Old World ceases. Wait until American music conservatories have age enough to become American and their faculties graduate American musicians. Wait until American philanthropic millionaires shall have given all America free music halls and the free public hearing of culturesome musical works; not omitting such a moneyed encouragement to American composers as would abate for them the bread-and-butter question's consideration, while they strive to make the best art-expression nature and their learning rendered possible for them to accomplish.

One has to but visit the American Academy of Design to realize what splendid progress toward the forming of an American sister art-school has already been affected. Wait until there is an American Academy of Music, with its yearly opportunities and inducements for exhibitions of American musical endeavor; and, with these opportunities and inducements in the hands of Americans who are sufficiently cultured and patriotic, and free enough from foreign prejudice and musical ambitions of their own to act intelligently and equitably in their disposition. West Point and her cadets have made the American war-art respectable the world over.

Though music is the language of the emotions—emotions common however to all mankind—yet those composers who have built up their respective national schools of music have done so less by giving a distinctive tone-language to their national legends, characteristics and exploits, than by giving their peculiar national tonal utterance to emotions common to all mankind, because of these composers' birth, heredity, education, and environments. Hence we find that the composers of all lands take, for the subjects of their great musical works, those themes and fancies that the world holds largely in common, as man's general, universal, heritage of sentiment. . . .

Let the Carnegies and Rockefellers and Goulds and Vanderbilts help struggling composers with yearly gifts of money, for a term of years, sufficient to enable them to study their art, here or abroad, or both, and to write great works. Let these millionaires help struggling American composers, as needy theological students are helped by the different American churches: helped through college, seminary, foreign university and into large-salaried pulpits, the helpers not knowing whether or not the helped have any talent in them beyond the desire to preach. Let these millionaires not limit their help to the younger struggling American composers; but extend it to those older ones who have been forced by bread-and-butter demands to neglect their art longings and smother work-germs within them which would, if written, enrich the treasury of American art and advance its cause in the world.

There never should be a struggling American Mozart or Wagner in this opulent land; and, even if a few hundred dollars may be wasted by these millionaires on a person whose career disappoints them, yet, let them continue their hospitality to art and artists; for, by so doing, they may entertain art-angels unawares. The way of the American theological student to the American pulpit has been made easy and pleasant. The way of the American musical student to the production of art works and their public hearing has been allowed to grow up in thorns and brambles, and obstacles often insurmountable. . . .

❋ ❋ ❋ ❋ ❋

❋ 1900 — HENRY I. KOWALSKI, MUSIC EDUCATOR AND WRITER ON MUSIC

From *National Conservatory: Educate Americans in America and Establish a Standard of Art* (San Francisco: Meese Print, ca. 1900), 3-16.

Writing from California, Henry I. Kowalski clearly had not kept up with activities in New York and Boston as they related to the conservatory movement. He, nonetheless, brought a passionate viewpoint to the topic. Kowalski insisted that the success of the national conservatory movement depended on its complete funding by the government; he is among the few who pointed out the economic benefits of keeping American music students in America.

The question most important that awaits an answer is: "When will the American nation, by and through its Government, establish institutions for the education of musical and art students?" The older and more prosperous we grow the more important becomes this question—a question so seldom thought of by the ordinary mind of the industrious dollar-seeking American, but which is so vital to the student who has run the gamut of the education afforded in this country through private resources; and when we come to consider the higher branches of art and music, then the darkness of the situation is appalling. . . .

It may be interesting to know that there are as many as 20,000 American students scattered through the great cities of Europe, studying music in every branch and likewise painting, sketching, and all the fine arts akin thereto. One-half of these students are either eking out a precarious existence as beggar students or are indulging in all kinds of self-denials in order that they may continue their studies until the time when they are competent to go forth and take up the battle for supremacy; and it is pitiful to hear the pathetic stories of struggle and self-abnegation the poor American student undergoes for the sake of achieving success in his chosen art; that the money he lives on [cannot] entirely be afforded by his family, who are in moderate circumstances; or the student who has worked and saved his earnings, or he who is doing some [menial] service in order to maintain an existence. These stories force upon the listener a blush of shame for our nation's neglect of the true genius and manhood suffering want and exile for the sake of art and to make the American name honored. . . .

Congress thinks little of appropriating $5,000,000 for a man-of-war, whose purposes are to destroy, whereas by the expenditure of $1,000,000 an institution can be reared to build up and perpetuate a lasting heritage for the glory of our nation.

The answer usually set forth and held up by some people as an excuse for our neglect in this direction is that we are a young nation, and a nation of business and not of art and music is neither logical nor tenable; it is not even good business policy. Is it good business to allow 20,000 of the youth of this country possessing genius and soul for art and music to leave America and for years to dwell abroad, divorcing themselves from our institutions, paying the foreign master for lessons and spending whatever money they may have in strange lands away from home and friends, accepting voluntary banishment for the sake of their art?

. . . Every American who loves music and loves his country ought to become an advocate of the establishment of an American conservatory of music under the Government patronage.

The location of the national conservatory of music should be placed according to the population, so that it might be accessible by all sections of the country in proportion to the numbers. A certain standard should be demanded, so as to make it the high finishing institution for the perfection of instrumental as well as vocal music. A regency should be established, non-political in character, for the production and promulgation of standard and classical music. Of course, at first it would necessitate the bringing here of well known masters from Europe, but in a few years the institutions would graduate [their] own teachers, and Americans would take pride in the American-born and American-educated musicians. . . .

The student who devotes himself to the severe and arduous labor in order to produce melodious sounds that give us great pleasure may bring great sacrifices; but we love and honor him. Success is most difficult even at the best, and when we know the hardships that must be borne before that end is attained, our nation can well afford to do its part to help the ambitious student to obtain the thorough education necessary to that end. We shall in sooth honor ourselves by honoring the noblest of all arts. Let the cornerstone of America's Temple of Arts be laid.

* * * * *

✻ 1901 — *THE DIAL*

From "Ten Years of Music," *The Dial* 30/357 (1 May 1901), 293-94.

> The unidentified writer for *The Dial* provided insights on the funding of the Chicago Symphony Orchestra, an institution developed by committee. It is important to point out the early emphasis on the orchestra as an educational institution and the unwillingness to alter repertoire simply to raise box office receipts.

The tenth season of the Chicago Orchestra has just come to an end, and the occasion seems to call for a few words of comment upon the history and purpose of this remarkable enterprise. When the Orchestra was organized in the autumn of 1891, and its support for three years was secured by a guaranty of fifty thousand dollars each year of that term, there were not many who were hopeful enough to believe that it was destined to become a permanent part of the higher life of Chicago. So many worthy movements had come to grief in the city, so many fresh enthusiasms had been chilled, so many commendable enterprises had suffered un-timely defeat from the caprices of fashion, that the argument from analogy seemed to indicate a like end for the newly-established Orchestra. When the three years of the original plan were ended, and the subscription plan had been overdrawn instead of being merely exhausted, the prospect was dark indeed, and it looked as if the work would have to be abandoned as a failure. But the forces which had led to its foundation proved equal to the new demands made upon them; the public-spirited founders of the organization renewed their subsidy, and the work has gone on ever since without any derogation from the fine artistic ideals that were set at its inception. The annual excess of expenses over receipts has fallen in the ten years from more than fifty thousand to less than twenty thousand dollars, but it still remains a charge upon the group of men who have borne it from the first, and who have, moreover, borne it ungrudgingly, conscious that they have been supporting one of the noblest of public causes. It is the gift of a third of a million dollars freely made by these men to the community during the past ten years, that has enabled Chicago to boast of the finest orchestral organization and equipment in America. We will not seek to praise these men as they deserve, for they would be the last to wish for such praise; it is perhaps the chief virtue of their gift to art and not for the sake of their personal reputations.

But in spite of the manifest devotion of these men to a higher ideal than that of money-getting, there are certain elements of public opinion so dense as to be incapable of realizing that the annual balance sheet of the orchestral organization is not the chief source of concern to its management. Every year, when the figures are given out, and the deficit once more stares the public in the face, a cry goes up from the newspapers to the effect that the loss might easily have been avoided by bringing the programs presented down a little nearer to the level of popular taste. Give us more "request programs," it is said, put in a few waltzes and medleys of operatic airs, and the public will crowd the concert hall. This is true, no doubt, but it is not the wish of the management to secure large audiences at such a cost. The Orchestra is first and foremost an educational enterprise, and the requirements of art are held paramount by Mr. [Theodore] Thomas and his supporters alike. Those who cannot understand how practical men may be actuated by such a motive should fall on their knees and pray for enlightenment, instead of assuming the injured air of persons whose good advice is ungratefully rejected. Yet the advice is proffered year after year by the same persevering critics, and it seems quite impossible to convince them that it is not wanted, or that the men who are responsible for the work of the Orchestra know quite as well as their critics that the concerts could be made to pay if it were thought desirable.

How well they have paid in a better than the commercial sense is apparent to every observer of musical conditions in Chicago during the past ten or twenty years. . . .

* * * * *

✻ 1902 — DAVID BISPHAM, BARITONE SINGER AND AMERICAN MUSIC ADVOCATE

From "Music as a Factor in National Life," *North American Review* 175/553 (December 1902), 786-99.

> The vision of Wagnerian baritone David Bispham (1857-1921) for a national conservatory was more comprehensive than Thurber's. His "University of Music" was conceived to attract talent nationally, to publish new music, to provide a music library for use by individuals nationwide, and to send students and faculty on recital tours across the country. Generally, Bispham, who was the first American to enjoy an international singing career, sought a more cosmopolitan, less nationalistic academy.

Nowhere more than in America is the disappearance of old-fashioned prejudices so distinctly marked, and the necessities and freedom of modern life have so widened the boundaries of what has been hitherto considered right for young men and women of birth and education, that the result of the adoption of music as one of the learned professions by thousands of these is having upon the public an effect which it is impossible to estimate. Still, there is an untrodden field for some benefactor yet to come, in founding what might be called The University of Music, which, having affiliations with all schools previously existing among us, could extend its influence throughout the country, by discovering, fostering and importing the best talent, and publishing and supplying the best music of all [compositional] schools to the public; by opening circulating libraries where all the compositions of noted composers of all times might be obtained; and by superintending, if not actually carrying on, the general instruction, not only of individuals, but of the masses. Such an institution, in order to make its work known and universally felt, would maintain a staff of singers and instrumentalists who might tour the country, or whose services could be obtained to perform at concerts and recitals of music of various kinds and countries, making it known historically before the countless audiences which would be only too glad to receive such enlightenment. From the Gregorian chant to the compositions of Palestrina, and the masses of Beethoven; from the lays [songs] of Troubadours and Minnesingers to the art songs of Germany; from the operas of Handel to those of Wagner, every phase of vocal art would be traversed. From the lyre to the harpsichord and the piano, from the viol to the string quartet, from "the instrument of ten strings" to the modern orchestra, the growth of music would be clearly demonstrated, its permanence as one of the most lofty, though most evanescent, of the liberal arts would be assured, the influence of the charlatan would be kept within bounds, and even the least attentive class of the population, unconsciously to themselves, attracted, cultivated, raised from the sordid affairs of the moment, soothed, cheered, ennobled, and inspired with fresh courage to face the problems of life.

To the mind awake to music in a land like ours its permanent value as a profound factor in Social Science cannot long remain hidden; for it is a civilizing influence of the most potent character.

* * * * *

⁂ 1906 — FRANK DAMROSCH, CHORAL CONDUCTOR, MUSIC EDUCATOR, AND MUSIC ADMINISTRATOR

From "The American Conservatory, Its Aims and Possibilities," *MTNA Studies in Musical Education, History and Aesthetics* (Cincinnati: Music Teachers National Association, 1906), 13-20.

> Frank Damrosch (1859-1937), the scion of a highly respected musical family and an important teacher in his own right, founded in 1905 the Institute of Musical Art (later the Juilliard School). He recognized that music in the home was vital to the continuation of music as a public institution. Damrosch sought better teacher training and hoped to engage all Americans in wholesome musical activities. In the end, though, he accepted the fact that music was not central to the lives of average Americans.

Were it not for the involuntary emphasis on the word *American*, the title of this discourse would give little incentive to renewed consideration or to discussion, for the story of the Conservatory of Music is old, its glory is of doubtful luster, and unless it be placed on a higher plane, its future is not encouraging. But, as in many other fields, old institutions implanted on new soil may bring forth finer fruits than they produced in the old, so the *American* Conservatory may find a richer soil, a more generous climate, more bracing air, and warmer life-giving sun, than its aunts and cousins of Europe, and a study of the conditions may therefore prove to be not unprofitable. . . .

Let us first take a glance at the so-called Conservatory, College, or University of Music which may be found in every American community, from the metropolis to the smallest town. It is usually organized by an individual whose commercial instincts are stronger than his musical conscience and who, banking on the dense ignorance of the average citizen in matters of art, offers what seems to be a great bargain in the acquisition of musical ability in one form or another. I need not describe the methods, for they are too well known, but this class of music school has done much harm to the development of true musical taste and training in America, and it is time that something were done to counteract and, if possible, destroy these agents for vulgar influences. Even in New York there are many such schools which seemingly flourish by the glittering, if empty, promises which they advertise. Some of them confer degrees, the humorous side of this feature being that one of the first Musical Doctor degrees conferred by the director of one of these schools was upon himself. But the time will come when, as Lincoln said, it will not be possible to fool all the people all the time. Indeed it seems as though this time [has] now arrived, and it behooves us to meet the requirements of an awakening people and to remember that in education the best is only just good enough. . . .

The first question to be settled is, can musical education be better given by a private teacher or a school? This requires, first, an answer to the question: What is a musical education? This assemblage of teachers will readily agree that it is not merely the ability to perform, but must include historical, aesthetical, and theoretical knowledge, together with such general academic and literary culture as is required to bring an intelligent understanding to bear on the work of art which may come under observation and study. A private teacher can only cultivate a part of such an education. It would take several good teachers of different special studies to produce the desired result, and the expense of such an arrangement would, in nearly all cases, be prohibitory. Do not grow pale, ladies and gentlemen, at the thought that I might advocate the abolishment and utter extinction of the private teacher. He has his good uses and a large field, no matter how many schools may be established, and, far from wishing him ill, I would rather do all in my power to raise his standing artistically and financially. Geologists say that the earth will be so cold in one hundred million years that it will no longer support life. I am willing to wager all I possess, with interest at five percent, that the last lingerer on this at present very warm sphere will be a private music teacher. My reason for this confident statement is that the last man or woman will have nothing else to do, and we all know that when people can't do anything else they give music lessons. Seriously speaking, however, we must depend upon the private teacher to carry music into the home, the true soil for musical culture, and it is to produce the best type of private teacher that must be one of the principal objects of a school of music. . . .

In my opinion the American School or Conservatory of Music should set itself three tasks. First, and most important, it should provide a thorough musical education to any and all who are culturally sufficiently advanced to desire to study seriously and who have the time and strength to do so. Such education should not be limited to those who want to follow music as a profession, but, as [with] the academic courses in college, should provide the foundation work for all musical pursuits, professional or amateur. The other two tasks may be looked upon as byproducts, but important ones, of any plant established for the first and primary object. They are, the leavening of the great mass of the people by encouraging musical effort in popular singing classes, by good concerts, by proper musical training in public and private schools and in the colleges and universities, and by the encouragement of home music. And, finally, its special care should be the development of real talent to its highest potentiality, and also the thorough training of teachers. . . .

The constant effort of the school should be to lead the mind of the student away from himself to the reverent appreciation and understanding of the art work. Most training is in the opposite direction. The student's aim should not be to get to the point when he can produce himself and exploit his talents, but to become capable of doing justice, by his adequate performance, to the mastermind which created the composition. The short-sighted will say that such an ideal conception will not tend towards paying the musician's board and lodging, but I am convinced that on the contrary such a musician will not only command the respect and admiration of music lovers, but will become more sought after and earn a better and more secure living than he who seeks to win money and fame by circus performances and advertising.

What, then, are the differences between the European and the American Conservatory as it should be? Briefly they may be found in the conditions of life, in student material and in the objects to be accomplished. In Europe, music forms a part of the life of the people. The folk song, the widespread musical culture through the military bands, through cheap opera and concerts in subsidized places of amusement and through the practice of the smaller forms of music in the home, are influences common to all the people, rich and poor. In America, there are, as yet, few such influences. Curiously enough, the chief promoters of musical culture among the masses are actuated by purely commercial incentives. I refer to the trolley companies, which open places of amusement near large cities, such as Willow Grove, near Philadelphia, or Ravinia Park, near Chicago, where such orchestras as the New York Symphony Orchestra are engaged to perform twice a day. Hundreds of thousands of people are thus enabled to become familiar with symphonic music of the highest order, excellently performed.

In Europe the conservatories devote themselves almost exclusively to the training of those who desire to become professional musicians. In America the conservatory must aim to make the mass musical, in order to rebuild its pyramid upon a broad foundation, upon which may then be built a structure that may pinnacle in the stars.

No one will deny that the quality of student material in America is of the highest order. American students in European schools and studios rank among the foremost. Our voices, our intelligence and perseverance are highly praised by European teachers. And with such material we will soon produce musicians of the highest rank in our schools. But what would this avail, if they were islands in an ocean of ignorance, if they preached to ears that hear not? In Europe the groove of activity is narrow, professions are crowded, class distinctions fetter every walk of life. Hence the training of the conservatory aims at some one specific line of work, the aim of the student is to be started in some definitely marked out career which will enable him to count upon a certain, if small competence.

In America, a whole continent, a vast people is yet to be brought to the recognition of music as a necessary part of life. There is room for everyone who is willing honestly to help in the missionary work of awakening this nation to the ameliorating, civilizing, spiritualizing influences of good music—each according to his talents. The broader his training, therefore, the better he will perform his mission.

The European conservatory has a valuable, useful, and important task to perform, but ours is greater, higher, nobler, because it does not seek to further the interests of only the individual, but aims at the heart of the whole people.

Why should we, then, fail to set our standards high when we realize the grandeur of our task[?] Our men of large means cannot do better than promote musical culture, for it will tend to improve the [human] race and, in the general social reorganization which is imminent, will do much to ameliorate the friction which is bound to ensue. Let us be exacting, however, and not rest satisfied with aught below the best attainable. He who waits and works for high aims will surely reach them in the end, while he who reaches out for only that which lies close at hand will not travel far nor soar high. Let our American Conservatory, then, be as the outer court of the temple in which the young votaries of music are fitted to become priests of the art, missionaries in its cause who will carry its true gospel of beauty and truth into the heart of every good American.

* * * * *

✻ 1913 — OSCAR G. SONNECK, MUSICOLOGIST AND LIBRARIAN

From "A Survey of American Music," *Suum Cuique: Essays in Music* (New York: Schirmer, 1916), 121-54. [From a lecture delivered in 1913.]

> Oscar G. Sonneck (1873-1928) acknowledged the importance of America's private music conservatories but encouraged the founding of a national one —built with government funds—that would show the world that the nation itself, not just a few wealthy philanthropists, was serious about the enterprise. Sonneck was an early advocate of tax-exempt status for the arts and was quick to note the positive effect that music had on the economy.

. . . For instance, there is the problem of municipal, state or federal subvention of music. Perhaps not as yet a really acute problem in our country, but one that will call for a solution one day and one to which several lectures might profitably be devoted. As you know, our musical life is based practically on what I have elsewhere called "Privatbetrieb," a term not fully covered by the translation "(under) private management." We belong with England and Italy to the small group of countries standing apart from other civilized countries, where the musical life depends on cooperation between private enterprise and the government's paternalistic interest and support. I had planned to convince you, if possible, that this mixed system is by far the better of the two and of necessity will produce the better results, but time forbids making propaganda here for my pet theories.

Not so many years ago the idea of governmental subvention of music would have met with the same shallow argument still hurled at our country at every progressive economic proposition tinged with so-called socialism, namely, that it is un-American. Well, a thing is un-American until it becomes American. I am glad to see the idea of governmental support of musical talent and interest in music–national assets just as much as potash deposits–spreading its roots throughout our country. The city of New York, for instance, is now spending considerable sums in that direction, and it would be a regrettable retrograde step if these sums were decreased instead of increased in the future. The time will yet come when our progressive municipalities will either own and manage their own opera houses or will exempt bona fide grand opera houses from taxation (as has been proposed in Boston), or in some other form will subvention opera not from mere sentimentality, but from the standpoint of civic business. And if one or more of our state universities find it necessary or desirable to include musical departments, I really cannot see why the idea of a National Conservatory of Music should meet with opposition. Of course, such one-sided and half-baked schemes as have been outlined recently will never do, especially no scheme which proposes to build up a *National* conservatory on private donations. The *raison d'etre* of a National Conservatory is the official recognition by a people of the higher professional training in music as a national asset, with all the educational, artistic and economic advantages to be derived therefrom. The most generously endowed private institution with a national name would be a rather poor substitute for the real thing. If such substitutes are offered simply because of fear of "graft" in a governmental institution, then the promoters should be reminded, on the one hand, of the fact that "graft" is not quite unknown in private business; on the other, of the fact that our Federal government is as clean as that of any other nation. Once the pressure behind Congress attains such an impetus as to put a National Conservatory within reach of our people, you may rest assured that it will be made an institution worthy of the name, provided the musical profession undermines the lobbying proclivities of petty schemers and sees to it that Congress entrusts the plans to a competent commission of experts. Such experts we have in plenty, and once the heads of our great private conservatories appreciate the certainty that the dignified competition of a National Conservatory will strengthen rather than weaken them in the pursuit of their educational ideals, our Government will find them ready to cooperate in the main difficulty; to put a National Conservatory speedily on the same level of efficiency with these great private institutions.

* * * * *

✻ 1914 — HENRY LEE HIGGINSON, BANKER AND FOUNDER OF THE BOSTON SYMPHONY ORCHESTRA

From Address to Members of the Boston Symphony Orchestra (27 April 1914); reprinted *The Life and Letters of Henry Lee Higginson*, ed. Bliss Perry (Boston: Atlantic Monthly Press, 1921), 291-96.

> Henry Lee Higginson (1834-1919) was a banking magnate who founded the Boston Symphony Orchestra. It was a heroic enterprise: not only did he understand that he would likely be obliged to shoulder the burden of annual deficits, but he harbored no expectations that the situation would change. This speech, which Higginson delivered to his musicians, gives some sense of the strain he experienced but also makes clear his devotion to the art.

Gentlemen:

Sixty years ago I wished to be a musician, and therefore went to Vienna, where I studied two years and a half diligently, learned something of music, something about musicians, and one other thing—that I had no talent for music. I heard there and in other European cities the best orchestras, and much wished that our own country should have such fine orchestras. Coming home at the end of 1860, I found our country in trouble, and presently in a great [Civil] war. Naturally I took part in the war, at the end of which time I did various things, and at last came to our present office [on] State Street, where I was admitted as a partner.

For many years I had hard work to earn my living and support my wife. Originally I had had a very small sum of money, which had been used up while studying in Vienna and during the war. All these years I watched the musical conditions in Boston, hoping to make them better. I believed that an orchestra of excellent musicians under one head and devoted to a single purpose could produce fine results, and wished for the ability to support such an undertaking; for I saw that it was impossible to give music at fair prices and make the Orchestra pay expenses.

After consulting with some European friends, I laid out a plan, and at the end of two very good years of business began concerts in the fall of 1881. It seemed best to undertake the matter single-handed, and, beyond one fine gift from a dear friend, I have borne the costs alone. All this is a matter of record, and yet it may interest you. It seemed clear that an orchestra of fair size and under possible conditions would cost at least $20,000 a year more than the public would pay. Therefore, I expected this deficit each year, and faced contracts with seventy men and a conductor. It was a large sum of money, which depended on my business each year and on the public. If the concert halls were filled, that would help me; if my own business went well, that would help me; and the truth is, that the great public has stood by me nobly.

In my eyes the requisites about the Orchestra were these: to leave the choice and care of the musicians, the choice and care of the music, the rehearsals and direction of the Orchestra, to the conductor, giving him every power possible; to leave to an able manager the business affairs of the enterprise; and on my part, to pay the bills, to be satisfied with nothing short of perfection, and always to remember that we were seeking high art and not money: art came first, then the good of the public, and the money must be an after consideration. . . .

Mr. [Charles A.] Ellis [the orchestra's business manager] suggested the summer concerts, in order to give more work to the members of the Orchestra; and this step met a want which was keenly felt. Mr. [Wilhelm] Gericke suggested the system of pensions, which was put in force and has given help to many past members of the Orchestra, and must be a comfort to you gentlemen of the Orchestra today as something to look forward to when you leave off work.

For the term of thirty-three years the total deficit is about $900,000. My friends have begged me again and again to stop the concerts because the strain was too great; but the work had gone on, and the result is the present beautiful Orchestra, of which we all are proud.

We had been driven out of the old Music Hall in Hamilton Place because the city planned to put a street through the hall, and I welcomed the change, as the old hall was not well aired, and was not very safe. Friends built the present hall, which I leased for a long term of years, as we must have it free for our use at all times. The hall is not rented so much as we could wish, the costs of keeping it in order are large, and therefore the yearly deficit ranges from $13,000 to $19,000.

Now what does each of us do for the Orchestra? Dr. [Karl] Muck chooses the music, prepares everything for the public, conducts the rehearsals and the concerts. Each of you gentlemen does his part excellently, and each of you is as well treated as lies in my power. My part is to run the risk of each year's contracts, and to meet the deficit, which will never fall below $20,000 yearly, and is often more. At present we have good luck in cities other than Boston, but it is a luck on which we cannot count, for good orchestras exist everywhere, and presently we may not be needed beyond our home. In Boston I have to take my luck, which thus far has been good; but there is always a chance, and you have only to reckon how many contracts I must sign, to see what a heavy burden would be on my shoulders if the concerts were not successful, and the audiences were small. . . .

* * * * *

✻ 1915 — DANIEL GREGORY MASON, COMPOSER AND MUSIC EDUCATOR

From "Music Patronage as an Art," *The New Republic* 4/42 (21 August 1915), 71-73. [Reprinted courtesy of the publisher]

> Composer and educator Daniel Gregory Mason (1873-1953) viewed the patronage of art music as one of the few solutions to the ever-increasing encroachment of popular culture. Only through generous patronage, Mason thought, could music of artistic merit continue to be produced in America. He also provided a list of qualities that should be sought in patrons.

It is a mistake to suppose, as the histories of music often seem to do, that the patronage system died out in the late eighteenth or early nineteenth century, within a generation or two after Mozart had been kicked downstairs by Archduke Hieronymus's underling, and that Beethoven was the last of the great composers whose way was smoothed by men like Archduke Rudolph and Prince Lobkowitz. . . . Today in America music needs intelligent, unselfish patronage as much as ever, perhaps more. What would happen if it were left entirely to the tender mercies of the people? The phonograph, the mechanical player, ragtime, and the Broadway "musical" comedy give the answer. But patronage is as difficult as it is necessary; to be a good patron one must have not only money and an interest in music, but what is rarer, tact; imaginative perception of other points of view, complete freedom from the wish to be personally conspicuous, and a greater love for art than for artists. What [Ralph Waldo] Emerson said of charity is even truer of patronage, that it is not enough to "abandon your money" to people, that your heart must go with it—that is, your sympathetic understanding of their artistic aims. . . .

In the matter of the composer, however—more important because the composer seems to be, after all, the prime mover who starts the endless give-and-take between his own activity and public receptivity out of which musical culture grows—the dubious elements in the [patronage] scheme seem fewer, the admirable points more incontestable. Each composer, states the program of the [Norfolk music] festival, "receives a handsome honorarium for his work, which remains his property for such disposition as he may elect, after the first performance at Norfolk."

This is exactly as it should be. The composer has to suffer no invasion of his privacy, but simply to sell a work that deserves to be public property. As he receives his money not before but after he completes his work, there is no element of charity in the transaction, and no harassing undefined obligation to torture his conscience. There is none of the subtle demoralization incident to charity, either; for inasmuch as he needs to give a *quid pro quo* for his money, he cannot forget that efficiency is demanded of him quite as of anyone else who proposes to be paid for a service rendered. On the other hand, he has a chance to hear his work adequately performed, with sufficient rehearsal—an immense benefit to his future workmanship; he gets the stimulus and encouragement of a public hearing; and he earns a fee that will enable him to devote time to new compositions.

The only comment left would seem to be that the young and unknown composer who specially needs such help might be crowded out by older, more established men. He might. That depends of course on the way the matter is administered. To find obscure merit is no easy task; it requires patience, independence, complete superiority to snobbery and conventional standards, and a catholic yet discriminating personal taste. Obviously few patrons will combine all these qualities in their own persons, and few will be sufficiently free from vanity to call in expert assistance. Thus we return to our original point—that music patronage is a delicate and exacting pursuit, and that the ideal patron must be quite as fine an artist in his way as the other artists it is his art to assist.

* * * * *

Czech composer Antonín Dvořák believed that the music of blacks and Native Americans could provide a basis for an American school of composition. Musician "Happy John" plays his banjo in this photograph by McCrary & Branson (ca. 1897).

Courtesy of the Prints and Photographs Division, Library of Congress: LC-USZ62-76294.

❊ 8 — Dvořák and American Musical Nationalism

1893 – Antonín Dvořák
From Letter to the Editor, *New York Herald*

1893 – William T. Mollenhauer
"A Reply to Dr. Dvořák and His Negro Melodies"

1895 – Antonín Dvořák
From "Music in America"

1904 – Richard Aldrich
From "Antonín Dvořák and His Music"

1908 – Lawrence Gilman
From *Edward MacDowell: A Study*

1914 – Henry Edward Krehbiel
From *Afro-American Folksongs: A Study in Racial and National Music*

The United States was not unaffected by the wave of nationalism that swept through Europe in the latter half of the nineteenth century. As nations—and cultures within nations—sought to define themselves in terms of their shared ethnic heritages, expression in art and music was inevitable. The problem for American composers was this: how can a democratic people of mixed races and ethnicities express a unified identity in music? For many the question was not worth asking; to them, music was a universal art, and nationalism was an imposed artifice. Others, however, thought that, by finding its own nationalistic "voice," America's musical independence from Europe could be won.

Philanthropist Jeanette Thurber (1841-1904) believed that Americans could gain by the example of Bohemian composer Antonín Dvořák, whose recognizably Czech music was widely admired. Thurber hired him to run her National Conservatory of Music in New York City but also to provide advice and inspiration for the formation of a school of composers whose music Thurber hoped would be uniquely American. Founded in 1885, the conservatory developed a reputation as a fine school, and its faculty boasted some of the city's best musicians. Dvořák was already a revered figure by the

1890s, and Thurber fully expected that, besides simply teaching and administering the conservatory, he would put a well-known face to her cause. In surprisingly short order, he declared that the music of blacks and Native Americans could serve as a foundation. His ideas—and the varied, often emotional reactions to them—comprise one of the more fascinating chapters in the history of American music.

❋ 1893 — ANTONÍN DVOŘÁK, VISITING CZECH COMPOSER

From Letter to the Editor, *New York Herald* (28 May 1893), 31.

The irony of enlisting a European composer to explore the possibilities of creating an American art was not lost on American musicians. Among Dvořák's first public statements was this lengthy letter to the editor of the *New York Herald*, which he wrote in response to an article published in that paper. He addressed two important themes: the professional education of musicians in America and the foundation of a national style of music based on African-American melodies. While the first generated little response, the second made a powerful impact on composers for years afterward.

I was deeply interested in the article in last Sunday's Herald, for the writer struck a note that should be sounded throughout America. It is my opinion that I find a sure foundation in the Negro melodies for a new national school of music, and my observations have already convinced me that the young musicians of this country need only intelligent directions, serious application and a reasonable amount of public support and applause to create a new musical school in America. This is not a sudden discovery on my part. The light has gradually dawned on me.

The new American school of music must strike its roots deeply into its own soil. There is no longer any reason why young Americans who have talent should go to Europe for their education. It is a waste of money and puts off the coming day when the Western world will be in music, as in many others, independent of other lands. In the National Conservatory of Music, founded and presided over by Mrs. Jeannette M. Thurber, is provided as good a school as can be found elsewhere. The masters are competent in the highest sense and the spirit of the institution is absolutely catholic. A fresh proof of the breadth of purpose involved in this conservatory is the fact that it has been opened without limit or reservation to the Negro race.

I find good talent here, and I am convinced that when the youth of the country realizes that it is better now to stay at home than go abroad we shall discover genius, for many who have talent but cannot undertake foreign residence will be encouraged to pursue their studies here. It is to the poor that I turn for musical greatness. The poor work hard; they study seriously. Rich people are apt to apply themselves lightly to music, and to abandon the painful toil to which every strong musician must submit without complaint and without rest. Poverty is no barrier to one endowed by nature with musical talent. It is a spur. It keeps the mind loyal to the end. It stimulates the student to great efforts.

If in my own career I have achieved a measure of success and reward it is to some extent due to the fact that I was the son of poor parents and was reared in an atmosphere of struggle and endeavor. Broadly speaking the Bohemians are a nation of peasants. My first musical education I got from my schoolmaster, a man of good ability and much earnestness. He taught me to play the violin. Afterward I traveled with him and we made our living together. Then I spent two years in the organ school in Prague. From that time on I had to study for myself. It is impossible for me to speak without emotion of the strains and sorrows that came upon me in the long and bitter years that followed. Looking back at that time, I can hardly understand how I endured the privations and labor of my youth.

Could I have had in my earlier days the advantages, freely offered in such a school as the National Conservatory of Music, I might have been spared many of my hardest trials and have accomplished much more. Not that I was unable to produce music, but that I had not technique enough to express all that was in me. I had ideas but could not utter them perfectly.

There is a great opportunity for musicians in America and it will increase when grand opera sung in English is more firmly established, with public or private assistance. At the present time this country needs also the materials for orchestral work. The dearth of good native performers on reeds and brass instruments is marked. Every one wants to sing or play the piano, violin or violoncello. Nobody seems to realize the importance of good cornetists, trombonists, clarinetists, oboists, flutists, trumpeters and the like. In Bohemia applicants for admission to the Conservatory are assigned to instruments according to the necessities of the time. Of course nearly every young musician wants to play the violin, but to encourage that tendency would be to undermine the orchestral system and leave composers without the means of properly presenting their works.

I do not agree with those who say that the air here is not good for vocalists. The American voice has a character of its own. It is quite different from the European voice, just as the English voice is different from the German and Italian. Singers like [Edward] Lloyd and [Barton] M'Guckin have an entirely different vocal quality from that of German singers and members of the Latin race. The American voice is unlike anything else, quite unlike the English voice. I do not speak of method or style, but of the natural quality, the timbre of the voice. I have noticed this difference ever since I have been in New York. The American voice is good; it pleases me very much.

Those who think that music is not latent in the American will discover their error before long. I only complain that the American musician is not serious enough in applying himself to the work he must do before he is qualified to enter upon a public career. I have always to remind my most promising pupils to the necessity of work. Work! work! work! to the very end.

The country is full of melody, original, sympathetic and varying in mood, color and character to suit every phase of composition. It is a rich field. America can have a great and noble music of her own, growing out of the very soil and partaking of its nature—the natural voice of a free and vigorous race.

This proves to me that there is such a thing as nationality in music in the sense that it may take on the character of its locality. It now rests with the young musicians of this country and with the patrons of music to say how soon the American school of music is to be developed. A good beginning has been made in New York. Honor to those who will help to increase and broaden this work.

* * * * *

❋ 1893 — WILLIAM T. MOLLENHAUER, MUSICIAN AND MUSIC EDUCATOR

From "A Reply to Dr. Dvořák and His Negro Melodies," *American Art Journal* 61/10 (17 June 1893), 224.

> Responses to Dvořák, particularly to his views about adopting "Negro" melodies as the basis for an American school of composition, were numerous, and William T. Mollenhauer's was typical. Objections usually centered around the same several themes: that Negro melodies are neither African nor American; that the music of the Africans is of a low sort; and that American composers could find better models for composition with only a little more effort. Racism is, of course, essential to an understanding of the dynamics of this debate. In many quarters black Americans were still thought of as strangers to this land, and unwelcome ones at that. But at the same time the call for nationalism in music was not entirely understood by musicians and critics; many thought it an unnecessary enterprise. To them, the aesthetic of music as a "universal language" held true, and any attempt to sort music by national types missed the point of artistic creativity and communication.

The idea of using Negro melodies as a basis for a new school of American music appears ridiculous. These melodies are so incipient and trivial that an American would be ashamed to derive his inspiration from such trash; besides the Negro is a Negro and belongs to Africa, not to America. These so-called Negro songs are not original; if they were, we would find them in their native land (which is not the case). They are derived from old Spanish, Dutch, French and English songs, reproduced by ear in a corrupted manner, and, moreover, many of them have been thumped out by chance on the piano by minstrels, like most popular so-called American songs . . . which were produced in like manner by people devoid of all musical science. Have we Americans so little talent that we must derive our inspirations from such sources? Besides, art belongs to the world, not to one nation; but if you must have an American school of composition, why not adopt Indian rhythms and melodies[?] They may be very crude, but they are at least American. To be sure, it is very difficult for a young American composer to become enthusiastic for his art when nothing will be acknowledged as great or praiseworthy unless it comes from foreign lands. Let some of our philanthropists come forward and offer substantial aid to those who have proved already to be highly gifted in the art—let it be composition, violin or piano. This would be an inducement for young artists to make themselves worthy of such acknowledgement. They would strive to attain the highest summit in art. Every talented man is ambitious; you crush by want or reverses his zeal [*sic*]; you stop the progress of his future greatness. Inspire him with your approval, and we will most assuredly accomplish more toward art than with the Negro melodies.

* * * * *

✻ 1895 — Antonín Dvořák, Visiting Czech Composer

From "Music in America," *Harper's New Monthly Magazine* 90/537 (February 1895), 428-34.

> By 1895 Dvořák was sufficiently familiar with America's musical scene to write the following lengthy article for *Harper's New Monthly Magazine*. "Music in America" was widely read, discussed, and debated sometimes ferociously. Here Dvořák provided a litany of observations on many topics, notably the education and development of composers, the role of government in the arts, the importance of folk elements in music, and the vital mission of music teachers in America. Most importantly, Dvořák expanded on his 1893 statements regarding the adoption of African-American melodies to forge a national school of composition. Here he elaborated on an idea he only alluded to earlier and gave a clearer idea about how this music may be used by composers of art music. Naturally, it was galling for some American composers, many of whom had been toiling at composition for years, to listen to a newly arrived Czech pontificate on how to form an American school of music. They were further irritated when he suggested that the foundation of American music could comfortably rest on the shoulders of black music. Most of Dvořák's audience, after all, was Northern, white, reasonably well-educated, and male; the music of black Americans was fairly distant from their everyday experience, and very few people had direct contact with the actual sources of this music.

It is a difficult task at best for a foreigner to give a correct verdict of the affairs of another country. With the United States of America this is more than usually difficult, because they cover such a vast area of land that it would take many years to become properly acquainted with the various localities, separated by great distances, that would have to be considered when rendering a judgement concerning them all. It would ill become me, therefore, to express my views on so general and all-embracing a subject as music in America, were I not pressed to do so, for I have neither traveled extensively, nor have I been here long enough to gain an intimate knowledge of American affairs. I can only judge it from what I have observed during my limited experience as a musician and teacher in America, and from what those whom I know here tell about their own country. Many of my impressions therefore are those of a foreigner who has not been here long enough to overcome the feeling of strangeness and bewildered astonishment which must fill all European visitors upon their first arrival.

The two American traits which most impress the foreign observer, I find, are the unbounded patriotism and the capacity for enthusiasm of most Americans. Unlike the more diffident inhabitants of other countries, who do not "wear their hearts upon their sleeves," the citizens of America are always patriotic, and no occasion seems to be too serious or too slight for them to give expression to this feeling. Thus nothing better pleases the average American, especially the American youth, than to be able to say that this or that building, this or that new patent appliance, is the finest or grandest in the world. This, of course, is due to that other trait—enthusiasm. The enthusiasm of most Americans for all things new is apparently without limit. It is the essence of what is called "push"—American push. Every day I meet with this quality in my pupils. They are unwilling to stop at anything. In the matters relating to their art they are inquisitive to a degree that they want to go to the bottom of all things at once. It is as if a boy wished to dive before he could swim.

At first, when my American pupils were new to me, this trait annoyed me, and I wished them to give more attention to the one matter in hand rather than to everything at once. But now I like it, for I have come to the conclusion that this youthful enthusiasm and eagerness to take up everything is the best promise for music in America. The same opinion, I remember, was expressed by the director of the conservatory in Berlin, who, from his experience with American students of music, predicted that America within twenty or thirty years would become the first [i.e., the best] musical country.

Only when people in general, however, begin to take as lively an interest in music and art as they now take in more material matters will the arts come into their own. Let the enthusiasm of the people once be excited, and patriotic gifts and bequests must surely follow.

It is a matter of surprise to me that all this has not come long ago. When I see how much is done in every other field by public-spirited men in America—how schools, universities, libraries, museums, hospitals, and parks spring up out of the ground and are maintained by generous gifts—I can only marvel that so little has been done for music. After two hundred years of almost unbroken prosperity and expansion, the net results for music are a number of public concert halls of most recent growth, several musical societies with orchestras of noted excellence, such as the Philharmonic Society of New York, the orchestras of Mr. [Theodore] Thomas and Mr. [Anton] Seidl, and the superb orchestra supported by a public-spirited citizen of Boston; one opera company, which only the upper classes can hear or understand, and a national conservatory which owes its existence to the generous forethought of one indefatigable woman.

It is true that music is the youngest of the arts, and must therefore be expected to be treated as Cinderella, but is it not time that she were lifted from the ashes and given a seat among the equally youthful sister arts in this land of youth until the coming of the fairy godmother and the prince of the crystal slipper?

Art, of course, must always go a-begging, but why should this country alone, which is so justly famed for the generosity and public spirit of its citizens, close its door to the poor beggar? In the Old World this is not so. Since the days of Palestrina . . . princes and prelates have vied with each other in extending a generous hand to music. Since the days of Pope Gregory the Church has made music one of her own chosen arts. In Germany and Austria, princes like Esterhazy, Lobkowitz, and Harrach, who supported Haydn and Beethoven, or the king of Bavaria, who did so much for Wagner, with many others, have helped create a demand for good music, which has since become universal, while in France all governments, be they monarchies, empires or republics, have done their best to carry on the noble work that was begun by Louis XIV. Even the little republic of Switzerland annually sets aside a budget for the furtherance of literature, music and the arts.

A few months ago only we saw how such a question of art as whether the operas sung in Hungary's capital would be of a national or foreign character could provoke a ministerial crisis. Such is the interest in music and art taken by the governments and people of other countries.

The great American republic alone, in its national government as well as in the several governments of the State, suffers art and music to go without encouragement. Trades and commerce are protected, funds are voted away for the unemployed, schools and colleges are endowed, but music must go unaided, and be content if she can get the support of a few private individuals like Mrs. Jeannette M. Thurber and Mr. H[enry]. L. Higginson.

Not long ago a young man came to me and showed me his compositions. His talent seemed so promising that I at once offered him a scholarship in our school, but he sorrowfully confessed that he could not afford to become my pupil because he had to earn his living by keeping books in Brooklyn. Even if he came just two afternoons in the week, or on Saturday afternoon only, he said, he would lose his employment, on which he and others had to depend. I urged him to arrange the matter with his employer, but he only received the answer: "If you want to play, you can't keep books. You will have to drop one or the other." He dropped his music.

In any other country, the State would have made some provision for such a deserving scholar, so that he could have pursued his natural calling without having to starve. With us in Bohemia, the Diet [government assembly] each year votes a special sum of money for just such purposes, and the imperial government in Vienna on occasion furnishes other funds for talented artists. Had it not been for such support I should not have been able to pursue my studies when I was a young man. Owing to the fact that, upon the kind recommendation of such men as [Johannes] Brahms, [Eduard] Hanslick and [Johann] Herbeck, the Minister of Public Education in Vienna on five successive years sent me sums ranging from four to six hundred florins, I could pursue my work and get my compositions published, so that at the end of that time I was able to stand on my own feet. This has filled me with lasting gratitude towards my country.

Such an attitude of the State towards deserving artists is not only kind but wise. For it cannot be emphasized too strongly that art, as such does not "pay," to use an American expression —at least, not in the beginning—and that the art that has to pay its own way is apt to become vitiated and cheap.

It is one of the anomalies of this country that the principle of protection is upheld for all enterprises but art. By protection I do not mean the exclusion of foreign art. That, of course, is absurd. But just as the State here provides for its poor, industrial scholars and university students, so it should help the would-be students of music and art. As it is now, the poor musician not only cannot get his necessary instruction in the first place, but if by any chance he has acquired it, he has small prospects of making his chosen calling support him in the end. Why is this? Simply because the orchestras in which first-class players could find a place in this country can be counted on one hand; while of opera companies where native singers can be heard, and where the English tongue is sung, there is none at all. Another thing which discourages the student of music is the unwillingness of publishers to take anything but light and trashy music. European publishers are bad enough in that respect, but the American publishers are worse. Thus, when one of my pupils last year produced a very creditable work, and a thoroughly American composition at that, he could not get it published in America, but had to send it to Germany, where it was at once accepted. The same is true of my own compositions on American subjects, each of which has had to be published abroad.

No wonder American composers and musicians grow discouraged, and regard the more promising conditions of music in other countries with envy! Such a state of affairs should be a source of mortification to all truly patriotic Americans. Yet it can be easily remedied. What was the situation in England but a short while ago? Then they had to procure all their players from abroad, while their own musicians went to the Continent to study. Now that they have two standard academies of music in London, like those of Berlin, Paris, and other cities, the national feeling for music seems to have been awakened, and the majority of orchestras are composed of native Englishmen, who play as well as the others did before. A single institution can make such a change, just as a single genius can bestow an art upon his country that before was lying in unheeded slumber.

Our musical conservatory in Prague was founded but three generations ago, when a few nobles and patrons of music subscribed five thousand florins which was then the annual cost of maintaining the school. Yet that little school flourished and grew, so that now more than sixfold that amount is annually expended. Only lately a school for organ music has been added to the conservatory, so that the organists of our churches can learn to play their instruments at home, without having to go to the other cities. Thus a school benefits the community in which it is. The citizens of Prague in return have shown their appreciation of the fact by building the "Rudolfinum" as a magnificent home for the arts. It is jointly occupied by the conservatory and the Academy of Arts and besides that contains large and small concert halls and rooms for picture galleries. In the proper maintenance of this building the whole community takes an interest. It is supported, as it was founded, by the stockholders of the Bohemian Bank of Deposit, and yearly gifts and bequests are made to the institution by private citizens.

If a school of art can grow so in a country of but six million inhabitants, what much brighter prospects should it not have in a land of seventy million? The important thing is to make a beginning, and in this the State should set an example.

They tell me that this cannot be done. I ask, why can't it be done? If the old commonwealths of Greece and Italy, and the modern republics of France and Switzerland, have been able to do this, why cannot America follow their example? The money certainly is not lacking. Constantly we see great sums of money spent for the material pleasures of the few, which, if devoted to the purposes of art, might give pleasure to thousands. If schools, art museums and libraries can be maintained at the public expense, why should not musical conservatories and playhouses? The function of the drama, with or without music, is not only to amuse, but to elevate and instruct while giving pleasure. Is it not in the interest of the State that this should be done in the most approved manner, so as to benefit all of the citizens? Let the owners of private playhouses give their performances for diversion only, let those who may, import singers who sing in foreign tongues, but let there be at least one intelligent power that will see to it that the people can hear and see what is best, and what can be understood by them, no matter how small the demand.

That such a system of performing classic plays and operas pleases the people was shown by the attitude of the populace in Prague. There the people collected money and raised subscriptions for over fifty years to build a national playhouse. In 1880 they at last had a sufficient amount and the "National Theater" was accordingly built. It had scarcely been built when it was burned to the ground. But the people were not to be discouraged. Everybody helped, and before a fortnight was over more than a million had been collected, and the house was at once built up again, more magnificent than it was before.

In answer to such arguments I am told that there is no popular demand for good music in America. That is not so. Every concert in New York, Boston, Philadelphia, Chicago or Washington, and most other cities, no doubt, disproves such a statement. American concert halls are as well filled as those of Europe, and, as a rule, the listeners—to judge them by their attentive conduct and subsequent expression of pleasure—are not a whit less appreciative. How it would be with opera I cannot judge, since American opera audiences, as the opera is conducted at present, are in no sense representative of the people at large. I have no doubt, however, that if the Americans had a chance to hear grand opera sung in their own language they would enjoy it as well and appreciate it as highly as the opera-goers of Vienna, Paris, or Munich enjoy theirs. The change from Italian and French to English will scarcely have an injurious effect on the present good voices of the singers, while it may have the effect of improving the voices of American singers, bringing out more clearly the beauty and strength of the timbre, while giving an intelligent conception of the work that enables singers to use pure diction, which cannot be obtained in a foreign tongue.

The American voice, so far as I can judge, is a good one. When I first arrived in this country, I was startled by the strength and the depth of the voices in the boys who sell papers on the street, and I am still constantly amazed at its penetrating quality.

In a sense, of course, it is true that there is less of a demand for music in America than in certain other countries. Our common folk in Bohemia know this. When they come here, they leave their fiddles and other instruments at home, and none of the itinerant musicians with whom our country abounds would ever think of trying their luck over here. Occasionally, when I have met one of my countrymen whom I knew to be musical in this city of New York or in the West, and have asked him why he did not become a professional musician, I have usually received the answer, "Oh, music is not wanted in this land." This I can scarcely believe. Music is wanted wherever good people are, as the German poet has sung. It only rests with the leaders of the people to make a right beginning.

When this beginning is made, and when those who have musical talent find it worth their while to stay in America and to study and exercise their art as the business of their life, the music of America will soon become more national in its character. This my conviction, I know, is not shared by many who can justly claim to know this country better than I do. Because the population of the United States is composed of many different races, in which the Teutonic element predominates, and because, owing to the improved method of transmission of the present day, the music of all the world is quickly absorbed in this country, they argue that nothing specially original or national can come forth. According to that view, all other countries which are but the results of a conglomeration of peoples and races, as, for instance, Italy, could not have produced a national literature or a national music.

A while ago I suggested that inspiration for a truly national music might be derived from the Negro melodies or Indian chants. I was led to take this view partly by the fact that the so-called plantation songs are indeed the most striking and appealing melodies that have yet been found on this side of the water, but largely by the observation that this seems to be recognized, though often unconsciously, by most Americans. All races have their distinctively national songs, which they at once recognize as their own, even if they have never heard them before.

When a Czech, a Pole, or a Magyar [Hungarian] in this country suddenly hears one of his folk-songs or dances, no matter if it is for the first time in his life, his eyes light up at once, and his heart within him responds, and claims that music as his own. So it is with those of Teutonic or Celtic blood, or any other men, indeed, whose first lullaby mayhap was a song wrung from the heart of the people.

It is a proper question to ask, what songs, then, belong to the American and appeal more strongly to him than any others? What melody could stop him on the street if he were in a strange land and make the home feeling well up within him, no matter how hardened he might be or how wretchedly the tune were played? Their number, to be sure, seems to be limited. The most potent as well as the most beautiful among them, according to my estimation, are certain of the so-called plantation melodies and slave songs, all of which are distinguished by unusual and subtle harmonies, the like of which I have found in no other songs but those of old Scotland and Ireland. The point has been urged that many of these touching songs, like those of [Stephen] Foster, have not been composed by the Negroes themselves, but are the work of white men, while others did not originate on the plantations, but were imported from Africa. It seems to me that this matters but little. One might as well condemn the Hungarian Rhapsody because Liszt could not speak Hungarian. The important thing is that the inspiration for such music should come from the right source, and that the music itself should be a true expression of the people's real feelings. To read the right meaning the composer need not necessarily be of the same blood, though that, of course, makes it easier for him. Schubert was a thorough German, but when he wrote Hungarian music, as in the second movement of the C-Major Symphony [No. 9, "Great"], or in some of his piano pieces, like the *Hungarian Divertissement* [D. 817], he struck the true Magyar note, to which all Magyar hearts, and with them our own, must forever respond. This is not a *tour de force*, but only an instance of how music can be comprehended by a sympathetic genius. The white composers who wrote the touching Negro songs which dimmed Thackeray's spectacles so that he exclaimed, "Behold, a vagabond with a corked face and a banjo sings a little song, strikes a wild note, which sets the whole heart thrilling with happy pity!" had a similarly sympathetic comprehension of the deep pathos of slave life. If, as I have been informed they were, these songs were adopted by the Negroes on the plantations, they thus became true Negro songs. Whether the original songs which must have inspired the composers came from Africa or originated on the plantations matters as little as whether Shakespeare invented his own plots or borrowed them from others. The thing to rejoice over is that such lovely songs exist and are sung at the present day. I, for one, am delighted by them. Just so it matters little whether the inspiration for the coming folk songs of America is derived from the Negro melodies, the songs of the Creoles, the red man's chant, or the plaintive ditties of the homesick German or Norwegian. Undoubtedly the germs for the best music lie hidden among all the races that are commingled in this great country. The music of the people is like a rare and lovely flower growing amidst encroaching weeds. Thousands pass it, while others trample it under foot, and thus the chances are that it will perish before it is seen by the one discriminating spirit who will prize it above all else. The fact that no one has yet arisen to make the most of it does not prove that nothing is there.

Not so many years ago Slavic music was not known to men of other races. A few men like Chopin, Glinka, Moniusko, Smetana, Rubinstein, and Tchaikovsky, with a few others, were able to create a Slavic school of music. Chopin alone caused the music of Poland to be known and prized by all lovers of music. Smetana did the same for us Bohemians. Such national music, I repeat, is not created out of nothing. It is discovered and clothed in new beauty, just as the myths and the legends of a people are brought to light and crystallized in undying verse by the master poets. All that is needed is a delicate ear, a retentive memory, and the power to weld the fragments of former ages together in one harmonious whole. Only the other day I read in a newspaper that Brahms himself admitted that he had taken existing folk songs for the themes of his new book of songs, and had arranged them for piano music. I have not seen nor heard the songs, and do not know if this be so; but if it were, it would in no wise reflect discredit upon the composer. Liszt in his rhapsodies and Berlioz in his *Faust* did the same thing with existing Hungarian strains, as for instance in the *Rákóczy March*; and [Robert] Schumann and [Richard] Wagner made similar use of the Marseillaise for their songs of the "Two Grenadiers." Thus, also, [Michael W.] Balfe, the Irishman, used one of our most national airs, a Hussite song, in his opera, *Bohemian Girl*, though how he came by it nobody has as yet explained. So the music of the people, sooner or later, will command attention and creep into the books of the composers.

An American reporter once told me that the most valuable talent that a journalist could possess was a "nose for news." Just so the musician must prick his ear for music. Nothing must be too low or too insignificant for the musician. When he walks he should listen to every whistling boy, every street singer or blind organ-grinder. I myself am often so fascinated by these people that I can scarcely tear myself away, for every now and then I catch a strain or hear the fragments of a recurring melodic theme that sounds like the voice of the people. These things are worth preserving, and no one should be above making a lavish use of all such suggestions. It is a sign of barrenness, indeed, when such characteristic bits of music exist and are not heeded by the learned musicians of the age.

I know that it is still an open question whether the inspiration derived from a few scattered melodies and folk songs can be sufficient to give a national character to higher forms of music, just as it is an open question whether national music, as such, is preferable. I myself, as I have always declared, believe firmly that the music that is most characteristic of the nation whence it springs is entitled to the highest consideration. The part of Beethoven's Ninth Symphony that appeals most strongly to all is the melody of the last movement, and that is also the most German. Weber's best opera, according to the popular estimate, is *Der Freischutz*. Why? Because it is the most German. His inspiration there clearly came from the thoroughly German sounds and situations of the story, and hence his music assumed that distinctly national character which has endeared it to the German nation as a whole. Yet he himself spent far more pains on his opera *Euryanthe*, and persisted to the end in regarding it as his best work. But the people, we see, claim their own: after all, it is for the people that we strive.

An interesting essay could be written on the subject [of] how much the external framework of an opera—that is, the words, the characters of the personages, and the general *mise en scene*—contributes toward the inspiration of the composer. If Weber was inspired to produce his masterpiece by so congenial a theme as the story of *Der Freischutz*, Rossini as undoubtedly similarly inspired by the Swiss surroundings of William Tell. Thus one might almost suspect that some of the charming melodies of that opera are more the product and property of Switzerland than of the Italian composer. It is to be noticed that all of Wagner's operas, with the exception of his earliest work, *Rienzi*, are inspired by German subjects. The most German of them all is that of *Die Meistersinger*, that opera of operas, which should be an example to all who distrust the potency of their own national topics.

Of course, as I have indicated before, it is possible for certain composers to project their spirit into that of another race and country. Verdi partially succeeded in striking Oriental chords in his *Aida*, while Bizet was able to produce so thoroughly Spanish strains and measures as those of *Carmen*. Thus inspiration can be drawn from the depths as well as from the heights, although that is not my conception of the true mission of music. Our mission should be to give pure pleasure, and to uphold the ideals of our race. Our mission as teachers is to show the right way to those who come after us.

My own duty as a teacher, I conceive, is not so much to interpret Beethoven, Wagner, or other masters of the past, but to give what encouragement I can to the young musicians of America. I must give full expression to my firm conviction, and to the hope that just as this nation has already surpassed so many others in marvelous inventions and feats of engineering and commerce, and has made an honorable place for itself in literature in one short century, so it must assert itself in the other arts, and especially in the art of music. Already there are enough public-spirited lovers of music striving for the advancement of this their chosen art to give rise to the hope that the United States of America will soon emulate the older countries in smoothing the thorny path of the artist and musician. When that beginning has been made, when no large city is without its public opera house and concert hall, and without its school of music and endowed orchestra, where native musicians can be heard and judged, then those who have hitherto had no opportunity to reveal their talent will come forth and compete with one another, till a real genius emerges from their number, who will be as thoroughly representative of his country as Wagner and Weber are of Germany, or Chopin of Poland.

To bring about this result we must trust to the ever youthful enthusiasm and patriotism of this country. When it is accomplished, and when music has been established as one of the reigning arts of the land, another wreath of fame and glory will be added to this country which earned its name, the "Land of Freedom," by unshackling her slaves at the price of her own blood.

* * * * *

✻ 1904 — RICHARD ALDRICH, MUSIC CRITIC AND WRITER ON MUSIC

From "Antonín Dvořák and His Music," *New York Times* (8 May 1904), III: 3.

> In an essay written one week after Dvořák's death, critic Richard Aldrich (1863-1937) observed that, although startling at the time, the Czech composer's accomplishments and his mission during his visit to the United States had been largely forgotten by 1904.

It may well be that Dr. Antonín Dvořák, who died a week ago today, will not be numbered among the immortals, with the company of great composers of whom Brahms was the last representative. But few will question that he was the greatest of these latest days. There were none left to contest the title with him. . . .

Dr. Dvořák's music had long been familiar to [the British] public when he came to New York in 1893 as the head of the National Conservatory of Music. His stay in this country was made memorable by the three profoundly interesting works that he produced here and the purpose he had in producing them—the symphony [No. 9] *From the New World*, the string quartet, and the string quintet, all under the same influence, that of the American folk song, as the composer found it in the negro melodies indigenous of this country. The strange controversy that arose over the fact of that influence, which the composer himself asserted to have been decisive with him, and so obviously embodying the elements and the essence of that folk song, is now well-nigh forgotten. These works, and the summons that he gave through them to American composers to pay heed to this potential element in their work, were the most important results of his stay here.

. . . Like other great champions of this element of strength and invigoration in artistic music he has used actual existing tunes with the utmost rarity; the form and the spirit are what have given the characteristic color to his work, and some of its most penetrating charm. How long that charm will keep its power is a question that cannot yet be answered. For its novelty and strength and freshness it has to pay the penalty of provincialism, of a certain primitiveness, of being the expression of a dialect. Through it he has reached a native eloquence that has fascinated and delighted the world, and through it he has given voice to one of the most spontaneous and naive promptings to music that the records of art can show. . . .

* * * * *

* 1908 — LAWRENCE GILMAN, MUSIC AND ARTS CRITIC AND WRITER ON MUSIC

From *Edward MacDowell: A Study* (New York: John Lane Company, 1908), 83-85.

> The monograph of music critic Lawrence Gilman (1878-1939) detailing the life and music of American composer Edward MacDowell (1860-1908) was a landmark work at the time as the first full-length study of the man generally regarded as America's finest composer and as one of the first volumes devoted exclusively to an American composer. Much of the author's account came from interviews with MacDowell himself. In this excerpt Gilman quoted MacDowell directly as the composer discussed Dvořák's views about the search for American nationalism.

A man is generally something different from the clothes he wears or the business he is occupied with; but when we do see a man identified with his clothes we think but little of him. And so it is with music. So-called Russian, Bohemian, or any other purely national music has no place in art, for its characteristics may be duplicated by anyone who takes a fancy to do so. On the other hand, the vital element of music—personality—stands alone. We have seen the Viennese Strauss family adopting the cross rhythms of the Spanish—or, to be more accurate, the Moorish or Arab—school of art. [Moritz] Moszkowski the Pole writes Spanish dances. [Frederic] Cowen in England writes a Scandinavian Symphony. [Edvard] Grieg the Norwegian writes

Arabian music; and, to cap the climax, we have here in America been offered a pattern for an "American" national musical costume by the Bohemian Dvořák—though what the Negro melodies have to do with Americanism in art still remains a mystery. Music that can be made by "recipe" is not music, but tailoring. To be sure, this tailoring may serve to cover a beautiful thought; but—why cover it? And worst of all, why cover it (if covered it must be: if the trade-mark of nationality is indispensable, which I deny)—why cover it with the badge of whilom slavery rather than with the stern but at least manly and free rudeness of the North American Indian? If what is called local tone color is necessary to music (which it most emphatically is not), why not adopt some of the Hindu *Ragas* and modes—each one of which (and the modes alone number over seventy-two) will give an individual tonal character to the music written according to its rules? But the means of "creating" a national music to which I have alluded are childish. No: before a people can find a musical writer to echo its genius it must first possess men who truly represent it—that is to say, men who, being part of the people, love the country for itself: men who put into their music what the nation has put into its life; and in the case of America it needs above all, both on the part of the public and on the part of the writer, absolute freedom from the restraint that an almost unlimited deference to European thought and prejudice has imposed upon us. Masquerading in the so-called nationalism of Negro clothes cut in Bohemia will not help us. What we must arrive at is the youthful optimistic vitality and the undaunted tenacity of spirit that characterizes the American man. This is what I hope to see echoed in American music.

* * * * *

✻ 1914 — Henry Edward Krehbiel, Music Critic and Writer on Music

From *Afro-American Folksongs: A Study in Racial and National Music* (New York: G. Schirmer, 1914), v-x [preface].

> **Critic Henry Krehbiel (1854-1923), writing on the music of black Americans, set out to describe and explain the structural nature of those works employing methods recognizable today in ethnomusicology. In addition, Krehbiel noted that several important American composers had taken up Dvořák's challenge to create a recognizably American style with African-American resources as the basis of inspiration.**

. . . The songs created by the Negroes while they were slaves on the plantation of the South have cried out in vain for scientific study, though "ragtime" tunes, which are their debased off-spring, have seized upon the fancy of the civilized world. This popularity may be deplorable, but it serves at least to prove that a marvelous potency lies in the characteristic rhythmical element of the slave songs. Would not a wider and truer knowledge of their other characteristics as well lead to the creation of a better art than that which tickles the ears and stimulates the feet of the pleasure-seekers of London, Paris, Berlin and Vienna even more than it does those of New York?

The charm of the Afro-American songs has been widely recognized, but no musical savant has yet come to analyze them. Their two most obvious elements only have been copied by composers and dance-makers, who have wished to imitate them. These elements are the rhythmical propulsion which comes from the initial syncopation common to the bulk of them (the "snap" or the "catch" which in an exaggerated form lies at the basis of "ragtime") and the frequent use of the five-tone or pentatonic scale. But there is much more that is characteristic in this body of melody, and this "more" has been neglected because it has not been uncovered to the artistic world. There has been no study of it outside of the author's introduction to the subject printed years ago and a few comments, called forth by transient phenomena, in the [New York] "Tribune" newspaper in the course of the last generation. This does not mean that the world has kept silent on the subject. On the contrary, there has been anything but a dearth of newspaper and platform talk about songs which the Negroes sang in America when they were slaves, but most of it has revolved around the questions whether or not the songs were original creations of these native blacks, whether or not they were entitled to be called American and whether or not they were worthy of consideration as foundation elements for a school of American composition.

The greater part of what has been written was the result of an agitation which followed Dr. Antonín Dvořák's efforts to direct the attention of American composers to the beauty and efficiency of the material which these melodies contained for treatment in the higher artistic forms. Dr. Dvořák's method was eminently practical; he composed a symphony, string quartet and string quintet in which he utilized characteristic elements which he had discovered in the songs of the Negroes which had come to his notice while he was a resident of New York. To the symphony which he gave a title—*From the New World*—which measurably disclosed his purpose; concerning the source of his inspiration for the chamber compositions he said nothing, leaving it to be discovered, as it easily was, from the spirit, or feeling, of the music and the character of its melodic and rhythmic idioms. The eminent composer's aims, as well as his deed, were widely misunderstood at the time, and, for that matter, still are. They called out a clamor from one class of critics which disclosed nothing so much as their want of intelligent discrimination unless it was their ungenerous and illiberal attitude toward a body of American citizens to whom at least must be credited the creation of a species of song in which an undeniably great composer had recognized artistic potentialities thitherto neglected, if not unsuspected, in the land of its origin. While the critics quarreled, however, a group of American musicians acted on Dr. Dvořák's suggestion, and music in the serious, artistic forms, racy of the soil from which the slave songs had sprung, was produced by George W. Chadwick, Henry Schoenberg, Edward R. Kroeger and others. . . .

The scope of my inquiry and the method which I have pursued may be set forth as follows:

1. First of all it shall be determined what are folksongs, and whether or not the songs in question conform to a scientific definition in respect of their origin, their melodic and rhythmical characteristics and their psychology.

2. The question, "Are they American?" shall be answered.

3. Their intervallic, rhythmical and structural elements will be inquired into and an effort be made to show that, while their combination into songs took place in this country, the essential elements came from Africa; in other words, that, while some of the material is foreign, the product is native; and, if native, then American.

4. An effort will be made to disprove the theory which has been frequently advanced that the songs are not original creations of the slaves, but only the fruit of the Negro's innate faculty for imitation. It will be shown that some of the melodies have peculiarities of scale and structure which could not possibly have been copied from the music which the blacks were privileged to hear on the plantations or anywhere else during the period of slavery. Correspondence will be disclosed, however, between these peculiarities and elements observed by travelers in African countries.

5. This will necessitate an excursion into the field of primitive African music and also into the philosophy underlying the conservation of savage music. Does it follow that, because the American Negroes have forgotten the language of their savage ancestors, they have also forgotten all of their music? May relics of that music not remain in a subconscious memory?

6. The influence of the music of the dominant peoples with whom the slaves were brought into contact upon the rude art of the latter will have to be looked into and also the reciprocal effect upon each other; and thus the character and nature of the hybrid art found in the Creole songs and dances of Louisiana will be disclosed.

* * * * *

Composer Horatio Parker, pictured here at his writing desk (ca. 1900), was one of the leaders of the group now referred to as the Second New England School of composers. Parker was one of the first American composers to establish a reputation abroad.

Courtesy of the George Grantham Bain Collection, Prints and Photographs Division, Library of Congress: LC-DIG-ggbain-06084.

❊ 9 — American Music Monuments

1876 – *The Atlantic Monthly*
From "Music"

1881 – Theodore F. Seward
From "Jubilee Songs: Preface to the Music"

1896 – A New York Critic
From "The Music of El Capitan"

1900 – Henry T. Finck
From *Songs and Song Writers*

1901 – Frederick R. Burton
From "The New Opera Judith"

1901 – *The New York Times*
From "The Philharmonic Society"

1902 – *Musical Courier*
From "Charles E. Ives' Concert and New Cantata,
'The Celestial Country' "

1908 – Henry T. Parker
From "Music and Drama–
Mr. Chadwick as a True American Composer"

1911 – *American Musician and Art Journal*
From "A Musical Novelty"

1912 – Daniel Gregory Mason
From "Recent Musical Happenings in New York: A Review"

1918 – *The New York Times*
From " 'Shanewis,' Indian Opera, Captivates"

The gradual formation of an American musical canon, particularly one comprising instrumental music and opera, is a central feature of the era under consideration. Although an impressive corpus of songs and hymn tunes had existed for more than a hundred years, an important body of art music was not forged until after the Civil War when a generation of young American composers trained in European conservatories returned home and began to ply their craft. This chapter considers eleven compositions that are cornerstones of this core repertoire.

❋ 1876 — *THE ATLANTIC MONTHLY*

From "Music," *Atlantic Monthly* 37/223 (May 1876), 633.

Although by no means the nation's first symphonist, John Knowles Paine (1839-1906) is widely recognized as the earliest American master of the genre. His First Symphony (Op. 23) was given its premiere in Boston by the Boston Symphony Orchestra in 1876. It, and a subsequent Second Symphony (*Im Frühling*), encouraged many New England composers and helped to forge what is often referred to as the Second New England School of composers. This "school," in fact a loosely connected group of individuals centered around Boston, included Amy Beach, George Whitefield Chadwick, Horatio Parker, and others. Paine's First Symphony in C Minor was inspired by Beethoven's great Fifth Symphony in the same key, but Paine's expansive work is more melodious, its harmonies are denser and lusher, and its palpable Romanticism reminds one more of Robert Schumann than of Beethoven. The following reviewer—probably John Sullivan Dwight—admitted the growing influence of "organicism" in music, that is, the concept through which musical forms evolve from their own materials. Later, as the composer's fame began to grow and his gifts began to be appreciated, Dwight quipped, "If you would give me pleasure, give me Paine."

Of the many important musical events of the past winter in Boston, Mr. John K. Paine's symphony claims our attention first. We heartily wish that we could put the extreme pleasure that two hearings of this work have given us into a more systematic form than it is actually possible to do. Had it been a sensational work (and there are sensational works in a high as well as in a low sense), an analysis of its effect upon us might have been comparatively easy, even after only one hearing. The mind is readier to grasp a composition full of strokes and strong hits than it is to separate into its various factors one in which the development is more purely organic. Absolute music, developing itself from a thematic germ, is a fair epitome of all organic and cosmic development in the physical world. If the theme be really vital, if it do really "contain the potency and power" of a living composition, its rational development will be beautifully gradual and uneventful. Whether this epitomizing of cosmic growth is the highest mission of music or not is apart from the present question. In considering any particular work of a man, it is impertinent to ask whether he has done the highest possible thing; all that we have a right to ask is whether he has done well the thing he palpably tried to do. To come more closely to the point, then, we are in no condition to analyze Mr. Paine's symphony (we have not even seen the score, much less studied it), but can only give our impressions of it. It gave us unalloyed enjoyment from beginning to end. It is melodious, natural, spirited, with that strength that comes from perfect equilibrium. Of dryness of detail we found not a trace; it is thoroughly genial throughout. One technical point we would mention, and that is that Mr. Paine has made a long stride in handling the orchestra since he wrote his [oratorio] *St. Peter* [Op. 20, 1872]. The orchestral coloring is throughout good, at times even peculiarly fascinating. We must all heartily thank Mr. [Theodore] Thomas for giving us a hearing of this work; both the performances were good, the second one even masterly.

* * * * *

* 1881 — THEODORE F. SEWARD, MUSIC EDUCATOR, COMPOSER, AND EDITOR OF MUSIC PERIODICALS

From "Jubilee Songs: Preface to the Music," in J. B. T. Marsh, *The Story of the [Fisk] Jubilee Singers with Their Songs* (Boston: Houghton, Mifflin, 1881), 121-22.

> The chorus known as the Jubilee Singers and comprised mostly of former slaves was formed in 1871 expressly to tour and raise funds for Fisk University in Nashville. Performances by the group represented for many whites their first exposure to the African-American spiritual. Although the music the ensemble sang was arranged in four parts, many of the essential aspects of the original performance practice, notably its remarkable rhythms and melodic inflections, were retained. In this essay Theodore F. Seward (1835-1902) detailed several noteworthy features, stressing how this music—a spontaneous religious expression—seemed to "spring into life." This writer, who was a serious collector and student of the Negro spiritual as well as the musical director of the Jubilee Singers during its second European tour, also expressed a clear appreciation of this music's uniqueness in America. As the century progressed, nevertheless, it became commonplace to try to relate the qualities of this repertoire to European and American "classical" music.

In giving these melodies to the world in a tangible form, it seems desirable to say a few words about them as judged from a musical standpoint. It is certain that the critic stands completely disarmed in their presence. He must not only recognize their immense power over audiences which include many people of the highest culture, but, if he be not thoroughly encased in prejudice, he must yield a tribute of admiration on his own part, and acknowledge that these songs touch a chord which the most consummate art fails to reach. Something of this result is doubtless due to the singers as well as to their melodies. The excellent rendering of the Jubilee Band [singers] is made more effective and the interest is intensified by the comparison of their former state of slavery and degradation with the present prospects and hopes of their race, which crowd upon every listener's mind during the singing of their songs. Yet the power is chiefly in the songs themselves, and hence a brief analysis of them will be of interest.

Their origin is unique. They are never "composed" after the manner of ordinary music, but spring into life, ready-made, from the white heat of religious fervor during some protracted meeting in church or camp. They come from no musical cultivation whatever, but are the simple, ecstatic utterances of wholly untutored minds. From so unpromising a source we could reasonably expect only such a mass of crudities as would be unendurable to the cultivated ear. On the contrary, however, the cultivated listener confesses to a new charm, and to a power never before felt, at least in its kind. What can we infer from this but that the childlike, receptive minds of these unfortunates were wrought upon with a true inspiration, and that this gift was bestowed upon them by an ever-watchful Father, to quicken the pulses of life, and to keep them from the state of hopeless apathy into which they were in danger of falling.

A technical analysis of these melodies shows some interesting facts. The first peculiarity that strikes the attention is in the rhythm. This is often complicated, and sometimes strikingly original. But although so new and strange, it is most remarkable that these effects are so extremely satisfactory. We see few cases of what theorists call *mis-form*, although the student of musical composition is likely to fall into that error long after he has mastered the leading principle of the art.

Another noticeable feature of the songs is the rare occurrence of triple time, or three-part measure among them. The reason for this is doubtless to be found in the beating of the foot and the swaying of the body which are such frequent accompaniments of the singing. These motions are in even measure, and in perfect time; and so it will be found that, however broken and seemingly irregular the movement of the music, it is always capable of the most exact measurement. In other words, its irregularities invariably conform to the "higher law" of the perfect rhythmic flow. . . .

❊ ❊ ❊ ❊ ❊

❊ 1896 — A NEW YORK CRITIC

From "The Music of El Capitan," *Musical Visitor* 25/6 (June 1896), 154.

> Today John Philip Sousa (1854-1932) is remembered almost solely for his impressive body of marches for band, but in his own time he was recognized as a gifted and far more versatile talent. The "March King," as he is often called, also composed nearly a dozen operettas, many of which were enormously popular. As a younger man, Sousa had been a theater violinist in Philadelphia. During that time he became well acquainted with the conventions of popular theater, which he managed to combine with his own unparalleled gift for melody. His tuneful and captivating operetta *El Capitan* (1895) exhibits many of the expected plot twists that accompany comic opera. Set in exotic Peru, *El Capitan* features disguised identity, forbidden love, revenge, and plenty of farce. Little wonder that it was so popular.

Sousa eschewed the notion that art could not be popular and indeed sought to gain the largest possible audience for his works. Following his service as leader of the United States Marine Band, Sousa formed his own ensemble, which performed worldwide until the onset of the Great Depression. The Sousa Band not only performed its namesake's music but was famous for its renderings of recognized masterpieces, which had been carefully arranged for the medium.

Of course everybody will go to hear Sousa's music. Sousa is real, Sousa is genuine, and his fame is not built on quicksands. Every maiden who knows the quick and sensuous joys of the ballroom adores Sousa, whose "two-steps" have worn out many a Parisian heel for her; and every jovial lad whose pulses have throbbed as he glided with a diaphanous partner over the polished floors of the summer hotels has offered up his thanks to the rhythmic bandmaster. *El Capitan* is Sousareque [*sic*] from beginning to end.

Of course the "enthusiasts," who are so completely educated that they prefer to read scores rather than to hear them, and to whom music is one of the ponderous and troublesome issues of the day, will tell you that Sousa's music is flippant and trivial. They don't even care to hear it. They know exactly what it is beforehand—all tumpty-tum and teety-tee. They will tell you that it is demoralizing and [emasculating], and they will run fat, Frankfort sausage fingers through tempestuous manes in sublime resignation to the worst.

Out upon them all, I say! Nobody need feel in the least ashamed to admit an admiration for Sousa. He caters to the pulses of the people. He is human. He writes intelligible music, because he sympathizes with his public. He is not a bit learned or technical. His tunes are not at all algebraic, and you can't imagine him sitting down to compose with an A-plus-B-equals-C cast of countenance. *El Capitan* is full of jolly, rollicking melody, and some capital choruses. . .

✻ ✻ ✻ ✻ ✻

✻ 1900 — HENRY T. FINCK, MUSIC CRITIC AND WRITER ON MUSIC

From *Songs and Song Writers* (New York: Charles Scribner's Sons, 1900), 239-49.

By the time he died, Edward MacDowell (1860-1908) was widely considered America's most accomplished composer of art music. He wrote a number of appealing, well-crafted orchestral works as well as a piano concerto that maintains a place in the contemporary repertoire, but during his lifetime he was also valued as an exceptional writer of songs. MacDowell's collection *Eight Songs* (Op. 47), published in 1893, was immediately recognized as a masterpiece. He used texts by Goethe and the American writer William Dean Howells, along with three of his own poems, to convey themes of love, loneliness, and nature. MacDowell's vocal lines are eminently suitable for performance by non-professionals, and he usually kept the piano parts accessible. His chord choices were often fresh and unexpected, as is noted in the review below by the prominent critic Henry T. Finck (1854-1926).

Thinkers are rare in all departments of mental activity, and thinkers in tones are rarest of all; but MacDowell is a thinker; you can see it in the portrait included in this volume, as well as you can hear it in his music; and with the faculty of meditation he unites the still rarer gift of originating ideas. . . . A regiment of soldiers could not make him write a stale melody or platitudinous succession of chords, such as constitute the stock in trade of most songwriters. One of the greatest charms of his music is that where you expect a certain chord as almost inevitable, he surprises you with quite another one. He has the faculty, peculiar to the highest order of genius, of evoking tears in the listener with a single chord or modulation. He never writes unless he has something new and interesting to say, and when he has said it he stops. A slow and hard worker himself, he wonders at the fertility of some of his colleagues who seem to shake compositions from their sleeves. But if these colleagues followed his example of writing only when they had something new to say, they would never write at all. . . .

Original and fascinating as are many of the songs so far considered, they are all surpassed by those comprised in the collection entitled Eight Songs (Op. 47), which cannot be too highly commended to those who are not yet aware or convinced that MacDowell belongs in the very front rank of songwriters. For three of them—songs of trees and birds and brown eyes and love—MacDowell has written his own poems, which have the same imaginative, romantic character as his music. The first of these, "The Robin Sings in the Apple Tree," with its subdued note of woe, is one of the most charming of modern love songs, to which concert-singers and amateurs have taken a great fancy of late. "Confidence" is a poetic refutation of the notion that love can die, enforced by the eloquence of fresh, buoyant music which puts the scoffers to flight. The third, "The West Wind Croons in the Cedar Trees," is another of those songs which have the initials E. A. M. stamped on every bar. MacDowell does not attend many concerts or operatic performances, for the reason that he fears being influenced unconsciously by the music of other composers. The song just named is one of many that prove the wisdom of this policy. It does not suggest any other composer, but is as original as a new orchid found by an explorer in a Brazilian forest. . . .

. . . But the greatest of these eight songs is "The Sea," which James Huneker has justly called "the strongest song of the sea since Schubert's 'Am Meer'." The rare poetic art with which [William Dean] Howells brings before our eyes the picture of the lover sailing away to sea, while the beloved stands on the shore and cries; followed by the picture of the wreck, and the lover lying asleep, far under, dead in his coral bed—is duplicated in the music, which shows a marvelous gift of emotional coloring in its harmonies, and is, in all other respects, a perfect song. It is not only the best of these Eight Songs, it is the best of all the MacDowell songs, of all American songs, one of the best hundred songs ever written, the world over. I shall never forget the eagerness and the delighted surprise with which [Ignaz] Paderewski read it over when I made him acquainted with it.

* * * * *

❊ 1901 — FREDERICK R. BURTON, ETHNOMUSICOLOGIST AND COMPOSER

From "The New Opera Judith," *New York Times* (29 September 1901), [magazine supplement]: 2.

George Whitefield Chadwick (1854-1931) completed his three-act "lyric drama" *Judith* in December 1900. A difficult work to categorize, it straddles the line somewhat uncomfortably between oratorio and opera and reveals a number of musical styles and influences. But what makes this opera significant in the American canon is not its polyglot musical language but its wholly unexpected and certainly unpuritanical subject matter. Presenting the apocryphal story of Judith and Holofernes, it is a passionate drama that features erotic seduction, a brutal beheading, exoticism, and triumph over the enemy. Chadwick's accompanying music is sometimes reserved, but at several important climactic points he offered some of his best writing. At *Judith*'s premiere—staged without action, costumes, or scenery—critics noted its power and intensity while also admitting flaws in the text and dramatic pacing. Nevertheless, the opera was generally assessed as an exceptional American work and received several more concert performances during Chadwick's lifetime.

Mr. George W. Chadwick's new work, *Judith*, gave uncommon distinction to the [Worcester, Massachusetts] music festival that came to an end last evening. . . .

Fortunately for the general cause of music, *Judith* was a success. It aroused no end of discussion among the visiting musicians—no end because the discussion bids fair to continue for a long time. This is not because Mr. Chadwick is a bold iconoclast, or because *Judith* is a startling innovation. It arises simply from the fact that the work is an opera. In recent times there have been presentations of opera in concert form, but it is hardly customary to introduce them to the public in that style, or to make a staid old oratorio society the vehicle. The first question, then, is, what is *Judith*? I have called it an opera. Mr. Chadwick and Mr. William Chauncy Langdon, the author of the "book," call it a lyric drama. Up to the present lyric drama means nothing definite. If *Judith* should be put up on the stage, it might immediately acquire a definite meaning, for the work would be quite unlike any operas now used. . . .

Mr. Chadwick has long been known as a skillful writer for chorus, and it seems to me that the best things in this work are the choruses. Some of them are massive and simple, with long passages *a cappella*; others are frankly in oratorio form, though nonetheless dramatic. There is a highly developed fugue in the first act that lends its structural peculiarities capitally to the requirements of the situation, theatrically speaking. It might be remarked in passing that when the word "theatrical" slips into this commentary it is not used in any disparaging sense. The music of *Judith* is not cheap; it includes few or none of the devices commonly stigmatized as theatrical, and it is quite possible that it would be found too reserved for success in the theater, but this is where it belongs, nevertheless, for, in the concert hall, while the musical sense is highly gratified, the imagination of the listener is too heavily burdened. He craves continually the assistance of spectacle and action.

There is an abundance of suave melody in the solo parts, and to some extent there is characterization. . . . The orchestration throughout is as rich as the most modern of moderns could desire. Altogether the impression made by the concert presentation of *Judith* is that it is a beautiful work, and that covers everything. . . .

❋ ❋ ❋ ❋ ❋

❋ 1901 — *The New York Times*

From "The Philharmonic Society" *New York Times* (21 December 1901), 8.

Henry Hadley (1871-1937) was a fine composer, an excellent conductor, and an unflinching advocate for music by American composers. Completed when he was only twenty-nine years old, his Symphony No. 2 (Op. 30, *The Four Seasons*) exhibits several important features. In it he emphasized programmaticism woven into the fabric of traditional forms, and he imbued the work with Indian-inspired themes. This last trait is particularly important, coming as it does only years after Dvořák's admonition regarding indigenous music that may be suitable for the creation of an American school of composition. The writer of the following review noted that Hadley's symphony bears a resemblance to Mendelssohn's music, but, in fact, it may be reasonably suggested that it bears a striking likeness to works by Chadwick. Hadley studied composition with Chadwick at the New England Conservatory, and there he became familiar with his teacher's light-hearted, melodic style. Not insignificantly, throughout the final decades of the nineteenth century Chadwick's music was also favorably compared to Mendelssohn's.

Mr. Hadley's symphony, *The Four Seasons*, was heard in its entirety yesterday for the first time anywhere. It is the work which was recently awarded the Paderewski and New England Conservatory prizes in composition for orchestral music. . . .

The symphony is in four movements, entitled "Winter, "Spring," "Summer," and "Autumn." This arrangement seems strained, but no doubt the composer was endeavoring to escape the obvious and the conventional in his distribution. Mr. Hadley is a thorough believer in program music, and he asks his hearer to follow him into the realm of his imagination. In his first movement he aims plainly to depict musically, first, the desolation, and, second, the wildness, of Winter. In his second movement he thinks of spring as a season of joy and the time of the awakening of nature. He hears the piping of birds and "the hum of the bees in immemorial elms," the breaking of waters from their winter bonds of ice, and the turning of a young man's fancy to thoughts of love.

In the "Summer" movement we are invited to think of a moonlight night in the west, and the themes are designed to sing the notes of an Indian love song and of the rising of the full-orbed moon. Together with these themes go certain chords intended to give a touch of mystery to the movement. The working up of the night theme brings into play the full resources of the orchestra, while toward the end of the movement the softer accents of the instrumental army are employed to leave the hearer with an impression of darkness and distance in his mind. . . .

The final movement, "Autumn," calls for more understanding on the part of the hearer. Mr. Hadley named this movement "The Death of the Leaves," and he begins it with a violin figure intended to portray the falling of the leaves in autumn. Together with this figure goes a theme meant to symbolize destiny. This melancholy part of the movement gives way to a lively allegro descriptive of the hunt, and this in turn yields again to the melancholy music with which the movement comes to an end.

The impression left at the end of the symphony is that the composer would have made a surer impression if he had followed the accepted order of the seasons and ended the work with his stirring movement descriptive of winter. For the rest it may be said that the detailed program, which was in the composer's mind, is not essential to an enjoyment of this work. As broad mood pictures, his four movements carry their titles with sufficient suitability. The symphony is a dignified and ambitious work and will add to Mr. Hadley's growing reputation. He is still a young man, and much may be expected from him in the future. He will undoubtedly in time cut loose from older models in phraseology and instrumentation, especially from Mendelssohn, whose influence is perceptible in many spots in this work. Furthermore, Mr. Hadley, who is well educated in the rules of form, will be in time a firmer master of that philosophy which underlies the rules. When he is such a master, he will know how to make his contrasts without open joints.

The symphony contains many beauties and some admirable orchestration. It is a credit to American music. . . .

❊ ❊ ❊ ❊ ❊

❊ 1902 — *THE MUSICAL COURIER*

From "Charles E. Ives' Concert and New Cantata, 'The Celestial Country'," *Musical Courier* 44/17 (23 April 1902), 34.

> Charles Edward Ives (1874-1954) is one of the more enigmatic figures in American music history. The son of a Connecticut bandmaster, Ives was introduced to music at an early age and developed eclectic, modernist tendencies far removed from other New England composers of his day. He was prolific but inexplicably kept his works mostly to himself as he toiled in the insurance business. He effectively stopped composing in the 1920s, but contact with musicians and the advocacy of friends gradually led to his "discovery" and ultimately to the appreciation of his gifts. He was awarded the Pulitzer Prize in 1947 for his Third Symphony, and there followed much interest in his life and works. This review of his early seven-movement cantata *The Celestial Country* (1898-99) is widely believed to have contributed significantly to his withdrawal from public musical life. Ives was a deep thinker, and his later compositions—with titles such as *The Unanswered*

Question and *Universe Symphony*—sometimes explored grand, philosophical topics. It seems likely that Ives thought that the following highly analytical review of *The Celestial Country* obscured his music's meaning and made it seem a pedantic exercise. He may also have concluded that, given the lack of critical enthusiasm of this rather tame cantata, his ideas about compositional innovation were certain to meet with failure.

At the Central Presbyterian Church last Friday night the organist, Charles E. Ives, a Yale graduate and pupil in music of Professor [Horatio] Parker, gave an invitation concert which had for its principal number a new cantata by Ives, *The Celestial Country*, words by Henry Alford, for solo quartet, chorus, organ and string orchestra, augmented by two horns.

The work shows undoubted earnestness in study and talent for composition, and was fairly creditably done, the thirty singers and players entering into the spirit of the thing with enthusiasm.

Beginning with a prelude, trio and chorus, with soft, long-drawn chords of mysterious meaning, picturing the far country, the music swells to a fine climax, various themes being heard, used later on. Indeed, throughout the work here is homogeneity, coming from the interweaving of appropriate themes. Following the opening chorus, there is a bass solo, sung on this occasion by the alto, however, Miss Emma Williams; it is lyric and full of grace, in B flat, and the low F's at the close came out finely.

There follows a quartet in D minor, difficult, with chromatic harmonies, and in the trio with alternating 3/4 and 4/4 time measures. It comes to a pianissimo close on the words, "Until the eve be light" most effectively. The "Intermezzo" for strings alone, con sordini, is song-like, with the first violin and later the viola singing the melody, and this, too, comes to a close in the softest tones. This "Intermezzo" the Kaltenborn Quartet will find useful for their concerts. It is full of unusual harmonies and [is] pleasing throughout.

The *a cappella* octet which follows has interwoven the principal theme of the quartet, followed by the tenor solo, one of the effective numbers of the cantata. This is in G major, well suited to a lyric tenor voice, with a graceful running figure in the accompaniment, the climax coming on the words "Till our faith be sight" on a high A, which rang out clear and true, sung by tenor E. Ellsworth Giles.

The finale is composed of a chorus, chorale and fugue. This shows some original ideas, many complex rhythms and effective part writing, the chorale in 4/2 time, the fugue built on the theme of the chorale. With an obbligato soprano on the high C, all voices fortissimo, the work comes to a triumphant close. . . .

An audience completely filling the church listened with expressions of pleasure, and at the close the composer was overwhelmed with congratulations, which he accepted in modest fashion.

* * * * *

⁜ 1908 — HENRY T. PARKER, MUSIC CRITIC

From "Music and Drama–Mr. Chadwick as a True American Composer," *Boston Evening Transcript* (10 February 1908), 11.

Although a prolific composer of vocal music, Chadwick is best known today for his instrumental music. Among his six multi-movement works for orchestra, *Symphonic Sketches* stands out for both its originality and the accolades it received in its own day. Not originally conceived as a single work, it was completed between 1895 and 1904 and draws on diverse musical materials, including Afro-Caribbean rhythms, pentatonic scales, and impressionistic harmonies. Its energetic and high-spirited moods appealed to audiences and critics alike, and its clever use of recognizable materials lent it a distinctively American sound. In the following review Henry T. Parker (1867-1934), a much-feared Boston critic, dwelt on Chadwick's Americanism and compared him to his contemporaries. With this composition Chadwick abandoned the formal symphony, perhaps perceiving that the development of the genre had run its course and was no longer appreciated by listeners. Here each movement is prefaced by brief lines of text intended to convey a mood. Chadwick opted to call these less severe, semi-programmatic movements "sketches," borrowing a term popular in contemporary literary circles.

Mr. Chadwick, as his *Symphonic Sketches* suggested once more at the [Boston] Symphony Concert of Saturday, is the most American of our composers, because oftener than with the rest his music in mood and spirit sounds distinctively American. For a composer to live permanently and work steadily in America is not to write American music. Mr. [Charles Martin] Loeffler, for example, so lives and works, but there is not an American trait so far as we can recall in his music. To have been born in America is no title to the writing of American music as the compositions of Templeton Strong, Arthur Bird and sundry other Teutonized Americans readily prove. In fact and in suggestion it is "made in Germany" as truly as though it were so invoiced from some musical custom-house. To write music from the melodies of primitive peoples, like the Indians or the Negroes, who happen to live on American soil, is to write music that is only geographically American. Dvořák was still a Czech when he wrote such a symphony and called it *From the New World*; Mr. [Arthur] Farwell and all his brethren are often only experimenting with an aboriginal music that has nothing to do with the American spirit today. Mr. [Edward] MacDowell was narrowly individual through and through, and he would have dreamed his dreams of Arthur's court, Celtic queens and Norse warriors anywhere, and shaped his *Woodland Sketches* or his sea-pieces as readily in Wiesbaden as in Boston.

And so forth and so on with other American composers. Russian music, with all allowance for its folk tunes and its other palpable Russian idiosyncrasies, is Russian because the mood and spirit of it is recognizable as such. . . . A score of other examples are as ready, to prove that the true test of nationality in music is not any comparatively extraneous circumstances, but its underlying, pervading and persuading spirit.

Mr. Chadwick's music seems so often American because it bears that test. Recall, for example, the scherzo in one of his symphonies [Symphony No. 2 in B-flat] . . . its mood is altogether American. Black, "buck" roustabouts dance on the wharf; an American composer watches them and puts into his music their soul and his. Recall the *Columbian Ode* for the World's Fair at Chicago—American in each succeeding mood of pride in the past, exultation in the present, and confidence in the future. Recall a movement here and there in Mr. Chadwick's chamber music, and again comes memory of a distinctly American spirit. Turn, in particular, to the *Symphonic Sketches* as Dr. [Karl] Muck and his men played them on Friday and Saturday. He is a German; they are of many nationalities, and, being foreigners, he and they perhaps sentimentalized the slow, contrasting passages of the first and last "sketches" more than a sensitive American conductor and band would do. Allow for this; and grant, too, that the nocturne of parental affection and longing of the second "sketch" is universal and not particular in spirit. The three other "sketches" remain and in them the mood is vividly, stirringly and, in two at least, irresistibly American. Americans "fool," Americans "jolly," and European observers are fane to lament these ingrained habits in us. Is Mr. Chadwick's final "sketch"—"The Vagrom Ballad" of "clay pipes and rum and broken heads and blackened eyes and thirty days to come"—anything else than musical "fooling" and musical "jollying," American in spirit and expression, and often at its loudest and most careless? [Then] comes the slow, mysterious, sober song near the end. The inevitable "contrasting passage," the merely academic might call it. As it seems to us [the writer], it is far more a just musical incarnation of the tendency in the American temperament to turn suddenly serious, and deeply and unaffectedly so, in the midst of its "fooling," to run away into sober fancies and moods, and then as quickly turn "jolly" again.

Return through the scherzo of "Hobgoblin," and it is bluff music with an unmistakable sturdy American tang. Mr. Chadwick has taken his boy-fairy out of English farm steads to set him in American farm houses. He is a Hobgoblin who musically sets his ten fingers to his nose like the American hobbledehoy that he is. Pass to the first "sketch" of "Jubilee." Here, as now and then elsewhere in Mr. Chadwick's later music, is the echo of Negro tunes; but the American quality of the music lies little in that. Rather it is in the high and volatile spirits of the music, the sheer rough-and-tumble of it at its fullest moments. As was said on Saturday, the music shouts because it cannot help it, and it sings because it cannot help it, and each as only Americans would shout and sing. And the intervening suaver passage, as in the last movement, is only the other face of this American volatility. No, Mr. Chadwick does not write American music because he was born in Lowell [Massachusetts] or because he lives and works in Boston, or because he now and then recalls an American folk tune. He writes it because it is often, and especially of late years, intrinsically American in mood, spirit, and appeal.

* * * * *

✻ 1911 — *AMERICAN MUSICIAN AND ART JOURNAL*

From "A Musical Novelty," *American Musician and Art Journal* (24 June 1911), 7.

With his success as the "King of Ragtime," Scott Joplin (1868-1917) longed for recognition on the operatic stage as well. His second opera, *Treemoni-*

sha, was completed in 1911 and first performed four years later without scenery or staging and with the composer accompanying his singers at the piano. A tale of superstition, deception, and ultimately forgiveness, the three-act opera features Treemonisha, a young girl who, as a child, was found under a "sacred" tree. Abducted by "conjurors," Treemonisha is saved by Remus but demands forgiveness for her captors, who are perilously close to being pounced upon by a riotous crowd. Treemonisha admonishes the crowd for its attempt to do evil to the evil-doers, and, once the rioters settle down, they realize that she possesses the qualities necessary to be their new leader. In this work Joplin utilizes many of the conventions associated with opera but adds a number of unique elements. *Treemonisha* features the jaunty rhythms of ragtime, African-American dialect, and a message of non-violence and forgiveness that had remained resonant a full generation after the Civil War.

Scott Joplin, well known as a writer of music, and especially of what a certain musician classified as "classic ragtime," has just published an opera in three acts, entitled *Treemonisha*, upon which he has been working for the past fifteen years. This achievement is noteworthy for two reasons: First, it is composed by a Negro, and second, the subject deals with an important phase of Negro life. . . .

Scott Joplin has not been influenced by his musical studies or by foreign schools. He has created an original type of music in which he employs syncopation in a most artistic and original manner. It is in no sense ragtime, but of that peculiar quality of rhythm which Dvořák used so successfully in the *New World* symphony. The composer has constantly kept in mind his characters and their purpose, and has written music in keeping with his libretto. *Treemonisha* is not grand opera, nor is [it] light opera; it is what we might call character opera or racial opera. . . .

There has been much written and printed of late concerning American opera, and the American composers have seized the opportunity of acquainting the world with the fact that they have been able to produce works in this line. Several operas by American composers have been produced recently, and there is promise of several others being heard next year, among which will be Professor [Horatio] Parker's *Mona*, which won the $10,000 Metropolitan Opera prize. Now the question is, Is this an American opera? And a correlative question is, Are the American composers endeavoring to write American operas? In other words, are they striving to create a school of American opera, or are they simply employing their talents to fashion something suitable for the operatic stage and satisfactory to the operatic management? If so, American opera will always remain a thing in embryo. To date there is no record of even the slightest tendency toward the fashioning of the real American opera, and although this work just completed by one of the Ethiopian race will hardly be accepted as a typical American opera for obvious reasons, nevertheless none can deny that it serves as an opening wedge, since it is in every respect indigenous. It has sprung from our soil practically of its own accord. Its composer has focused his mind upon a single object, and with a nature wholly in sympathy with it has hewn an entirely new form of operatic art. . . .

*****

✻ 1912 — DANIEL GREGORY MASON, COMPOSER AND MUSIC EDUCATOR

From "Recent Musical Happenings in New York: A Review," *The Outlook* (13 April 1912), 806-08.

Daniel Gregory Mason (1873-1953) was himself a composer and long-time professor of music at Columbia University. A self-described "conservative" musician, Mason was an adherent of the traditional compositional styles represented during the late nineteenth century by Brahms. In this review of Horatio Parker's three-act opera *Mona* (Op. 71, 1910), Mason chided Parker for having "forsaken" himself and for having "out-Wagnered Wagner." It is true that Parker's best-known works were sacred and therefore generally conservative and restrained. But in *Mona* Parker applied lush scoring and dense harmonies to create an unexpectedly sensual work. Significantly, *Mona* won the $10,000 prize offered by New York's Metropolitan Opera, which also mounted its premiere in 1912. Set in ancient Britain and recalling the plot of Bellini's *Norma* (1831), *Mona* presents the story of a warrior princess torn between her allegiance to her country and her love for the disguised Gwynn, who she later learns is the son of the ruling Roman governor against whom Mona has been battling. Following a number of sordid encounters, she kills Gwynn, only to be captured and executed by the Romans.

What is really worth finding out is not whether America is producing music that is worthy of being preserved alongside of that by European masters, but whether the art of music is really making progress in America; and, if so, whether that progress is discernible in the works of American composers.

That is what must be borne in mind in forming any estimate of such a work as Horatio Parker's opera, *Mona*.

As a composer Professor Parker has already made a creditable place for himself in the annals of American music. Very few American compositions are so well known outside of this country as his [oratorio] *Hora novissima* [Op. 30]. The music that he has composed for the service of the church has both distinction and beauty. In his work there has generally been evidence of that restraint without which the highest art in music cannot be achieved. One does not naturally think of Professor Parker as a composer of opera. Perhaps that fact whetted the curiosity of those who waited to hear the music of *Mona*. It proved to be very different from the music that has come from his pen heretofore. The writer of massive choral music has transformed himself into an extreme exponent of music drama. The idiom of the English church musician is forsaken for the idiom of Wagner. Into his choral writing, particularly in that for the church, Horatio Parker has succeeded in infusing something of his own personality. Almost any one of his anthems, for example, leaves the impression that only Horatio Parker could have written it. Now in his conversion to opera he seems to have forsaken not only his old style, but also himself. One has the feeling that, except for occasional passages of individuality, almost anybody of Professor Parker's attainments might have written *Mona*.

Nevertheless, the opera *Mona*—which is not really an opera at all, but a music drama—is in many respects impressive. In the first place, Professor Parker has in Mr. Brian Hooker's dramatic poem an unusual libretto. . . .

The story of *Mona* is the story of many twentieth-century women. Indeed, sometimes it seems as if it were the story of twentieth-century woman. And in this poem of Brian Hooker's it is told with great dramatic power. As a libretto for an opera it is not by any means perfect; but it is so far superior in substance, and even in form, to what serves as a framework for most operas, that it is safe to say that whatever success *Mona* secures will be in large measure to Mr. Hooker's book.

In writing the music for this drama, Professor Parker has out-Wagnered Wagner in his observance of the rule that the music should serve simply to intensify the dramatic movement. It is hard to imagine that any one would ever care to hear this music apart from the opera, any more than one would care to go to the Metropolitan Opera House simply to look at the stage scenery. This does not mean that the stage scenery is not beautiful. In many respects it is unusually so. But it served its purpose when it gave an adequate setting to the play. So much with the music; it served its purpose insofar as it contributed to the expression of the feelings implicit in the drama itself.

In handling his material, Professor Parker showed that he understood his medium. He knows how to write for the voice, and he knows how to write for the orchestra. There is nothing uncertain or amateurish about his workmanship. In that respect he has set an example that it will not be easy for other American composers to follow. It is natural to compare *Mona* with the one other opera by a native American produced on the Metropolitan stage—Frederick S. Converse's *The Pipe of Desire*. As a whole, *Mona* is much the more successful. This is partly due to the fact that the Yale composer, Professor Parker, seemed to hold his forces in hand better than his Harvard compeer, Mr. Converse. On the other hand, there was more individuality and distinction in the material of the earlier opera than in that of *Mona*. . . .

* * * * *

❋ 1918 — *THE NEW YORK TIMES*

From "'Shanewis,' Indian Opera, Captivates," *New York Times* (24 March 1918), I: 19.

Henry F. B. Gilbert (1868-1928) became known for a number of so-called "Negro works" with such titles as *Comedy Overture on Negro Themes*, *Humoresque on Negro Minstrel Tunes*, and *Negro Rhapsody*, among others. Few of his compositions are as evocative as his symphonic poem, *Dance in Place Congo* (1908). Place Congo, or Congo Square (now within Louis Armstrong Park), was New Orleans's famous Sunday gathering spot for slaves and free blacks in the eighteenth and nineteenth centuries. Here they were allowed to associate, sing, play instruments, and dance. This Metropolitan Opera Company performance of Gilbert's work occurred on a program with *Shanewis*, an "Indian" opera by Charles Wakefield Cadman (1881-1946). Gilbert added dance numbers to his original score to make it more appropriate for the stage. A native New Englander and former student of Edward MacDowell, Gilbert was inspired by writer George Washington Cable (1844-1925), whose stories of New Orleans and southern Creole and Black cultures were widely read. A New Orleans native, Cable was recognized for crafting stories that exuded local color and energy and provided readers a brush with the unfamiliar, exotic Deep South.

Midway in the matinee bill Mr. Gilbert's *The Dance in Place Congo* shared interest out of all proportion to its little length, less than twenty minutes, but enough to keep dancing feet busy all that time and as many times more as the season allows. A scene, not of the old New Orleans waterfront square of famous slave revels, but out across the river or bayou, with the city's spires in the sunlit distance, and black folk coming from the "quarters" under the shady cottonwood trees, was the work of [designer] Livingston Platt, as were the costumes, a banzai sunburst of bandannas. Ottokar Bartik, who worked out Mr. Gilbert's bit of love story in low life, had been to New Orleans for local color, and what was better, he had introduced traditional figures, at least one Uncle Tom, and a half-dozen Simon Legrees. The ballet "chorus" distinguished itself once when it not only danced but sang.

Mr. Gilbert's music, expanded forty bars in one instance to let in the booming bell of slavery's workdays with its whiplash obbligato, is for all its realism as genial a piece of symphonic writing as has come to local hearing in some time. Like Mr. [Charles Wakefield] Cadman, he has also told the sources of his tunes, and some he did not need to tell. The "Bamboula," borrowed by Gottschalk many years before Coleridge-Taylor, is universally known in the West Indies and the South, while Louisiana long ago furnished its mate in "Michie Bainjo," and the love song, "Ma Mourri," as well as the only air actually sung near the end yesterday, the "One, Two, Three, Caroline," of a good old darky breakdown.

Something of George W. Cable's story to which Mr. Gilbert set music and action may have evaded the grasp of trained dancers in conventional ballet, but the dances, not the darky love affair, were the main thing, and they set the stage awhirl. Mr. Bartik made a point of the villain's consultation of the fortune teller. Mr. Benfiglio gave sufficient evidence of a passion for the quadroon girl. Miss Galli, who within a fortnight had become a staged-center star in [the] Russian *Coq d'Or* [Rimsky-Korsakov's *The Golden Cockerel*], achieved an astonishing transformation to the kinky-haired, black-faced vixen of the *Place Congo*. Her climax of the dance, a trance-like orgy ending with much writhing and mopping of a carpet spread on Massa's cold, cold ground, was a tarantella of terpsichorean virtuosity, the last word in dancing on the Metropolitan stage or anywhere else since [Anna] Pavlova's Manhattan *Carmen*.

* * * * *

During this era the musical landscape was transformed by innovations in technology developed by such men as Thomas Edison. His phonograph laboratory in Orange, New Jersey is pictured above in an 1892 photograph by W. K. Dickson.

Courtesy of the Prints and Photographs Division, Library of Congress: LC-USZ62-15292.

※ 10 — Music and Technology

Capturing Sound

1874 – *Church's Musical Visitor*
From "The Inventor's Opportunity"

1878 – *Scientific American*
From "The Phonograph"

1878 – Thomas A. Edison
From "The Phonograph and its Future"

1878 – *Scientific American*
From "The Phonograph Wins a Victory"

1888 – Thomas A. Edison
From "The Perfected Phonograph"

1890 – *The New York Times*
From "Before the Phonograph"

1893 – *The Manufacturer and Builder*
From "The Latest Developments in the Art of Recording and Reproducing Speech and Music"

1906 – John Philip Sousa
From "The Menace of Mechanical Music"

1918 – Horatio Parker
From "Our Taste in Music"

Mechanical and Electronic Instruments

1882 – *Church's Musical Visitor*
From "Musical Telegraphy for Concert Purposes"

1886 – F. O. Jones
From "Mechanical Orguinette,"
A Handbook of American Music and Musicians

MUSIC AND THE MOTION PICTURE

1914 –Mrs. Florence Currier Pillsbury
From "A Wonderful Opportunity for Carrying Good Music to the General Public through Moving Picture Houses"

1915 – Carl Van Vechten
From "Music for the Movies" in Red: Papers on Musical Subjects

The history of the development of sound recording is also the story of the typically American love / hate relationship with technological innovation. From the scientist's perspective, sound recording offered a new world of practical applications, from dictation to family reminiscence to entertainment. But to the American composer it was a more ominous force. Not only was American copyright law wholly unprepared for the new recorded artistic medium, but many decried the burgeoning technology as soulless, utterly incapable of reproducing the humanity that is the very essence of music.

CAPTURING SOUND

❋ 1874 – *CHURCH'S MUSICAL VISITOR*

From "The Inventor's Opportunity," *Church's Musical Visitor* (August 1874), 9.

The concept of capturing a "record" of sound was one that resonated throughout Europe and in the United States during the mid-nineteenth century. Experiments had been made on both continents with minimal results until American inventor Thomas Alva Edison (1847-1931) succeeded in developing his "phonograph" in 1877. In 1874 *Church's Musical Visitor* made an early plea for the complete development of the new science of sound recording.

Readers of the Visitor have been informed of the discovery of a method by which music may be photographed, as it were, which for a time engaged the minds of musicians. Why does not some slumbering genius awake and bring this valuable idea into shape and force? In moments of enthusiasm and inspiration exquisite music is often produced, which vanishes like a rainbow when, in calmer moments, the author sits downs and endeavors to recall the tones and fix the notes upon paper. They are lost beyond the power of resuscitation. It is obvious that an instrument or machine which could catch these fleeting tones and hold them, would be of incalculable value. It is an invention whose need has long been felt, and for more than a century, attempts have been made to construct such a machine. . . .

And it appears that such a contrivance was actually constructed in a satisfactory manner, by a person in Berlin, but it was neglected and thrown aside, until, without any further attempts at improvement on the first attempt, this curious and ingenious piece of workmanship was destroyed by fire, and never until recently has the project of making anything like it been renewed.

Why, if as we are told, the instrument was really complete, it should have been neglected, we can hardly understand. It may be that it was in some way difficult to be used, clumsy to make, or easily put out of working order; for it is only after a great length of time that any invention of importance is brought to a high state of perfection, however perfect the conception may be. In those days, too, people received with caution any new thing, and the struggles of the greatest inventors to obtain the favorable notice of the public is familiar to all. A century ago a patent-right for every invention under the sun, however trivial, was not to be obtained. But now, in this age of the world, the person who should be able to construct such a machine would acquire both reputation and remuneration, and that speedily.

* * * * *

* 1878 — *SCIENTIFIC AMERICAN*

From "The Phonograph," *Scientific American* 38/13 (30 March 1878), 193. [Reprinted courtesy of the publisher]

> In 1878 the journal *Scientific American* provided to its readers a description of Edison's machine, commenting on its simplicity and its capacity for future improvement.

It is a peculiar feature of the [Thomas A.] Edison phonograph that no mere description can impart any really adequate idea of its performances. Fully familiar as we are and have been with the machine since its inception, it is still impossible for us to listen to it without a feeling of astonishment and a well-defined doubt that our senses are not deceiving us. The extreme simplicity of the contrivance enhances the notion. . . .

If accurate and clearly enunciated repetition of the sounds made in it are the *ultima Thule* [i.e., the great unreachable place] of the phonograph's capabilities, then it has already attained that point. Where it is open to improvement, and to this the attention of the inventor is now being devoted, is in augmenting the intensity of the sound. In form it is substantially the same as when it was first described in these columns . . . .

As it is, even now, the phonograph will meet the most sanguine anticipations of any one that hears it. The first model that was brought to our notice certainly talked, that is, it produced sounds, the timbre of which was unquestionably that of the human voice; but . . . it required some previous knowledge to distinguish what was said. The speech was the lispings of infancy. At present previous explanation is wholly needless. The machine repeats the voice with perfect articulation and with every inflection, so that the tones may be recognized as those of the speaker who made them.

Through the courtesy of Mr. W. S. Applebaugh, who has charge of the apparatus now on exhibition in this city, we have been able to make as thorough an examination of all its peculiarities as we could desire. At our request the exhibitor sang into the machine an entire verse, and it was repeated as often as the cylinder was readjusted. Sounds of coughing, clearing the throat, knocks, noises of all kinds, were as accurately reproduced. A curious effect is produced by whistling, the apparatus giving forth every note clearly and fully; but more remarkable still is to hear two voices at once come from the machine. . . .

The only means now used for magnifying the sound as it is emitted is the funnel-shaped resonator . . . attached to the speaking orifice. Mr. Edison, however, is busily experimenting upon some adaptation of compressed air, by which the sound waves, he thinks, may be intensified. He says that he can in time make the machine talk so loudly that it can be used on vessels to warn off other ships during fogs, and his last astonishing proposal is that he shall construct a huge phonograph to go in the great bronze statue which is to be erected in New York Harbor. . . .

* * * * *

✻ 1878 — THOMAS A. EDISON, INVENTOR

From "The Phonograph and Its Future," *North American Review* 126/262 (May/June 1878), 527-36.

> Edison himself provided a lengthy and detailed account on the subject of his invention to the popular periodical *North American Review*. It was a surprising gesture for Edison, who generally did not elaborate on his work. But as an intensely practical man he envisioned many varied uses for his "phonograph," a term he coined. He not only explored technical and engineering issues related to the re-creation of sound, but he also grappled with such mundane issues as how the recordings may be mailed.

Of all the writer's inventions, none has commanded such profound and earnest attention throughout the civilized world as has the phonograph. This fact he attributes largely to the peculiarity of the invention which brings its possibilities within the range of the speculative imaginations of all thinking people, as well as to the almost universal applicability of the foundation principle, namely, the gathering up and retaining of sounds hitherto fugitive, and their reproduction at will.

From the very abundance of conjectural and prophetic opinions which have been disseminated by the press, the public is liable to become confused, and less accurately informed as to the immediate result and effects of the phonograph than if the invention had been one confined to certain specific applications, and therefore of less interest to the masses. The writer has no fault to find with this condition of the discussion of the merits and possibilities of his invention; for, indeed, the possibilities are so illimitable and the probabilities so numerous that he—though subject to the influence of familiar contact—is himself in a somewhat chaotic condition of mind as to where to draw the dividing line. In point of fact, such [a] line cannot with safety be defined in ordinary inventions at so early a stage of their development. In the case of an invention of the nature and scope of the phonograph, it is practically impossible to indicate it today, for tomorrow a trifle may extend it almost indefinitely.

There are, however, certain stages in the developing process which have thus far been actually reached; certain others which are clearly within reach; and others which, though they are in the light of today classed as possibilities, may tomorrow become probable and a little later actual achievements. It is the intention of the writer in this article to confine himself to the actual and the probable, to the end that a clearer conception of the immediate realizations of the phonograph may be had. He concedes to the public press and the world of science the imaginative work of pointing and commenting upon the possible. It is in view of the liberal manner in which this has already been done, and the handsome treatment he has received at their hands, that he for the first time appears *in propria persona* [in his own guise] to discuss and comment upon the merits of one of his own inventions.

In order to furnish a basis upon which the reader may take his stand, and accept or combat the logic of the writer in his presentment of the probabilities of the phonograph, a few categorical questions are put and answers given upon the essential features of the principles involved:

1. Is a vibrating plate or disk capable of receiving a complex motion which shall correctly represent the peculiar property of each and all the multifarious vocal and other sound-waves?

The telephone answers affirmatively.

2. Can such complex movement be transmitted from such plate, by means of a single embossing-point attached thereto, to effect a record upon a plastic material by indentation, with such fidelity as to give such indentations the same varied and complex form; and, if so, will this embossing-point, upon being passed over the record thus made, follow it with such fidelity as to transmit to the disk the same variety of movement, and thus effect a restoration of reproduction of the vocal or other sound waves, without loss of any property essential to producing upon the ear the same sensation as if coming direct from the original source?

The answer to this may be summed up in a statement of the fact that, by the application of power for uniformity of movement, and by attention to many seemingly unimportant and minor details, such as the *form* and material of the embossing-point, the proper *dampening* of the plate, the character of the material embossed, the formation of the mouth-piece over the plate, etc., the writer has at various times during the past weeks reproduced these waves with such [a] degree of accuracy in each and every detail as to enable his assistants to read, without the loss of a word, one or more columns of a newspaper article unfamiliar to them, and which were spoken into the apparatus when they were not present. The only perceptible loss was found to be in the quality of the utterance—a non-essential in the practical application of the apparatus. Indeed, the articulation of some individuals has been very perceptibly improved by passage through the phonograph, the original utterance being mutilated by imperfection of lip and mouth formation, and these mutilations eliminated or corrected by the mechanism of the phonograph.

3. Can a record be removed from the apparatus upon which it was made, and replaced upon a second without mutilation or loss of effective power to vibrate the second plate?

This is a mere mechanical detail, creating no greater obstacle than having proper regard for the perfect interchangeableness of the various working parts of the apparatus—not so nice a problem as the manufacture of the American watch.

4. What as to facility of placing and removing the record-sheet, and as to its transcription by mail?

But ten or fifteen seconds suffice for such placing or removal. A special envelope will probably be required for the present, the weight and form of which, however, will but slightly increase the cost of postage.

5. What as to durability?

Repeated experiments have proved that the indentations possess wonderful enduring power, even when the reproduction has been effected by the comparatively rigid plate used for their production. It is proposed, however, to use a more flexible plate for reproducing, which, with a perfectly smooth stone point—diamond or sapphire—will render the record capable of from 50 to 100 repetitions, enough for all practical purposes.

6. What as to duplication of a record and its permanence?

Many experiments have been made with more or less success, in the effort to obtain electrotypes of a record. This work has been done by others, and, though the writer has not as yet seen it, he is reliably informed that, very recently, it has been successfully accomplished. He can certainly see no great practical obstacle in the way. This, of course, permits of an indefinite multiplication of a record, and its preservation for all time.

7. What are the requisite force of wave impinging upon the diaphragm and the proximity of the mouth to the diaphragm to affect a record?

These depend in a great measure upon the volume of sound desired in the reproductions. If the reproduction is to be made audible to an audience, considerable force is requisite in the original utterance; if for the individual ear, only the ordinary conversational tone (even a whisper has been reproduced). In both cases the original utterances are delivered directly in the mouthpiece of the instrument. An audible reproduction may, however, be had by speaking at the instrument from a distance of from two to three feet in a loud tone. The application of a flaring tube or funnel to collect the sound-waves and the construction of an especially delicate diaphragm and embossing-point, etc., are the simple means which suggest themselves to affect this. The writer has not yet given this stage of development much attention, but sees no practical difficulty in gathering up and retaining a sectional part of the sound-waves diffused about the original source, within a radius of, say, three feet (sufficiently removed not to be annoying to a speaker or a singer).

The foregoing presentment of the stage of development reached by the several essential features of the phonograph demonstrates the following as *faits accompli*:

1. The captivity of all manner of sound-waves heretofore designated as "fugitive," and their permanent retention.

2. Their reproduction with all their original characteristics at will, without the presence or consent of the original source, and after the lapse of any period of time.

3. The transmission of such captive sounds through the ordinary channels of commercial intercourse and trade in material form, for purposes of communication or as merchantable goods.

4. Indefinite multiplication and preservation of such sounds, without regard to the existence or non-existence of the original source.

5. The captivation of sounds, with or without the knowledge or consent of the source of their origin. . . .

* * * * *

✻ 1878 — *SCIENTIFIC AMERICAN*

From "The Phonograph Wins a Victory," *Scientific American* 38/25 (22 June 1878), 384. [Reprinted courtesy of the publisher]

> Written at approximately the same time as Edison's essay in *North American Review,* the author of this article provided an eyewitness report on what the phonograph could accomplish.

The phonograph has been distinguishing itself lately in this city [New York City] by its remarkably accurate reproductions of the cornet solos of Mr. [Jules] Levy, the famous performer on that instrument. Mr. Levy possesses the phenomenal ability of getting notes out of the cornet which, he says, "are not there," or in other words, he plays airs in notes an octave lower than any one else has succeeded in producing on the cornet, and thus he has extended the range of his instrument over four full octaves. The phonograph, however, not only follows Levy, but surpasses him, by reproducing cornet notes in entirely new octaves of its own origination, proving itself to have a compass of extraordinary range, if not especial tunefulness and brilliancy.

At a very pleasant reception given to Mr. [Thomas A.] Edison recently . . . a most interesting conflict between Levy and the phonograph occurred. Messrs. Edison and Johnson ably seconded the phonograph, and of course none but Levy could scientifically manipulate the cornet. Fresh tin foil being adjusted on the cylinder, the bell of the cornet was placed near the mouth piece, and "Yankee Doodle," first plain, then garnished with variations of the most decorative character, assumed the form of dots on the foil. Without the loss of a note, the phonograph repeated it, and not only this, but even the peculiar expression imparted by the player, and the triumphant kind of a flourish which brought the tune to a conclusion, were reproduced with wonderful accuracy. After several other popular airs had been similarly replayed, Mr. Edison showed the effect of turning the cylinder at different degrees of speed, and then the phonograph proceeded utterly to rout Levy by playing his tunes in pitches and octaves of astonishing variety. It was interesting to observe the total indifference of the phonograph to the pitch of the note it began upon with regard to the pitch of the note with which it was to end. Gravely singing the tune correctly for half a dozen notes, it would suddenly soar into regions too painfully high for the cornet even by any chance to follow it. Then it delivered the variations on "Yankee Doodle" with a celerity that no human fingering of the cornet could rival, interspersing new notes, which it seemed probable were neither on the cornet nor on any other instrument–fortunately. Finally the phonograph recited "Bingen on the Rhine" after its inventor, then repeated the poem with a whistling accompaniment, then in conjunction with two songs and a speech, all this on one tin foil, though by this time the remarks began to get mixed. Just here Levy returned to the charge, and played his cornet fiercely upon the much indented strip. But the phonograph was equal to any attempts to take unfair advantage of it, and it repeated its songs, and whistles, and speeches, with the cornet music heard so clearly over all, that its victory was unanimously conceded, and amid hilarious crowing from the triumphant cylinder the cornet was ignominiously shut up in its box. . . .

* * * * *

✻ 1888 — THOMAS A. EDISON, INVENTOR

From "The Perfected Phonograph," *North American Review* 146/379 (June 1888), 641-50.

In 1888 Edison offered another article wherein he gave an update on the phonograph's evolution and on its numerous applications.

Ten years ago I contributed . . . a paper on the "Phonograph and its Future," in which I sketched the solution of certain problems accomplished by my invention, and predicted some of the uses to which it would be put. Other weighty matters engaged much of my time and attention after that article was published, but the future of which I then spoke has now arrived, and the predictions which I made at that time are now verified. For, when these words appear in print, the demonstration of the phonograph's practical adaptability to the purposes mentioned by me will have been completed, and the perfected instrument itself will be in the hands of the public, to be tested and employed by them at will. Rumors, I understand, have been circulated to the effect that, subsequently to my announcements made ten years ago, I allowed the phonograph to go adrift, leaving its further development to chance and to the tender mercies of such disinterested persons, not connected with me, as might conceive that they were doing me a favor by claiming to have developed my idea. Those who may have been taken in by these rumors would do well to inform themselves concerning the prolonged labor involved in carrying out important inventions. They are also referred to my former statements in this Review, as proof that the signer of those statements at least knew clearly what he was talking about and predicted only that which he has now fulfilled. . . .

The history of the phonograph as it was then [late 1870s] devised and manufactured in small quantity, merely for the purposes of public exhibition and explanation, need not be repeated here. The idea occurred to me in the Spring of 1877, and, according as I could get leisure, I gave my attention to preparing the few exhibition machines which were placed before the public in 1878, and then universally recognized by scientific men and every one else as an absolute novelty. These machines, of course, exemplified only a small part of the capacity of the phonograph. I was hard at work describing and noting down the various parts of the machine as it would appear when perfected, and making drawings of them in various forms.

As it was impossible to drop my work and sit down to tell the public what I was doing every day, I noted briefly [in 1878] . . . some of the things which I proposed to accomplish. The details of the electric light and other inventions afterwards absorbed much of my time and attention. My laboratory was converted into a factory in order to supply the demand for the electric light, and my progress in carrying out my ideas about the phonograph, though continuous, was necessarily retarded. For months past, however, I have had a special factory in operation, producing the component parts of the perfected phonograph, so as to bring the machine within the reach of the public in the form which I originally designed it to take.

It may be of interest, here, to contrast briefly the perfected phonograph with the mere exhibition models shown, all over the world, in 1878. Those models were large, heavy machines which purposely sacrificed distinctness of articulation, in order to secure a loud tone which could be heard in a large room when emitted through a funnel-shaped transmitter. Tinfoil was used as the material on which the indentations were to be made. The cylinders were revolved by hand, or by clockwork; and there were numerous other details of construction which differed from those of the instrument as now completed. At that time I had made various designs for a special kind of electric motor, differing from all others, to run the machine, in place of clockwork; and the phonograph as we now manufacture it is provided with such a motor, which turns the cylinder noiselessly, uniformly and easily. Instead of tinfoil, I now use a cylinder of wax for receiving the record of sound-pulsations, as in the original experiment. . . .

A single wax cylinder, or blank, may be used for fifteen or twenty successive records before it is worn out. But if the record is to be kept, the wax blank must not be talked upon again, and is simply slipped off from the metal cylinder and filed away for future reference. It may be fitted on to the metal cylinder again at any time, and will at once utter whatever has been registered on it. One of these wax blanks will repeat its contents thousands of times with undiminished clearness. Further, we are able to multiply to any extent, at slight cost, phonographic copies of the blank, after the talking, or music, or other sounds have been put upon it once. . . .

Any one sitting in his room alone may order an assorted supply of wax cylinders inscribed with songs, poems, piano or violin music, short stories, anecdotes, or dialect pieces, and, by putting them on his phonograph, he can listen to them as originally sung or recited by authors, vocalists or actors, or elocutionists. The variety of entertainment he thus commands, at trifling expense, and without moving from his chair, is practically unlimited. Music by a band, in fact whole operas, can be stored up on the cylinders, and the voice of [Adelina] Patti singing in England can thus be heard again on this side of the ocean, or preserved for future generations. . . .

* * * * *

✻ 1890 — *THE NEW YORK TIMES*

From "Before the Phonograph," *New York Times* (14 December 1890), 11.

> The anonymous author of this news report from 1890 attested to the popularity that the phonograph had already achieved by this time. The "phonogram craze" was not soon to subside, and that collectors were already hoarding recorded sound seemed a positive sign for the infant technology's future.

The phonograph, since Mr. [Thomas A.] Edison has succeeded in bringing it somewhat near perfection as a reproducer of the human voice, has become a welcome inmate of thousands of houses in this city and throughout the country, where it serves as a perpetual source of entertainment. As yet it has not been extensively adopted in New York for business purposes as it has in the Western cities, where it is used by merchants, bankers, and other businessmen as an excellent substitute for the stenographer, but it is gradually being introduced here in this relation, and Mr. Edison is looking forward to the time when businessmen will fill cylinders with letters and have them transferred to paper by their typewriters instead of dictating to shorthand experts. . . .

In the meantime, the phonograph as a source of entertainment has become exceedingly popular in New York. A photograph of the human voice is much more valuable to the curious collector than a picture of the face, even when accompanied by an autograph. There is something peculiarly weird and attractive in the idea of calling up at will some old friend or famous character and listening to an exact reproduction of his or her voice. If the person is dead it is like resurrecting him from the grave, and many collectors of phonograms now possess records of this kind which are extremely valuable. A favorite phase of the "phonogram craze" is the collection of specimens of recitations or singing from popular artists of the stage, and one gentleman of this city has secured cylinders representing vocally nearly every artist of any note who has been seen here for the last year. The collection is unique, because many of the records have no duplicates in existence, and the owner can give a six-hours' entertainment in his own house at any time, presenting the different artists, whose voice he has "bottled up," so to speak, in some of their most popular and successful roles. . . .

* * * * *

✻ 1893 — *THE MANUFACTURER AND BUILDER*

From "The Latest Developments in the Art of Recording and Reproducing Speech and Music," *The Manufacturer and Builder* 25/1 (January 1893), 15.

> Edison was not the only scientist involved in the pursuit of recorded sound. German inventor Emile Berliner (1851-1929) had been working since the 1880s. He hoped to replace Edison's fragile wax cylinder apparatus and placed his recording on a flat disc, which came to be known as a "gramophone" record. Berliner's system had the advantages of greater permanence and improved reproducibility, but Edison's machine did not immediately disappear—the two inventions competed vigorously for public favor well into the twentieth century. As is now well known, Berliner won.

Several years ago, Emile Berliner, a gentleman noted as an ingenious inventor in the electrical field, devised an apparatus for making a permanent record of musical sounds and articulate speech, and of reproducing the same in a reproducing device adapted for the purpose. This invention at the time attracted much attention from its extreme originality; but although the principle of its operation was universally admitted to be correct, the results obtained by it at that time were no more remarkable than those obtainable with the phonograph, and for some time nothing further was heard of it

A few words in explanation of the construction and mode of operation of this system of recording and reproducing sounds and articulate speech will be appropriate at this point, and we can give this best by making a comparison with the phonograph, with which our readers are presumably all familiar.

In the phonograph in its present improved form, the record-making stylus is made to cut into the smooth surface of a cylinder of wax, or some composition of similar nature; the point of the stylus moves at right angles to the wax surface and makes its cut squarely into it. In the gramophone, a sheet of polished zinc, coated with a very thin film of wax composition, is prepared by flowing over the metal surface a solution of the compound, which, on evaporation of the solvent, leaves the wax film behind. The point of the stylus in the gramophone moves parallel to this waxed surface, in contradistinction to the perpendicular movement of the stylus of the phonograph. In the case of the latter, the stylus meets with increasing resistance according to the depths of its cut; in the case of the gramophone, the resistance is absolutely uniform at all times, no matter what may be the amplitude of the vibration of the stylus point. To those who know how difficult it is to retain in a mechanical record of sounds the peculiar property termed "quality," the radical difference in the manner of making the record in the two cases will immediately impress them in favor of the method of Mr. Berliner as being the scientifically correct one.

Further, the wax cylinder record of the phonograph may be duplicated at will, but it must be admitted that it lacks one important element inherent in the nature of the materials—namely, permanence. The record made by the stylus of the gramophone remove[s] the delicate film of wax covering the zinc surface, leaving the metal exposed in the path it has traversed. The zinc plate in this condition is placed in an etching liquid, and in about fifteen minutes the acid will have eaten its way through the metal where it has been exposed by the stylus, and we have a permanent record of the sounds etched into the metal. By a simple process of electrotyping which it will be unnecessary to describe here, this original record may be duplicated ad libitum in metal or in hard rubber, losing thereby nothing of its character, so that any one of the duplicate plates, placed in the reproducing apparatus, will render back the speech, song or music with such accuracy that one cannot be distinguished from the other, or from the original. The fact that these records have the quality of practical permanence to a degree unapproachable by the phonograph record, gives to the gramophone record a very decided superiority over the former.

Finally, we come to the question of the character of the reproduction. Those who are familiar with the phonograph will generally admit that it leaves much to be desired, both in respect of the quality of the sounds reproduced and in distinctness and loudness. The reproduction of the gramophone record, on the other hand, when reinforced by the aid of a flaring mouth trumpet, can easily be heard over a large audience room, and while the quality of the reproduced sounds presents that of the original so faithfully that the effect is absolutely startling. Both the distinctness and the quality of the reproduced sounds or speech suffer somewhat by the use of the trumpet; but when the ear tubes are used, the sound or speech is loud, sharply defined, and rendered with a fidelity that leave nothing to be desired. In brief, the improved gramophone is mechanically operated on more correct scientific principles, and the quality of its performance is greatly superior to that of the phonograph.

At a recent meeting of one of our prominent scientific societies, there was given an exhibition of the gramophone, in the course of which the capabilities of the instrument were demonstrated so successfully as to arouse the critical audience that saw and heard the performance to the point of enthusiasm.

Finally, it will be interesting to our readers to know that the gramophone is about to be manufactured and placed upon the market at so low a price that it cannot fail to come into general use as a source of popular entertainment, as well as for the more serious applications for which it is adapted. In its present form, the gramophone represents the highest development of the art of recording and reproducing musical sounds and articulate speech, and Mr. Berliner must be congratulated on having achieved a notable success.

* * * * *

✻ 1906 — JOHN PHILIP SOUSA, BANDMASTER AND COMPOSER

From "The Menace of Mechanical Music," *Appleton's Magazine* 8/3 (September 1906), 278-84.

> John Philip Sousa (1854-1931) was not the only individual to consider recorded sound a "menace," but he was certainly the most notable musical celebrity to proclaim it so in such a public way. To Sousa, recorded music, or "canned music" as he called it, took humanity out of the equation. This left listeners to confront a heartless, soulless, and ultimately unsatisfactory artistic creation. Sousa admired the human imagination and the technology that went into the creation of the phonograph and gramophone, but he believed that they would not support music—rather, that they would supplant it.

Sweeping across the country with the speed of a transient fashion in slang or Panama hats, political war cries or popular novels, comes now the mechanical device to sing for us a song or play for us a piano, in substitute for human skill, intelligence, and soul. Only by harking back to the day of the roller skate or the bicycle craze, when sports of admitted utility ran to extravagance and virtual madness, can we find a parallel in which these ingenious instruments have invaded every community in the land. . . .

On a matter which I feel so deeply, and which I consider so far-reaching, I am quite willing to be reckoned an alarmist, admittedly swayed in part by personal interest, as well as by the impending harm to American musical art. I foresee a marked deterioration in American music and musical taste, an interruption in the musical development of the country, and a host of other injuries to music in its artistic manifestations, by virtue—or rather by vice—of the multiplication of the various music-reproducing machines. When I add to this that I myself and every other popular composer are victims of a serious infringement on our clear moral rights in our own work, I but offer a second reason why the facts and conditions be made clear to everyone, alike in the interest of musical art and of fair play.

It cannot be denied that the owners and inventors have shown wonderful aggressiveness and ingenuity in developing and exploiting these remarkable devices. Their mechanism has been steadily and marvelously improved, and they have come into very extensive use. And it must be admitted that where families lack time or inclination to acquire musical technique, and to hear public performances, the best of these machines supply a certain amount of satisfaction and pleasure.

But heretofore, the whole course of music, from its first day to this, has been along the line of making it the expression of soul states; in other words, of pouring it into the soul. . . .

From the days when the mathematical and mechanical were paramount in music, the struggle has been bitter and incessant for the sway of the emotional and the soulful. And now, in this twentieth century, come these talking and playing machines, and offer again to reduce the expression of music to a mathematical system of megaphones, wheels, cogs, disks, cylinders, and all manner of revolving things, which are as like real art as the marble statue of Eve is like her beautiful, living, breathing daughters. . . .

Step by step through the centuries, working in an atmosphere almost wholly monopolized by commercial pursuit, America has advanced art to such a degree that today she is the Mecca toward which journey the artists of all nations. Musical enterprises are given financial support here as nowhere else in the universe, while our appreciation of music is bounded only by our geographical limits.

This wide love for the art springs from the singing school, secular or sacred; from the village band, and from the study of those instruments that are nearest the people. There are more pianos, violins, guitars, mandolins, and banjos among the working classes of America than in all the rest of the world, and the presence of these instruments in the homes has given employment to enormous numbers of teachers who have patiently taught the children and inculcated a love for music throughout the various communities.

Right here is the menace in machine-made music! The first rift in the lute has appeared. The cheaper of these instruments of the home are no longer being purchased as formerly, and all because the automatic music devices are usurping their places.

And what is the result? The child becomes indifferent to practice, for when music can be heard in the homes without the labor of study and close application, and without the slow process of acquiring a technique, it will be simply a question of time when the amateur disappears entirely, and with him a host of vocal and instrumental teachers, who will be without field or calling. . . .

When a mother can turn on the phonograph with the same ease that she applies to the electric light, will she croon her baby to slumber with sweet lullabies, or will the infant be put to sleep by machinery?

Children are naturally imitative, and if, in their infancy, they hear only phonographs, will they not sing, if they sing at all, in imitation and finally become simply human phonographs—without soul or expression? Congregational singing will suffer also, which, though crude at times, at least improves the respiration of many a weary sinner and softens the voices of those who live amid tumult and noise.

The host of mechanical reproducing machines, in their desire to supply music for all occasions, is offering to supplant the illustrator in the classroom, the dance orchestra, the home and public singers and players, and so on. Evidently they believe no field too large for their incursions, no claim too extravagant. But the further they can justify these claims, the more noxious the whole system becomes. . . .

The country dance orchestra of violin, guitar, and melodeon had to rest at times, and the resultant interruption afforded the opportunity for general sociability and rest among the entire company. Now a tireless mechanism can keep everlastingly at it, and much of what made the dance a wholesome recreation is eliminated.

The country band, with its energetic renditions, its loyal support by local merchants, its benefit concerts, band wagon, gay uniforms, state tournaments, and the attendant pride and gayety, is apparently doomed to vanish in the general assault on personality in music.

There was a time when the pine woods of the north were sacred to summer simplicity, when around the camp fire at night the stories were told and the songs were sung with a charm all their own. But even now the invasion of the north has begun, and the ingenious purveyor of canned music is urging the sportsman, on his way to the silent places with gun and rod, tent and canoe, to take with him some disks, cranks, and cogs to sing to him as he sits by the firelight, a thought as unhappy and incongruous as canned salmon by a trout brook. . . .

* * * * *

* 1918 — HORATIO PARKER, COMPOSER, MUSIC EDUCATOR, AND MUSIC ADMINISTRATOR

From "Our Taste in Music," *Yale Review* 7 (1918), 777-88.

> As composer and teacher Horatio Parker (1863-1919) further demonstrated in this essay, not all reactions to sound recording were positive. Writing in 1918, long after the machine had become part of the American musician's reality, Parker lamented its very existence.

It is increasingly difficult to avoid mechanical music records of many kinds. For a sober music lover they seem like specimens, stuffed creatures, or at best reminders. The immature can love a china dog or a teddy bear–[but] not grown people. I once heard a parrot whistle with orchestral accompaniment, but did not think my musical experience enriched thereby. The phonograph is like Echo in the Latin phrase, "Vox, et praeterea nihil" ["Sound, and nothing else"]. Even if the melodic outline be clear, pure, and tolerable in tone quality, the rich background which we demand in art music is sketched with a few mechanical squeaks, squawks, and grunts. Piccolo and banjo come out faultlessly, but the violin is always perfectly wooden, and there is no bass. Such canned music is quite dead, but is not necessarily bad. It is not fair to say that a man is bad because he is dead–there is a proverb to the contrary; but his usefulness is distinctly limited. Music to fulfill its destiny must tend to produce more music. Can we credit such records with the power to stimulate original effort? We must agree that dead things are unsuitable for procreation. And I think the usefulness of records in cultivating preferences may easily be overestimated. They are suspiciously cheap and painless in their demands. We don't get anything for nothing, and we get mighty little for sixpence.

* * * * *

MECHANICAL AND ELECTRONIC INSTRUMENTS

❊ 1882 — *CHURCH'S MUSICAL VISITOR*

From "Musical Telegraphy for Concert Purposes" [Open Letter to Alexander Graham Bell with a Reply], *Church's Musical Visitor* (May 1882), 211.

> American inventors maintained a strong interest in developing new instruments or improving old ones, particularly given the advances in electricity and engineering that occurred in the latter part of the nineteenth century. Dr. Hachenburg's "musical telegraphy" displayed a captivating vision and enthusiasm although it is unclear if Alexander Graham Bell (1847-1922) realized further progress.

[To] Prof. Alexander G. Bell – Sir: Permit me to draw your attention to my system of Musical Telegraphy for concert purposes. I watched with much interest your experiments on the subject, as well as those from other eminent electricians. I have anticipated from these experiments, based upon telephonic principles, doubtful results.

More than thirty years ago my attention was directed to musical telegraphy. You may well imagine what precedence I had to go upon. So primitive was telegraphing then that the first part of my invention was the nomenclature itself. In my first studies on the subject, I associated the waves of sound with the current of electricity—that is, the transmission of sound by electricity. As a factor for my research, I took it for granted that such a thing was practicable in nature; but I soon discovered that electricity, as a sound carrier, would serve me no good, practical results, and then and there I dropped it. My final conclusion was, that the only way that musical telegraphy can be developed to render favorable results, is mainly to depend on electro-dynamic operations, or a combination of musical instruments electronically connected, controlled by one performer. The most available instruments for this purpose are pianos, organs, bells, etc. The expression—or, rather, the individuality—of this electro-music is not rendered by the performer, but by a musical director who, through a keyboard of his own, makes and breaks the electrical communication between the instruments to impart volume and expression to music. . . .

Without going into any details, the use of these instruments to play accompaniments in vocalization would have the most wonderful effect of all. By a telephonic arrangement the singing could be transmitted through the different instruments with a most pleasing harmonic effect, even if the instruments were not in action.

But even to know all this is not sufficient to fathom the strange results of musical telegraphy from our present position. But with these premises on your mind, set your imagination to work on any well executed instrumental music, what the same would be rendered, say, from ten pianos electrically conducted, with sounds reaching the tympanum from different points, with its various expressions. Follow this music, but have a place for each note in this electrical circle of instruments. You will not make this experiment very often before you will catch a study in it that the mind will dwell upon with intense interest. You will light on a science that some day will revolutionize the art of music! . . .

[To] Dr. Hachenberg, Austin, Texas - Dear Sir: I have read with much interest your communication to me . . . concerning musical telegraphy for concert purposes, and have no doubt that very beautiful and wonderful effects would be produced by a combination of musical instruments electrically connected and controlled by one performer, as you suggest.

Your letter does not give me any idea of the details of your proposed arrangement, but I am so much interested in the matter that I shall examine, at the earliest possible moment, the publications to which you have referred me. . . .

* * * * *

✻ 1886 — F. O. Jones

From "Mechanical Orguinette," *A Handbook of American Music and Musicians* (Canaseraga, N.Y.: F. O. Jones, 1886), 97.

> F. O. Jones's concise handbook describes a variety of mechanical instrument that portends the player piano, which was not developed until the 1890s. Jones's description of its users is as captivating as his description of the instrument itself.

Mechanical Orguinette. The name of a certain class of mechanical musical instruments, which have lately sprung into existence. They are constructed of every size, from that of a small square box up to that of a diminutive pipe organ, and of many different styles, some resembling reed organs and some resembling pianos. The music is produced automatically, in the smaller sizes by turning a crank and in the larger sizes by pedals, by passing sheets of paper perforated in a certain manner through the instruments, the mechanism being so arranged that whenever a perforation comes in the right place a small lever passes through, opens a valve, and produces the required note. The tone of these instruments, though of course not equaling that of the reed organ, is not bad. They may be of service in some cases where musicians cannot be obtained, or where persons are too stupid or too lazy to learn music, but they have no permanent artistic value.

* * * * *

MUSIC AND THE MOTION PICTURE

✻ 1914 — MRS. FLORENCE CURRIER PILLSBURY, ACCOMPANIST

From "A Wonderful Opportunity for Carrying Good Music to the General Public through Moving Picture Houses," *Etude* 32/12 (December 1914), 925.

> Although recorded sound did not accompany motion pictures until the 1920s, music performed by live musicians had been common in movie theaters since their inception. By 1914 Florence Currier Pillsbury could express the

hope that the proliferation of the movies, considered by some to be a detrimental force on the culture, could exert a positive influence on the musical education of Americans.

[Mrs. Pillsbury's article reveals a condition of which we have been aware for some time. In the thousands and thousands of moving picture theaters in the United States huge armies of people assemble every day. At first the music of the moving picture house was as cheap and as trashy as it possibly could be. Then someone discovered that good music—even the best of music went well—that is the public liked it, was impressed by it and wanted more. Consequently we find picture houses installing organs costing small fortunes, putting in the finest of pianos and even introducing orchestras that would do credit to a small European opera house. There is only one reason why the manager does this. He has no interest in educating the public to do anything more than become regular visitors to his box office. Good music pays and Mrs. Pillsbury tells how she has employed *The Etude* to good effect as have thousands of other musicians in moving picture theaters.—Editor of *The Etude*.]

The time has most certainly passed when people looked furtively about the entrance of a picture theater and then sneaked cautiously in as though they were doing something to be ashamed of in such a glare of light. It is hardly a half a century since some of our puritanical forefathers looked upon reading a novel as a kind of petty crime. One who does not know the good novels now is put down as ignorant and as the art of moving picture-play producing advances in the hands of masters such as Gabriele d'Annunzio there may come a time when moving pictures will be a part of the education of every good and proper young person. Now the public marches up to the box office window and deems himself fortunate if he can secure a seat. It is this same Mr. Public who will in time remove whatever there may have been that was bad in moving pictures and also demand better and better music.

The time is passing too when the mechanical operations of a ragtime pianist can still induce patrons to remain in a picture theater. There is as much real comment today on the proper music for films, as there is on the films themselves, and if the photoplay is to live, especially in the smaller up-country houses, much depends on the proper musical settings. I do not refer to the ragtime player again, who plays "rags" and dirges to everything shown on the screen, but to the real musician, who is willing and anxious, to read the advance synopsis of each number on the program and to introduce the right music so subtly into each reel as it is shown, so as to lend a perfect background to the story itself. Recently we had one of the best of feature plays at our picture house, the play was accompanied by a musical score, and yet I found the selection in a recent number of *The Etude* so much better than a certain part of that score, that I substituted it on the second run of the picture and found it much more appropriate and pleasing than the original.

In some houses a wonderful chance to educate the American people to the right grade of music is being neglected because probably it is safe to say that the actual picture attendance of one night, in our country, is as great as the total attendance of a year to all our public recitals. At present there is in the country more actual money in playing for a good picture house where the patrons appreciate the right kind of music, than in teaching the same number of hours, and good interpreters of the photoplays are as hard to find as are good teachers of piano. But it does not interfere with teaching, in fact it is a help, if the player is allied with a manager who believes, that, as a musician, you are in a position to know more than he does about the proper musical settings. In some circles, of course, doing anything outside of teaching would not be desirable, but in others playing in a theater means no loss of caste—often it actually brings pupils. Remember we are not all teaching in Carnegie Hall or the Musical Art Building. . . .

At a very conservative estimate there are at least five thousand of us who are playing in the smaller picture houses of our country where the piano alone is used, and some of us are trying very hard to interpret the photoplays and adapt the right kind of music to each one of them. . .

* * * * *

✱ 1915 — CARL VAN VECHTEN, WRITER, ARTS CRITIC, AND PHOTOGRAPHER

From "Music for the Movies," *Red: Papers on Musical Subjects* (New York: Alfred A. Knopf, 1925), 48-59. [Essay dated 10 November 1915]

> Carl Van Vechten (1880-1964), one of the most astute, observant, and modern-sounding writers of the era, saw the need for the movies to establish their own compositional and performance aesthetic. This essay shows that Van Vechten, an early proponent of music composed to fit the movie it accompanied precisely, was well ahead of his time.

Although it would appear that the moving picture drama had opened up new worlds to the modern musician, no important composer, so far as I am aware, has yet turned his attention to the writing of music for films. If the cinema play is in its infancy, as certain enthusiasts would have us believe, then we may be sure that the day is not far distant when moving picture scores will take their places on musicians' bookshelves alongside those occupied by operas, symphonies, masses, and string quartets. In the meantime, completely ignorant of the truth (or oblivious to it, or merely helpless, as the case may be) that writing music for moving pictures is a new art, which demands a new point of view, the musical directors of the picture theatres are struggling with the situation as best they may. Under the circumstances, it is remarkable on the whole, how swiftly and how well the demand for music with the silent drama has been met. Certainly the quality of the music is on a level with, or even better than, the type of entertainment offered. Nevertheless, the directors have not squarely faced the issue: they still continue to try to force old wine into new bottles, arranging and rearranging melodies and harmonies contrived for quite other occasions and purposes. Even when scores have been written for pictures the result has not shown any imaginative advance over the arranged scores. It is curious that it seems to have occurred to no one that the moving picture demands a *new* kind of music. . . .

In some theaters, the chef d'orchestre [leader of the orchestra] strikes an attitude of total disrespect towards the picture. He makes up his musical program as if he were giving a concert, not at all with the view of effectively accompanying the action on the screen. In a theater on Second Avenue in New York for example, I have heard an orchestra play the whole of Beethoven's First Symphony as an accompaniment to Irene Fenwick's performance of *The*

Woman Next Door. As the symphony came to an end before the picture, it was supplemented by [Emil] Waldteufel's waltz, "Les Patineurs." . . .

Waiting the birth of authentic moving picture music, which a new composer must rise to invent, the safest way (not necessarily the best) is the middle course, one method for this film, another for that. One of the difficulties which arises is the necessity of arranging the score for a theater with a large band, where the leader must plan his accompaniment, or have it planned for him, for an entire picture before his men can play a note. Music cues must be definite: twenty bars of "Alexander's Ragtime Band," seventeen of "The Ride of the Valkyries," ten of "Vissi d'arte," etc. . . .

The single man orchestra, the player of the upright piano, need not make so many preparatory gestures. He may with impunity, if he be of an inventive turn of mind or if his memory be good, improvise his score as the picture unreels itself for the first time before what may very well be his astonished vision; after that, he may vary his accompaniment, as the shows of the day progress, improving it here or there, or not, as the case may be, but keeping generally as near to his original performance as possible. . . .

It will not be long before an enterprising director engages an enterprising musician to compose music for a picture. For the same reason that [Gabriele] d'Annunzio, very early in the career of the moving picture, wrote a scenario for a film, I should not be surprised to learn that Richard Strauss was under contract to construct an accompaniment to a screened drama. It will be very loud music and it will require a band of one hundred and forty three men to interpret it. Probably Strauss himself will conduct the first performance; later, excerpts will be played by the Boston Symphony Orchestra and the critics will say, in spite of Philip Hale's diverting program notes, that this music should never be performed save in conjunction with the picture for which it was written. [Pietro] Mascagni is another composer who should find an excellent field for his talent in writing tone poems for pictures, although he would contrive nothing more daring than a well-arranged series of illustrative melodies.

But put Igor Stravinsky, or some other modern genius, to work on this problem and see what happens! The composer of the future should revel in the opportunity the moving picture affords him to create a new form. . . . The swift flash from scene to scene, the cutback, the necessary rapidity of the action, all these are adapted to inspire the future composer to brilliant effort; a tinkle of this and a snatch of that, without working-out or development; illustration, comment, piquant or serious, that's what the new film music should be. The ultimate moving picture score will be something more than a sentimental accompaniment.

* * * * *

Richard Strauss, pictured here circa 1905, was considered by many American composers and critics to be the most controversial of the modern composers prior to World War I.

Courtesy of the George Grantham Bain Collection, Prints and Photographs Division, Library of Congress: LC-DIG-ggbain-21003.

⁂ 11 — Reception of Modern Music

Mainstream Moderns

1862 – John Sullivan Dwight
From "Concerts"

1899 – James Gibbons Huneker
From "Strauss and Nietsche,"
Mezzotints in Modern Music

1904 – Lawrence Gilman
From "Charles Martin Loeffler,"
Phases of Modern Music

1904 – *The New York Times*
From " 'Symphonia domestica,' with Composer Leading"

1907 – Reginald De Koven
From "The Modern Revolt in Music"

1910 – Horatio Parker
From "Contemporary Music"

1912 – John C. Griggs
From "Claude Debussy"

1914 – Lawrence Gilman
From "Music and Drama: The Irrubrical
Schoenberg and His Extraordinary Music"

1915 – Hiram K. Moderwell
From "On Acquiring New Ears"

1915 – James Gibbons Huneker
From "The Seven Arts: Leo Ornstein"

1915 – Carl Van Vechten
From "Music after the Great War,"
From "Igor Stravinsky: A New Composer,"
Music after the Great War and Other Studies

1917 – *The New York Times*
From "Ernest Bloch's Music"

1918 – [James Gibbons Huneker]
From "Serge Prokofiev A Virile Pianist"

RAGTIME AND JAZZ

1915 – Hiram K. Moderwell
From "Ragtime"

1916 – *Variety*
From "Cabarets"

1918 – Edward Baxter Perry
"'Ragging' Good Music"

1918 – Daniel Gregory Mason
From "Music in America," *Contemporary Composers*

Those few Americans fortunate enough to hear orchestral music in the first three quarters of the nineteenth century were by and large treated to music by Classical and early-Romantic composers such as Mozart, Schubert, and, especially, Beethoven. But as the turn of the new century approached, American orchestras—most of which were newly-established—began to explore more adventuresome repertoire. Then as now, conductors and musicians enjoyed the technical challenges often associated with contemporary music, and the difficulty of the newest compositions paired nicely with the increasing virtuosity of the ensembles. Naturally, audiences and critics were not always enthusiastic. This chapter presents essays concerning several of the most important "modernist" composers of the period. It also grapples briefly with two uniquely American genres, ragtime and jazz, which, while original and beautiful to many, were completely repellent to others.

❋ 1862 — JOHN SULLIVAN DWIGHT, MUSIC CRITIC AND JOURNAL EDITOR

From "Concerts," *Dwight's Journal of Music* 31/1 (5 April 1862), 6.

Composer Franz Liszt's symphonic poem *Les preludes* was premiered in Germany in 1854 and made its Boston debut only five years later. A second Boston performance, in 1862, prompted Boston music critic John Sullivan Dwight (1813-1893) to pen the following review in which he confirmed the impressions made by his first hearing of it. Dwight is often chided for "conservative" ideals that are reflected in his deep love of abstract and formalist music represented in works by Haydn, Beethoven, Schubert, and others. Here Dwight expressed cautious admiration for Liszt, but he was quick to point out the formal weakness of his "program music." A central idea in music of the Classical era is "organicism," in which entire compositions are built on a single idea or motive. As Romantic era composers altered that aesthetic and shifted toward compositions with extra-musical content (i.e., programs), Dwight was bothered by what he perceived as a lack of unity and formal clarity in the music. For Dwight, musical form was paramount; other elements, especially mere "expression," were disdained.

Liszt's [*Les*] *preludes* was first brought out here . . . in December 1859; the impression which it then produced on us, and on musical persons generally, we think, was recorded in terms which we venture to recall now, since they serve precisely to describe the new impression of last Saturday evening:

Liszt has now written, it is said, his nine—not symphonies, but "symphonic poems"—so called (and in this sense pertaining to the Wagner or "Music of the Future" direction) because they have not an exclusively and purely musical reference, and do not therefore cling to the usual symphonic form, but take their texts from and propose to illustrate some poem, or passage from a poem, or some poet's life, or some picture, or what not. . . .

These themes [inspired by Lamartine's *Meditations Poetiques*] came up one by one in a moving panorama, as it were, of tone-pictures, painted on a great breadth of orchestral canvas, with a richer scale than usual of colors; thus there were *three* flutes; four horns; a huge ophicleid thundering through the other storm of brass; and a harp part. You heard first the tolling, and mysterious solemn harmonies, vague yearning questionings, etc., as at thought of the great hereafter; there were some strange and large effects, more physically imposing than beautiful sometimes. . . .

The real merit of the work appeared to us to lie in the remarkable talent shown for instrumentation. It is full of striking, original, sometimes exquisite effects: there were chord-phrases and blendings of instruments in it which almost opened a new sense. But these seem rather the accumulations of separate efforts, than the spontaneous, and at the same time logically necessitated outgrowth from one central and all-vitalizing thought, as in the real imaginative works of genius. It has a certain outward and well managed unity, we own; but not that sort of unity which great works of Art have, where the whole is implied and felt in each successive part, or rather each unfolding phrase. . . .

* * * * *

✻ 1899 — JAMES GIBBONS HUNEKER, MUSIC CRITIC AND WRITER ON MUSIC

From "Strauss and Nietsche," *Mezzotints in Modern Music* (New York: Charles Scribner's Sons, 1899), 143-59.

Like Liszt's music, that of Richard Strauss (1864-1949) proved controversial to critics and audiences in the United States. Strauss's efforts to convey precise thought and meaning through his music took Liszt's notion of program music a step farther and necessitated a near-total abandonment of formal principles that thrust Americans well beyond their comfort zone. By the time respected writer James Huneker (1857-1921) authored this book, several generations of American composers had been schooled in the formal procedures of composition at German conservatories, and American audiences were accustomed to (and expected) something rather more sedate—Beethoven, Mendelssohn, and Raff, for example—than they found in Strauss.

Tchaikovsky went far, but Richard Strauss has dared to go further. He first individualized, and rather grotesquely, *Don Juan* [1889], *Till Eulenspiegel* [1895], *Macbeth* [1888]; but in *Death and Apotheosis* [*Tod und Verklärung*; 1889] and in *Also Sprach Zarathustra* [1896] he has attempted almost the impossible; he has attempted the delineation of thought, not musical thought, but philosophical ideas in tone. He has disclaimed this attempt, but the fact nevertheless remains that the various divisions and subdivisions of his extraordinary work are attempts to seize not only certain elusive psychical states, but also to paint pure idea–the "Reine Vernunft" [pure reason] of the metaphysicians. Of course he has failed, but his failure marks a great step in the mastery over the indefiniteness of music. Strauss's German brain with its grasp of the essentials of philosophy, allied to a vigorous emotional nature and a will and imagination that stop at nothing, enabled him to throw into high relief his excited mental states. That these states took unusual melodic shapes, that there is the suggestion of abnormality, was to be expected; for Strauss has made a flight into a country in which it is almost madness to venture. He has, on his own opinions and purely by the aid of a powerful reasoning imagination, sought to give an emotional garb to pure abstractions. Ugliness was bound to result but it is characteristic ugliness. There is profound method in the madness of Strauss, and I beg his adverse critics to pause and consider his aims before entirely condemning him. . . .

Strauss is a man of rare and powerful imagination; the tentacles of his imagination are restlessly feeling and thrusting forward and grappling with material on most dangerous territory. The need of expression of definite modes of thought, of more definite modes of emotion, is a question that has perplexed every great composer. With such an apparatus as the modern orchestra–in Strauss's hands an eloquent, plastic and palpitating instrument–much may be ventured and, while the composer has not altogether succeeded–it is almost a superhuman task he sets himself to achieve–he has made us think seriously of a new trend in the art of discoursing music. Formalism is abandoned–Strauss moves by episodes; now furiously swift, now ponderously lethargic, and one is lost in amazement at the loftiness, the solidity and general massiveness of his structure. The man's scholarship is so profound, almost as profound as Brahms's; his genius for the orchestra so marked, his color and rhythmic sense so magnificently developed that the general effect of his rhetoric is perhaps too blazingly brilliant. He has more to say than Berlioz and says it better, is less magniloquent and more poetical than Liszt, is as clever as Saint-Saëns, but in thematic invention he is miles behind Wagner.

His melodies, it must be confessed, are not always remarkable or distinguished in quality, setting aside the question of ugliness altogether. But the melodic curve is big and passional [*sic*]. Strauss can be tender, dramatic, bizarre, poetic and humorous, but the noble art of simplicity he sadly lacks–for art it is. His themes in this poem [*Also Sprach Zarathustra*] are often simple; indeed the waltz is distinctly commonplace, but it is not the Doric, the bald simplicity of Beethoven. It is rather a brutal plainness of speech.

Strauss is too deadly in earnest to trifle or to condescend to ear tickling devices. The tremendous sincerity of the work will be its saving salt for many who violently disagree with the whole scheme. . . .

* * * * *

✻ 1904 — LAWRENCE GILMAN, MUSIC CRITIC AND WRITER ON MUSIC

From "Charles Martin Loeffler," *Phases of Modern Music* (New York: Harper & Brothers, 1904), 61-71.

French-born violinist and composer Charles Martin Loeffler (1861-1935) was a fixture in musical Boston from his arrival in the early 1880s until his death. Following more than twenty years as assistant concertmaster in the Boston Symphony Orchestra, Loeffler retired to devote himself to composition in 1903. Although not a prolific composer, he created works considered well-crafted and generally attractive. Loeffler was one of the first composers on American soil to take up the impressionist techniques of Debussy and other French composers, eschewing both the formalism and the programmaticism of the German school. Loeffler's music was routinely performed in Boston; his better known compositions, *La mort de Tintagiles* (1900), *La villanelle du diable* (1901) and *Pagan Poem* (1906) offer an aesthetic of calm reflection and thoughtfulness, desired traits in an increasingly modern world beginning to take notice of Germany's growing militarism. Critic Lawrence Gilman (1878-1939) served as an advocate of contemporaneous French musical practice as well as the "classics" of the Germanic tradition.

Mr. Charles Martin Loeffler, an Alsatian by birth but a Bostonian by profession, occupies a peculiar place, entirely of his own creation, in the field of contemporary music. He is a seeker after the realities of shadowy and dim illusions, an artist in grays and greens and subtle golds. The opulent purples in which Richard Strauss delights, with the exuberance of his fiery temperament, have no attraction for Mr. Loeffler. The insistent appeal, the expected richness, the continual iridescence of Strauss's schemes are quite absent from the strange and intimate music of this tonal [Paul] Verlaine. . . .

That serenity, that innocence of intention, is, indeed, remarkable. After the plangent splendors, the torrential rhetoric, of the amazing Strauss, the music of Mr. Loeffler, owning something of the subdued and elusive beauty of antique tapestries, addresses the spirit with a unique appeal. Where Strauss is challenging, importunate, Mr. Loeffler persuades—not with the personal concern of the advocate, for his detachment, and, as I have said, his innocence of intention, are as entire as they are sincere—but, as it were, in spite of himself. . . .

In his musical style, Mr. Loeffler has a certain kinship with the school of contemporary France; he is of a kind with Debussy, with Vincent D'Indy, with [Gabriel] Faure, with Pierre de Breville, and with the dead master, César Franck—the school whose capital traits are finesse, a passion for the recondite, a scrupulous avoidance of too definite, too facile patterns, an exquisite mastery of harmonic and orchestral color. With Mr. Loeffler these traits are a most conspicuous possession. He is, in his artistic constitution, pre-eminently Gallic—so far as the term is a signal for fastidiousness, for dexterity, for sensibility. The overwhelming impact of Wagner's genius seems, happily, not to have involved him in any appreciable degree; what little of the Teutonic tradition he has inherited is connoted by occasional touches in his work of a quality which one knows only in Brahms—and Brahms, let it be remarked, at his best, his most admirably Teutonic.

Mr. Loeffler, then, owing something to the subtlest and most sensitizing influences in the musical art of today, is himself an influential force of definite potency. . . . He has given us an art in which the declaration is of an emotion within emotion, an alembicated eloquence—an eloquence which prevails through its very passivity. But you will not know its spell at once, for its beauty issues from remote and hidden sources.

* * * * *

✻ 1904 — *The New York Times*

From "'Symphonia domestica,' with Composer Leading," *New York Times* (22 March 1904), 5.

> Strauss conducted the premiere of his new *Symphonia domestica* (Op. 53) on 21 March 1904 during his first American sojourn. Ostensibly an attempt to describe the events of his private life at home, *Symphonia domestica* created quite a commotion in New York City's musical circles. Utilizing a large orchestra that includes four saxophones and a number of unusual harmonic twists, this composition was originally supplied with program notes written by Strauss himself, who purported to describe musically—and in minute detail—a number of routine daily activities. Although Strauss later withdrew the notes, hoping that the music would speak for itself, the damage had been done. Debate raged in the this country and abroad about the limits of program music, and Strauss's reputation as the most adventuresome of modern composers persisted.

More than twenty years ago Richard Strauss's Symphony in F (Op. 12), the work of an unknown young German composer, was first brought before the world by a performance in this city. Last night the latest composition of Dr. Richard Strauss, the foremost man of the day in music, his *Symphonia domestica*, was also given its first public performance here. It was in Carnegie Hall, and was the climax and culminating point of Dr. Strauss's visit to this country. . . .

. . . The *Symphonia domestica* is, like all his music, deeply interesting, in some respects fascinating. It is full of new effects, and many of his old ones are repeated with a supreme mastery of technical manipulation that seems raised to a higher power than ever. The thematic development is carried to the furthest limit. The combination of themes—counterpoint, if there were only that regard for euphony which it is the function of counterpoint to protect—are bewildering. The cacophony upon which the harmony sometimes enters is recklessness.

The composer is as unsparing as ever of his listener's ears in this respect. The instrumentation is scarcely more natural than it is in some of his previous works–there is much forging of instruments into impossible registers and heart-breaking demands upon their technique. There are enormous difficulties, and the ensemble is most exacting. . .

Is not the hearer constantly impressed, in hearing this one, that something of apparently tremendous import is going on of which rightful knowledge is denied him? Is he not tantalized by sounds that are plainly meant to be to the mind something more than they seem to the ear? It was very difficult to perceive for Dr. Strauss's performance of this enormously complex and detailed piece of program music without a word of explanation any sufficient cause. Even with a knowledge of all his intentions, the *Symphonia domestica* does not reach complete success in characterization, notwithstanding all its prodigious cleverness. Without that knowledge the music rarely explains itself or justifies itself as music. The fact that his program has served his own purpose in inspiring him to its production is not sufficient. Their experience last evening ought to be full of suggestion to all who heard the *Symphonia domestica* as to the philosophy of program music.

* * * * *

* 1907 — REGINALD DE KOVEN, COMPOSER

From "The Modern Revolt in Music," *North American Review* 186/624 (November 1907), 360-69.

> An American composer and music critic himself, Reginald De Koven (1859-1920) recognized that music by Strauss and other "ultra-modern" composers was swiftly breaching the boundaries of traditional composition. Although De Koven, known principally as a creator of operettas and theatrical music, probably seemed to many at the time to be an alarmist, in retrospect his sense that a musical revolution was brewing was prescient.

During the past few years, the works of a group of ultra-modern composers, foremost among whom is Richard Strauss, have attracted an attention, and compelled a consideration, which, in view of their inherent characteristics, and revolutionary tendencies, are in the highest degree significant. Throwing musical tradition and convention over the moon, and all previously accepted theory and practice of the art to the four winds, these composers, by works so far, perhaps, more remarkable for manner than matter, have succeeded in arousing among their admirers a spirit of extravagant enthusiasm, a rabidly zealous partisanship, which bids fair to become a cult, and recalls the early days of frenetic Wagnerism.

It is not the intention here to discuss Richard Strauss . . . as a melodist or a harmonist; to extol his marvelous orchestration, or decry his less marvelous cacophony; to assign him a present place as a composer among the great ones of the earth, or to predict his particular niche in some future Temple of Fame. Critics, alive today, who characterized as "Katzen Musik" [useless music], and cacophonic, passages in Wagner which now appear almost obvious in their simplicity, stand as a warning to the dangers and pitfalls of premature critical judgement; while, in view of recent developments, the term "cacophony" is one to be handled with extreme caution and reserve. . . .

And so by degrees, and little by little, the chains of tradition were loosened, the fetters of convention and arbitrary theory broken; this limitation disappeared, that restriction ceased to bind; and, failing any generally recognized law as to what constitutes beauty in music from a purely aesthetic standpoint, the theory of "Wohlklang" [euphony], or whatever sounds well, is right, became of almost universal acceptance among musicians.

But this doctrine of Wohlklang, once accepted, carries with it a further corollary, namely: Whatever sounds *at all* is right, when one is accustomed to it.

And this is no extravagant statement; for the most advanced thinkers claim that the human ear may be trained and cultivated to the extent of receiving a pleasurable sensation from any sound or a series of sounds, so long as an emotional impression is conveyed thereby; that, psychologically considered, concord and discord are meaningless terms, musical form is superfluous, and all harmonic theory [is] a delusion and a snare. And after Strauss's *Salome*, who shall say them nay?

But there is another aspect of what we have styled the modern Revolt in Music, a psychological, emotional and temperamental aspect, which has been, perhaps, the most powerful factor in determining the scope and direction of the revolt against hidebound tradition and formal theory now under discussion. Music is first and foremost an emotional art; and those who practice it are more often swayed by their feelings than by their faculties. Who among the army of brain-workers in many fields has not felt and writhed under the lash of the arbitrary "Thou shalt not" [?] Who has not felt the despair of the inevitable, the tragedy of routine, sink like iron into his very soul? Some such feeling as actuated the man who committed suicide because he was tired of getting up, and going to bed, has come to every brain-worker possessed of even a spark of the divine fire. Imagine, then, the creative musician, with soul afire, seeking an outlet for thoughts beyond words, hemmed in, bound down by forbidden intervals and prohibited progressions, harmonies not allowed, chords interdicted, and resolutions proscribed; the chains and fetters, centuries old, of monastic scholiasts. Imagine a poet, or essayist, compelled to end each verse or paragraph with some set phrase such as "This is the end"! . . .

One may scoff, sneer at and deride even the idea of the revolution foreshadowed in this modern revolt; may call it impossible, impracticable and useless. The same was said of the electric telegraph little more than half a century ago; and today the phonograph and wireless telegraphy are but ordinary incidents in our daily life. But, say what we will, think as we may, believe or doubt as our attitude of mind is liberal or narrow, progressive or reactionary, the modern revolt in music, as typified in the works of the arch-innovator Richard Strauss, is with us, and advancing in importance and influence with giant strides.

And because of it, the musical world today is confronted with an unusual dilemma. Either we must accept the music of Strauss and all that it implies, and thereby admit the possibility, at least, of such consequent organic changes in the art as have been outlined above; or we must reject it as outside the proper limitations of music, and admit that the boundary line which cannot be passed has been reached, the last word in musical form and expression spoken, and that, after two centuries of constant sequential development, music has become a dead art.

No; a thousand times, no!

Even a cursory glance at existing musical conditions is sufficient to show that, at the present moment, music is farther than ever from being a dead art. The whole musical atmosphere is charged with the unrest of progress, the desire of new things; and, unless all signs fail, it can hardly be doubted that we stand today on the threshold of a revolution involving a reconstruction of our present scale, so important and far-reaching that it bids fair to change the face of the musical world.

* * * * *

* 1910 — HORATIO PARKER, COMPOSER, MUSIC EDUCATOR,

From "Contemporary Music," *North American Review* 191/653 (April 1910), 517-26.

> Horatio Parker (1863-1919) was a leading member of the group of Boston-based composers collectively known as the "Second New England School." He was an equally talented essayist; several of his articles are penetrating. Here Parker compared two of the leading modernist composers of the day—Strauss and Debussy—and exposed his own Teutonic prejudices and predilections, a close reflection of the opinions of most Boston composers of the day. Parker's expectation of "warm dissent" probably masked a surer expectation for heated argument on this issue.

The musical vocabulary of the two men differs immensely. Many admirers of the modern French school think Strauss's music vulgar because it really has tunes and because you can almost always tell what key it is in. In the French music the continual evasion of everything we consider obvious becomes monotonous and furiously unimportant after an hour or two. One longs in vain for a tonal point of departure, for some drawing [extra-musical illustration], but there is nothing but color. . . .

But to compare Strauss and Debussy. Other men might be found, but these two are most influential and both are typical. Each composer has a rich, individual, personal melodic and harmonic vocabulary; each offers new and satisfying rhythmic discoveries; each shows us a wealth of new and beautiful color. The differences in melody lie in the greater directness of Strauss's work. His tunes are sometimes garish in their baldness and simplicity. This is never true of Debussy, to whom a plain tune like the principal dance tune in [Strauss's] *Salome* would seem utterly common and hateful. Polyphony is regarded as the highest, the ultimate development of melody. There seems to be infinitely more polyphonic and rhythmic vitality in Strauss's work than in that of Debussy. . . .

. . . Total absence of form is inconceivable in music, and form implies inevitably some degree of formality. This element is always clearly present in Strauss and always purposely absent in Debussy, who steadfastly avoids the indicative mood and confines himself apparently to the subjunctive. At great climaxes Strauss ordinarily seeks a simple triad, Debussy some more than usually obscure and refined dissonance. The harmonic element in Strauss is, perhaps, less refined, but less subtle. In Debussy it is less direct and less beautiful, but quite distinctly less obvious, if less varied.

That Strauss may be a positive and Debussy a negative force in music, the one greatest in what he does, the other in what he avoids, may invite the warmest kind of dissent. . . .

* * * * *

✻ 1912 — JOHN C. GRIGGS, VOICE TEACHER AND CHOIRMASTER

From "Claude Debussy," *Yale Review* 1/3 (April 1912), 484-94.

> John C. Griggs's rumination on Claude Debussy (1862-1918) was probably occasioned by the Boston Opera's performance of the French composer's opera *Pelleas et Melisande* in Boston in January of 1912. Debussy's musical style stood in stark contrast to the Germanic styles that dominated America's classical music terrain. Griggs's sensitive analysis admitted that it was too early to predict Debussy's contribution to art in the long-term, but he recognized that his music was indeed original. Griggs (1865-1932) studied at Yale, earned a doctorate in Leipzig, and, interestingly, was a long-time friend of Charles Ives.

Claude Debussy, by his novelty and elegance of form, perplexing subtlety of thought, unerring sense of musico-dramatic diction, and exquisite vision of certain hitherto unseen beauty, has challenged the critical attention of the world of art. He is still in middle life, and styled a young composer. Whether he shall prove a prophet of the larger future, or merely a brilliant by-product of the onward course of tonal expression, may not yet be safely said. That he is a master of his craft, skilled in all the learning, tradition, and resource of the schools, cannot be gainsaid any more than can the fertility and facility of his imagination, and the easy distinction of his utterance. He has much to say, and says it in a polished style, at once supremely idiomatic and unquestionably artistic.

Whether what he says is worth saying at all, and whether his individual idiom is worth apprehending, are the points of dispute between his many admirers and the contemptuous detractors, good men all, who dismiss his content as vapid and his manner as merely grotesque.

The first impression of Debussy's music may be compared to the effect of a newly discovered picture gallery where not only colors, drawing, and subjects, but also frames and walls are strange. The floor even seems perhaps a bit billowy, until sight becomes adjusted and our senses assure us that we are still in the world of reality, with solid foundation. . . .

His art contains no platitude set forth with diagram and deadly distinctness, no grandiloquent impositions upon an inactive imagination. Yet there is no ultimate evasion. Thought is contained in seductive glow, not beckoning glitter; in languorous sentiment, not without the occasional full-bodied voice of a man. While he does not lay bare every last quivering nerve with a cruel tweak or acid twinge of a Strauss or a [Max] Reger, Debussy no less surely gains the intensity of soul experience, and that in a manner neither nervous nor nerveless. . . .

Whether his subtle, complex, and novel work shall prove a large force in modern musical development cannot yet be safely said. Opinions differ greatly as to the value of both his content and of his expressional methods. Alluring and strong as they appear to many, to others his content appears trivial and his new methods unprofitable. . . .

* * * * *

✻ 1914 — LAWRENCE GILMAN, MUSIC CRITIC AND WRITER ON MUSIC

From "Music and Drama: The Irrubrical Schoenberg and His Extraordinary Music," *North American Review* 199/700 (March 1914), 452-58.

> The critic Lawrence Gilman (1878-1939) discussed a recent New York performance of the String Quartet No. 1 in D minor (Op. 7, 1905) by Arnold Schoenberg (1874-1951), a leading figure in the first decades of the twentieth century. Composed near the end of his tonal period, the quartet is marked by a hyper-Romanticism that emphasizes melody and gradually decreases the importance of a tonal center. The quartet is among the last works the Viennese master composed before embarking on what musicologists call his "expressionist" period, a dozen-year span during which his music explored complete atonality. One senses here that Gilman was trying to convince himself that the art of music was not dying.

The most difficult problem that Art presents to the human intelligence is one that is never permanently solved: we mean the problem of the innovator, the pathbreaker, the smasher of idols. It is a problem of unexampled difficulty because it is eternally recurrent. . . . Those who, a quarter-century ago, welcomed, extolled, and promoted the heterodoxies of Wagner, who yesterday were shamefacedly uneasy over Richard Strauss and [Claude] Debussy, today are openly and vehemently hostile to the irrubrical Arnold Schoenberg—who happens to be the conspicuous idol-breaker of our time. There is no help for it; the difficulty is inevitable. However responsive, however flexible, however hospitable we may be, there is bound to come an hour when some new voice will speak out of the art that is contemporary with us in a tongue that is alien and repugnant; and we shall find ourselves exclaiming against it as passionately, with as sincere a conviction that we are defending the most sacred and immutable canons of art against a ruthless violator, as did our grandfathers against the iconoclast who is to us classic. What is being said today of Schoenberg—that he is "lifting the art of music from its ancient foundations, which have upheld it since the night of time, and setting it upon new ones"—is what, in substance, has been said of every innovator of the past.

What is one to do about it? Nothing—except to petition the gods for wisdom and forbearance and spiritual humility, while the one utters frankly, after due fasting and prayer, the conviction that is within the soul.

For example, there is the case of Schoenberg, the idol-breaker whom we have already mentioned. Let us confess at once that we hold no brief for Schoenberg; we are not of the cult. Nor are we of the opposition. We should like nothing better than to be thrilled by this extraordinary music-maker, though as yet—but we shall come to that later. The point is that Schoenberg (who is a sober and industrious Viennese of forty) is causing many of us, his contemporary auditors, to display precisely the same spiritual rigidity, to indulge in precisely the same opposition and contumely, for which we so complacently upbraid those who, half a century ago, witnessed the unsettling procedures of Richard Wagner; the only difference being that we have an uncomfortable suspicion that we may be making asses of ourselves, whereas the anti-Wagnerites of fifty years ago had no such self-conscious and morbid misgiving, but went about their solemn business of upholding the eternal verities of art with a perfect and invincible assurance of rectitude. . . . Which brings us to some consideration of the occasion of these remarks: the recent performance by the Flonzaley Quartet (a performance of incredible virtuosity) of Schoenberg's string quartet in D minor, opus 7.

Schoenberg is easily the most "modern" of the moderns—the most venturesome, the most flagrant in his disregard of all the rules of the game. He has been called a madman. He has passionate adherents, and equally passionate opponents. . . . As to the D minor quartet—the first characteristic example of Schoenberg's writing that has been heard in New York—there is this to be said at the start: parts of it, as the adagio and the final pages, are beautiful with a beauty that is as an open book—a beauty that no sensitive hearer will fail to perceive; a beauty that is grave and exquisite, that enlarges the spirit and lingers in the heart. These pages we can all gladly and uncompromisingly acclaim—as the perplexed and angry public of Wagner's lifetime used to except and accept, with a relief that is now comically pathetic. . . . But it is not this aspect of Schoenberg that is in question—it is not because of such things as these that he is an "issue," a Burning Question, in contemporary music. The essential, the problematical, Schoenberg is to be found in the first section of this quartet in—as Mr. [Kurt] Schindler meticulously warns us—"the opening ten minutes" (the quartet takes fifty-two minutes to perform). It is while listening to these initial pages that even the most imperturbable of "modernists" receives a shock. . . .

We have tried to like this music . . . we have earnestly desired to be moved by it, to find in it power or eloquence or beauty; but we have not succeeded. It seems to us immeasurably dull. We do not say that it is ugly, for ugliness in music is often fascinating; we say merely that it is dull, flat, homely, and insipid. . . .

Is Schoenberg, then, a revolutionary genius, or is he not? We are uninformed. We have not a trace of hostility toward him. He does not fill us with alarm, or outrage our convictions. We do not know whether he is upsetting the ancient foundations of musical art or not, and we do not care—we should not mind if he turned them upside down, so long as he stirred us, or filled us with awe, or made us dream. Our chief, indeed our only, objection to him is that we find him dull.

* * * * *

✻ 1915 — HIRAM K. MODERWELL, MUSIC CRITIC

From "On Acquiring New Ears," *The New Republic* 4/44 (4 September 1915), 119-21. [Reprinted courtesy of the publisher]

A critic of little renown, Hiram K. Moderwell (1888-1945) was, in fact, an astute observer of modern and popular music. In this essay Moderwell observed the advent of the newest music, called "futurist" by some, and defended it as another step in the evolution of the art. His theme of "acquiring new ears" was one that resounded among the more eclectic consumers of music.

I remember a concert I once heard in Vienna, where there were three fist fights going on at once, a composer standing in one of the boxes shouting insults at the audience, a uniformed policeman dashing from group to group to separate belligerents, tearful wives entreating violent husbands to master their anger, and a hubbub of voices that made the rafters shake. Finally the police were called to clear the hall by force. And I remember another concert, this time in Paris, where hoots, guffaws and hisses drowned the music, and the audience was presently divided into groups of men chattering in frenzy and knots of awed foreigners studying local manners and customs. . . . The *causus belli* [i.e., the cause of war] in both cases was a new kind of music. It has been dubbed, by common consent, futurist music.

This music has come to America. It has not come with a crash, as cubist and post-impressionist art came, nor will any music ever provoke a fist fight in this land of free opinion. . . .

What then is futurist music? Actually it has no more right to a single name than the labor unrest or the present anti-materialistic trend in philosophy. It comes from many men, some of them strangers to each other in name and in influence. It has antecedents as various as the French salon and the Siberian steppe. Its several composers could not possibly agree on a theory or a manifesto. Yet it needs a name. It has a more than superficial homogeneity. It is born of one stage of musical evolution. It has certain uniformity in point of technical means. And, what is much more important, it has manifested itself to the man in the street as a music of a definite type—that which consists solely of discords. So we may as well continue for the present to lump the new music in one and call it "futurist." . . .

To appreciate this new music we must acquire a new set of ears. We must neglect the norms and standards with which we listened to Bach and adopt new ones from the new music itself. Whether or not we "should" do this may be decided by the critics at their leisure. But the fact is that if we are to make head or tail of the new music, we have got to. For this music is, at its extreme, almost unrelated to the music which went before. . . .

Though most of the futurist composers violently repudiate any system, [to] be sure we shall discover uniformities in their work, type words and phrases, even a growing syntax of logic and form. Out of these we shall make our new ears. We shall discover units of "color" in the chords which now seem undifferentiated in their ugliness. We shall perhaps learn to listen, as ears have not listened for a century, to the rich and diverse inner voices. With a new harmony there seems to be coming a new and freer polyphony. And gradually, as we become accustomed to the new materials, somebody—probably the composer—will whisper in our ear that this or that type of dissonance or polyphony "expresses" love or envy or longing. Such suggestion will probably suffice to give the music meaning. The suggestion will become forever associated with the music, just as in speech the image is associated with the word. And presently this new, ugly, abstract music will have become familiar, beautiful and poetic! So it goes in this disconcerting business of acquiring new ears. At the first hearing the thing is ugly; at the second, interesting; and at the third—if the gods so will—beautiful.

* * * * *

✻ 1915 — JAMES GIBBONS HUNEKER, MUSIC CRITIC AND WRITER ON MUSIC

From "The Seven Arts: Leo Ornstein," *Puck* (17 April 1915), 11.

> Russian-born pianist Leo Ornstein (1893-2002) was on the cusp of a spectacular career as a conventional concert artist when he turned to composition. Among his most famous works is the early *Danse sauvage* (ca. 1915), a modernistic, sometimes bizarre, "futuristic" work that was simultaneously reviled and admired by press and public. Although he is little remembered today, that work and others vaulted Ornstein onto the international stage, where he was not always viewed in a positive light. Here critic James Gibbons Huneker described his first encounter with Ornstein and his works.

I had heard of Leo Ornstein. I had read some of his compositions. I even attempted to play them. In London he received columns of comment several years ago. But I had never seen, never heard Leo Ornstein. My curiosity, both optical and aural, was gratified, as the Music League of America was considerate enough to send me seats for his fourth recital given in the pretty little Bandbox Theatre on East 57th Street. The auditorium is small, but ideal for an intimate piano recital. And Leo Ornstein is nothing if not intimate. I confess I went, if not to mock, at least in a rather skeptical mood; but I remained to applaud; a sad commentary on my critical consistency. . . .

However, when Leo smites the keys he is not in the least anemic. That glowing apparition, the young Siegfried—Percy Grainger—is a muscular artist, who crashes chords with the energy of a sun god. Compared with Ornstein on the rampage, Grainger is as mellifluous as mother's milk. Nor is the Ornstein scale of dynamics limited. He has a liquid singing touch, his tone is rich, massive, his color-scheme varied, his phrasing musical, subtle. An unquestionable piano talent, I should say, tortured by perverse dogmas. He can ripple. Always a pressure touch in pianissimo. He can explode. A veritable siege-gun in action. I'm sure, without having heard him in Chopin or Schumann, that he can interpret those masters with sympathy and intelligence. But, as he wishes to present the latter-day composers, we must accept him at face value. . . .

Here is where we hit a snag. Leo Ornstein composes; furthermore, he is unafraid as to their publicity. I appreciated the original flavor of his performance. I never thought I would live to hear Arnold Schoenberg sound tame; yet tame he is, almost timid and halting, after Ornstein—who is, most emphatically, the only true-blue genuine Futurist composer alive. Excruciating to ears attuned to the plangent progressions of Schoenberg are the Burlesques, Preludes, and Moods of Leo the Intrepid. Like two amorous felines in a moonlit backyard is the dialogue of his love pieces. I was dazzled. I was stunned; especially after the *glissandi* that ripped up the keyboard, and fizzed and foamed over the stage. He was supposed to depict Angels, Peace, Joy—but I could detect only Rage and Hell, and again, Hell let loose. And suffusing it all a diabolical humor, a frenzied humor that bruised one's very bones. The softer emotions, including the erotic, have been squeezed out to the last rag by the older masters; now it is the turn for the uglier, nastier "reactions" in art and music. Ornstein exposes the psychology of a sea-shell, a glow-worm, and a policeman. As an oldster, I'm all at sea in these newer manifestations. I recognize the art involved in playing on your naked nerves, and I will endure much dissonance if the mood expressed be an authentic one, yet I do bewail the murderous means of expression with which Leo Ornstein patrolled the piano; he stormed its keys, scooping chunks of slag and spouting scoriae like a vicious volcano. Heavens! with what orgiastic abandon he played his own "Wild Man's Dance" [*Danse sauvage*]. He, no doubt, said to himself, a dance of wild men is not a cradle song, but a crazy carnival of legs and rum. And so it is. That he is apt to become the rage next season in the musical world would not surprise me, despite his "eccentricities" and "mannerisms." He is that rare thing–an individual pianist. . . .

❋ ❋ ❋ ❋ ❋

❋ 1915 — CARL VAN VECHTEN, COMPOSER, NOVELIST, FILM MAKER, AND PHOTOGRAPHER

From "Music after the Great War," *Music after the Great War and Other Studies* (New York: Schirmer, 1915), 3-25.

> Like Moderwell, Carl Van Vechten (1880-1964) had a soft spot for modernism. He viewed current developments as only the latest manifestation of musical progress and thought that the onset of war would not compel a return to the formal structures or the sentimentality of the nineteenth century. In this essay Van Vechten also considered the popularity of American music. He was among the few who argued that American composers had received a fair hearing.

Since the beginnings of music, as an art form, there has always been a complaint that contemporary composers could not write a melody. Beethoven suffered from this complaint; Wagner suffered from it; we have only recently gone through the period when Strauss and Debussy suffered from it. The reason is an obvious one. Each new composer has made his own rules for composition. Each has progressed a step further in his use of harmony. Now it is evident that in this way novelty lies, for an entirely new unaccompanied melody would be difficult to devise. It is in the combination of melody and harmony that a composer may show his talent at invention. It is but natural that any advance in this direction should at first startle unaccustomed ears, and it is by no means uncertain that this first thrill is not the most delicious sensation to be derived from hearing music. In time harmony is exhausted–combinations of notes in ordered forms–but there is still the pursuit of disharmony to be made. We are all quite accustomed to occasional discords, even in the music of Beethoven, where they occur very frequently. Strauss utilizes discords skillfully in his tonal painting; in such works as *Elektra* and [*Ein*] *Heldenleben* they abound. The newer composers have almost founded a school on disharmony.

To me it seems certain that it is the men who have given the new impetus to tonal art in the past five years who will make the opening for whatever art music we are to hear after the war, and I am referring even to occasional pieces after the manner of Tchaikovsky's overture, *1812*, in which the Russian National Anthem put to rout the Marseillaise. . . . Perhaps it will be Karol Szymanowski of Poland (if he is still alive) or a new César Franck in Belgium who will rise to write of the intensity of suffering through which his country has struggled. But it seems to me beyond a doubt that music after the Great War will be "newer" (I mean, of course, more primitive) than it was in the last days of July, 1914. There will be plenty of disharmonies, foreshadowed by Schoenberg and Stravinsky, let loose on our ears, but . . . I submit that these disharmonies are a steady progression from Wagner, and not a freakish whim of an abnormal devil. I do not predict a return to Mozart as one result of the war. . . .

I shall not hesitate [to write] on the music of America, because in a country that has no ante-bellum music—one cannot speak with too great enthusiasm of Ethelbert Nevin and Edward MacDowell—there is no immediate promise of development. However, in a digression, I should like to make a few remarks on the subject of the oft-repeated charge, re-echoed by Holbrooke in relation to British musicians, that American composers are neglected and have no chance for a hearing in their own country. Has ever a piano piece been played more often or sold more copies than MacDowell's "To a Wild Rose," unless it be Nevin's "Narcissus"? Probably "The Rosary" has been sung more times in more quarters of the globe than "Rule Britannia." Other American songs which have achieved an international success and a huge sale are "At Parting," "A Maid Sings Light," "From the Land of the Skyblue Water," and "The Year's at the Spring." Orchestral works by Paine, Hadley, Converse, and others, are heard almost as soon as they are composed, and many of them are heard more than once, played by more than one orchestra. Of late years it has been the custom to produce an American work at the Metropolitan Opera House, a custom fortunately abandoned during the season just passed. No it cannot be said that the American composer has been neglected.

From "Igor Stravinsky: A New Composer," *Music after the Great War and Other Studies* (New York: Schirmer, 1915), 85-117.

Van Vechten (1880-1964) generally disdained impressionism. He saw Stravinsky as a legitimate heir to Strauss and appreciated the Russian's creativity in both harmony and rhythm.

This young Russian has appeared in an epoch in which the ambition of most composers seems to be to dream, to write their symbolic visions in terms of the mist, to harmonize the imperceptible. Stravinsky sweeps away this vague atmosphere with one gesture; his idea of movement is Dionysian; he overwhelms us with his speed. One critic has referred to him as the "whirling dervish of his art." His gifts to future composers are his conciseness, his development of the complexities of rhythm, and his invention of chord formation. His use of dissonance is an art in itself. Richard Strauss has employed dissonance in obvious development of Richard Wagner's polyphonic and chromatic style. Pushed to its furthest, his system is one of inversion. With Stravinsky the use of dissonance is invention itself. He improvises new chords, while Strauss is taking recognized chords apart to make something else of them. So this new figure stands for something in advance of what has already been expressed. He is, perhaps, the most vital of the modern forces in the music world.

* * * * *

✻ 1917 — *THE NEW YORK TIMES*

From "Ernest Bloch's Music," *New York Times* (4 May 1917), 11.

> The music of Ernest Bloch (1880-1959) still holds a small place in the modern repertoire. One of a wave of musicians displaced to America by the Great War, the Swiss-born Bloch was the first composer to gain widespread acclaim for the use of Jewish musical materials. Several of his compositions not only communicate the Jewish experience, as does his *Three Jewish Poems* of 1913, but they also often employ a sometimes severe modernism.

The Society of Friends of Music did a friendly and generous thing last evening–one of the things that have given a reason for its existence in New York–by offering a concert in Carnegie Hall of works by Ernest Bloch. Mr. Bloch is a Swiss musician whom the war has sent to this country. One of his compositions, a string quartet, had already been performed here by the Flonzaley Quartet. Others have been played in Boston by the Boston Symphony Orchestra. The concert last evening gave a hearing to *Three Jewish Poems* for orchestra. . . .

Mr. Bloch had already shown musical talent and distinction as a composer in his quartet, and the same power and originality were amply revealed in this concert. It was called a "Jewish Cycle," and in his music Mr. Bloch avows that he wishes to give expression to the Jewish racial spirit, as well as to his own individuality. He does this with small use of existing traditional Jewish melody. Yet the conclusion can hardly be avoided that his musical inspiration has been influenced to a greater or less[er] degree by this melody and by certain intervals and melodic forms that are recognized as Oriental [i.e., middle Eastern]. As a harmonist, Mr. Bloch goes to the limit of modern procedure and writes much that is drastic and mordant discord. He has a remarkable command of orchestral technique, and there is much that is extremely striking. . . .

The intense sincerity and the frequently profound and stirring expressiveness of Mr. Bloch's music are evident. It is, with scarcely an intermission, somber, gloomy, the utterance of lamentation; and this lamentation sometimes becomes shrill. . . .

In truth, this concert of Mr. Bloch's music suffered from the monotony of style and expression inevitable in the work of one man so wholly under the sway of one idea as he is; and especially one whose methods make so heavy demands upon the listener. The audience was large, distinguished in its quality, and very appreciative of Mr. Bloch's work. . . .

* * * * *

✻ 1918 — [JAMES GIBBONS HUNEKER], MUSIC CRITIC AND WRITER ON MUSIC

From "Serge Prokofiev A Virile Pianist," *New York Times* (21 November 1918), 13.

One of America's most prolific critics, James Gibbons Huneker (1857-1921) was generally appreciative of contemporary composition. This early review of Serge Prokofiev (1891-1953) as pianist and composer revealed Huneker's wide knowledge of modern trends. He sounded the familiar theme that "new ears" are required, but regarding Prokofiev he made no declarations that the Russian's music would stand the test of time.

New ears for new music! The new ears were necessary to appreciate the new music made by Serge Prokofiev in his first pianoforte recital at Aeolian Hall yesterday. He is younger looking than his years, which are patriarchal, almost twenty seven. He is blond, slender, modest as a musician, and his impassibility contrasted with the volcanic eruptions he produced on the keyboard. We have already one musical anarch here, Leo Ornstein, yet that youth's *Wild Man's Dance* is a mere exercise in euphony, a piece positively Mozartian, in comparison with the astounding disharmonies gentle Serge extorted from his suffering pianoforte; the young man's style is orchestral, and the instruments of percussion rule in this Scythian drama.

He is an individual virtuoso with a technique all his own. He can create big sonorities, sometimes mellow to richness [*sic*], more often brittle and raucous. His fingers are steel, his wrists are steel, his biceps and triceps steel, his scapula steel. . . .

As a composer he is cerebral. His music is volitional and essentially cold, as are all cerebral composers. At first you are stunned by the overwhelming quality of his music; presently a pattern is noted. The lyric themes are generally insipid. The etude form, and there is a well defined one, predominates. Immense technical difficulties deafen one to the intrinsic poverty of ideas in his music. . . .

Prokofiev uses, like Arnold Schoenberg, the entire [range of] modern harmonies. The House of Bondage of normal key relationships is discarded. He is a psychologist of the uglier emotions: hatred, contempt, rage—above all rage—disgust, despair, mockery and defiance legitimately serve as models for moods. Occasionally there are moments of tenderness, exquisite jewels that briefly sparkle and then melt into seething undertow. The danger in all this highly spiced music is manifest: it almost exhausts our facility of attention; . . .

A parterre of pianists greeted the newcomer with dynamic applause. Of his instant success there can be no doubt. Whether he will last—Ah! New music for new ears. Serge Prokofiev is very startling.

* * * * *

RAGTIME AND JAZZ

✻ 1915 — HIRAM K. MODERWELL, MUSIC CRITIC

From "Ragtime," *The New Republic* 4/50 (16 October 1915), 284-86. [Reprinted courtesy of the publisher]

The art of "ragging" music, or applying heavily syncopated rhythms against a comparatively steady bass line, had existed in an early form since the mid-nineteenth century. Scott Joplin's enormously popular "Maple Leaf Rag," published in 1899, helped to vault ragtime into American homes despite the music's close association with the African-American community as well as notorious societal elements (bars, brothels, and the like). In the following sympathetic essay Hiram K. Moderwell (1888-1945) summed up many of the era's contradictions with regard to this art form, and, as he often did, Moderwell proved himself an enlightened critic with an uncanny ability to identify styles with lasting value.

It has been nearly twenty years, and American ragtime is still officially beyond the pale. As the one original and indigenous type of music of the American people, as the one type of American popular music that has persisted and undergone constant evolution, one would think it might receive the clammy hand of fellowship from composers and critics. There is very little evidence that these gentlemen have changed their feeling about it in the last ten years. Then they asserted that it was "fortunately on the wane"; now they sigh that it will always be with us. That is the only difference.

I can't feel satisfied with this. I can't help feeling that a person who doesn't open his heart to ragtime somehow isn't human. Nine out of ten musicians, if caught unawares, will like this music until they remember that they shouldn't. . . .

The taste of the populace is often enough toward the shoddy and outworn. But when the populace creates its own art without official encouragement, then let the artists listen. I haven't a notion whether ragtime is going to form the basis of an "American school of composition." But I am sure that many a native composer could save his soul if he would open his ears to this folk music of the American city.

But the schools have their reply. "Ragtime is not new," they say. "It is merely syncopation, which was used by Haydn and Mozart, Beethoven and Brahms, and is good, like any other musical material, when it is used well." But they are wrong. Ragtime is not "merely syncopation." . . . Ragtime has its flavor which no definition can imprison. No one would take the syncopation of a Haydn symphony to be American ragtime. "Certainly not," replies the indignant musician. Nor the syncopation of any recognized composer. But if this is so, then ragtime *is* new. You can't tell an American composer's "art song" from any mediocre art song the world over. . . . You can distinguish American ragtime from the popular music of any nation at any age. . . .

I cannot understand how a trained musician can overlook its purely technical elements of interest. . . . It has established subtle conflicting rhythms to a degree never before attempted in any popular or folk music, and rarely enough in art music. It has shown a definite and natural evolution—always a proof of vitality in a musical idea. It has gone far beyond most other popular music in the freedom of inner voices (yes, I mean polyphony) and of harmonic modulation. And it has proved its adaptability to the expression of many distinct moods. Only the trained musician can appreciate the significance of a style which can be turned to so many distinct uses. . . .

As you walk up and down the streets of an American city, you feel in its jerk and rattle a personality different from that of any European capital. This is American. It is in our lives, and it helps to form our characters and condition our mode of action. It should have expression in art, simply because any people must express itself if it is to know itself. No European music can or possibly could express this American personality. Ragtime I believe does express it. It is today the one true American music.

* * * * *

✻ 1916 — *VARIETY*

From "Cabarets," *Variety* (27 October 1916), 12.

> This brief notice in *Variety*, the trade magazine of the American entertainment industry, was among the first to print the word "jazz." The writer was quick to note that improvisation and versatile instrumentation are important features of this burgeoning art form. The possibility that jazz bands might replace "classical orchestras" proved prescient.

Chicago, the home of "Walkin' the Dog," "Ballin' the Jack" and sundry other cabaret features, has added another innovation to its list of discoveries in the so-called "Jazz Bands." The Jazz Band is composed of three or more instruments and seldom plays regulated [i.e., notated] music. The College Inn and practically all the other high class places of entertainment have a Jazz Band featured, while the low cost makes it possible for all the smaller places to carry their [own] jazz orchestra. A number of the organizations [i.e., jazz bands] are reported to be considering the possibilities of invading New York, and it would not be surprising to note the disappearance of the classical orchestras for the syncopated groups.

* * * * *

✻ 1918 — EDWARD BAXTER PERRY, PIANIST, PIANO TEACHER, AND AUTHOR OF PEDAGOGICAL STUDIES

From "'Ragging' Good Music," *The Etude* 36/6 (June 1918), 372.

> An article by blind pianist Edward Baxter Perry (1855-1924), a prominent figure in the education of piano teachers and their students, was one of many in the Great War era to lambaste ragtime, but his observation that classical works were being subjected to the "ragging" process has significance. Although ragtime is differentiated from jazz by its reliance on notation (whereas jazz's most notable feature is its basis in improvisation), after the War the two become more intertwined, and many jazz musicians began look to classical music, particularly to its harmonic traits, for inspiration.

It is no uncommon thing in these days of rampant frivolity and seemingly almost universal imbecility, to hear in hotels and other places of public gathering not only a continuous series of the trashiest ragtime pieces played on a mechanical piano, but even well known good compositions by recognized composers of high standing perverted and distorted out of all semblance to the original works and vulgarized beyond the power of language to express by being changed and twisted into cheap ragtime rhythms.

Only lately I heard in the dining room of a first-class hotel in a large city the *Traumerei* by [Robert] Schumann and a few other equally exquisite and well-known gems played in ragtime throughout by an orchestra composed of fairly good executants, which might have been good if it had confined itself to legitimate work instead of attempting to cater to the present ragtime mania. If the distance between us had not been so great I certainly should have thrown my dishes, with their contents, at the head of the director. But I was afraid to trust my aim.

If musicians, so called, will insist on prostituting their art, whatever talent they possess, there is plenty of cheap stuff they might give without desecrating the works of the masters. I have heard that there were in New York surgeons who advertised to operate for the ragtime mania, and I should be willing to contribute something to encourage such an attempt. But I doubt if they could find within the skulls of such musicians or their voluntary listeners sufficient brains on which to operate.

Ragtime is syncopation gone mad, and its victims, in my opinion, can only be treated successfully like the dog with rabies, namely, with a dose of lead. Whether it is simply a passing phase of our decadent art culture or an infectious disease which has come to stay, like la grippe and leprosy, time alone can show. But so long as the general public insists upon hearing it I regret to say there will be plenty of musicians, again so-called, who will be quite ready to furnish it at so much per night. What they do with their self-respect, if they ever had any, in the meantime is a problem for the psychologist to wrestle with, but which is wholly beyond my power to solve.

We have musical unions in many of our cities, and one of the first rules they should pass is that any member found guilty of what is called "ragging" a classic should be dismissed from the organization in disgrace . . . .

Unfortunately, the bureaus and lyceum managements realize the trend of public taste and cater to it instead of attempting to elevate it. With them it is purely a business proposition. They engage by the season the attractions which they can get for the least money and sell for the most, because they are what are known as "Box Office Propositions." . . . Unless the local managements of lyceum courses take a firm and decided stand in the matter and find some way to work together there will soon be no artists at all worthy of the name, only bureaus and the players of "Good Gravy Rag," whom they send out and foist upon the helpless public. And then what becomes of good music, with its educational and artistic uplift?

If, however, worst comes to worst, and cheap music and vaudeville kill the concert and the theater, as is already being done, let us at least make a stand together in the interest of the few who really care and insist that ragtime effects shall be obtained from ragtime writers or the rag-bag or any other available and suitable source, and that really good music shall not be mutilated, degraded and disgraced by being subjected to the "ragging" process.

* * * * *

✻ 1918 — DANIEL GREGORY MASON, COMPOSER AND MUSIC EDUCATOR

From "Music in America," *Contemporary Composers* (New York: Macmillan, 1918), 231-90.

This belated response of Daniel Gregory Mason (1873-1953) to Moderwell admitted that ragtime was expressive of the American character—but only one aspect of it. And Mason believed that it was an undesirable one at that. A highly-educated musician and composer of impressive pedigree, Mason showed himself to be a disciple of John Sullivan Dwight. Mason, like the Boston journalist, disdained the ephemeral nature of popular music and longed for the reflection and craft that accompanies music that aspires to art.

In the discussions of "American music" that go on perennially in our newspapers and journals . . . a sharp cleavage will usually be observed between those whose interest is primarily in the music itself, wherever it comes from, and those in whom the artistic considerations give way before patriotic ardor, and propaganda usurps the place of discrimination. One group, in uttering the phrase, "American music," places the stress instinctively on the noun and regards the adjective as only qualification; the other, in its preoccupation with "American," seems to take "music" rather for granted. . . .

What, then, is the precise value we ought justly to ascribe to that word "American" as applied to music, and wherein have those we may call champions of the adjective been inclined to exaggerate it? If we analyze their attitude, we shall find them the prey of two fallacies which constantly falsify their conclusions, and make them dangerous guides for those who have at heart the real interests of music in America. The first of these fallacies is that which confuses quantity with quality, and supposes that artistic excellence can be decided by the vote of the majority. The second is that which identifies racial character with local idioms and tricks of speech rather than with a certain emotional and spiritual temper. Both lead straight to the oft-repeated conclusion that "ragtime" is the necessary basis of our musical art. . . .

Thus the technical limitations of ragtime which we have tried to analyze are seen to be in the last analysis the results and indices of a more fundamental shortcoming—an emotional superficiality and triviality peculiar to it. Ragtime is the musical expression of an attitude toward life only too familiar to us all, an attitude shallow, restless, avid of excitement, incapable of sustained attention, skimming the surface of everything, finding nowhere satisfaction, realization, or repose. It is a meaningless stir-about, a commotion without purpose, an epilepsy simulating controlled muscular action. It is the musical counterpart of the sterile cleverness we find in so much of our contemporary conversation, as well as in our theater and our books. No candid observer could deny the prominence in our American life of this restlessness of which ragtime is one expression. It is undoubtedly what most strikes superficial observation. The question is whether it is really representative of the American temper as a whole, or is prominent only as the froth is prominent on a glass of beer. Mr. Moderwell thinks the former. . . .

Here is a music, local and piquantly idiomatic, and undeniably representative of a certain aspect of American character—our restlessness, our insatiable nervous activity, our thoughtless superficial "optimism," our fondness for "hustling," our carelessness of whither, how, or why we are moving if only we can "keep on the move." If this were all of us, if the first impression which foreigners get of us, summed up for them oftentimes in our inimitably characteristic "Step lively, please," were also the last, and there was nothing more solid, sweet, or wise in America than this galvanic twitching, then indeed ragtime would be our perfect music. But every true American knows that, on the contrary, this is not our virtue but our vice, not our strength but our weakness, and that such a picture of us as it presents is not a portrait but a caricature. And similarly, as soon as we examine ragtime at all critically we discover its essential triviality. Its melodies are commonplace, its harmonies cheap, shoddy, and sentimental. Even its rhythm, as we have seen, is a clever formula rather than a creative form, a trick for giving ordinary movement a specious air of animation. . . .

* * * * *

As during the Civil War, music was considered vital to the morale of troops during the Great War. This poster, created circa 1917, solicits donations of gramophone recordings, which then could be sent to American soldiers abroad.

Courtesy of the Prints and Photographs Division, Library of Congress: LC-USZC4-10035.

※ 12 — MUSIC AND THE GREAT WAR

OPPORTUNITY KNOCKS

1914 – *The New York Times*
From "New York as an Art Center"
From "America Has Opportunity: Musical Supremacy May Be Won During War Abroad, Says Seagle"

1915 – John Galsworthy
From "Art and the War"

1917 – Olin Downes
From "Making a Singing Army"

1918 – Edwin Litchfield Turnbull
From "Musicians Needed to Help Win War"

THE GERMAN PROBLEM

1914 – *The New York Times*
From "Neutrality in Music"

1917 – *The New York Times*
From "Halt German Opera at Metropolitan"

1917 – Fritz Kreisler
From "Fritz Kreisler in a Statement of Great Frankness Tells of His Conduct in the War"

1917 – *The New York Times*
From "Philharmonic Facts"

1918 – *The New York Times*
From "Philharmonic Bars German Composers"

THE CONTROVERSY SURROUNDING DR. MUCK

1917 – *The New York Times*
From "Orchestra and Muck Condemned"

From "Threat to Disband Boston Symphony"
From "A Musician Makes a Mistake"
From "An Artists Grave Indiscretion"

1917 – David Stanley Smith
From "National Anthem's Place"

1917 – *The New York Times*
From "Muck Blameless, Higginson Insists"
From "Ex-Gov. Warfield Would Mob Muck"
From "Baltimore Forbids Dr. Muck's Concert"
From "Denounce Muck at Rally"
From "Dr. Muck, Citizen of Switzerland"

The idea of a war for "musical supremacy," its relation to artistic creation, and the implications of such a struggle had resonated in some American quarters since at least the mid-nineteenth century. Despite years of substantial gains in all spheres of music—the rise of institutions for learning and for performance, the advent of a generation of respected composers and critics, increased access to music by way of technology, and laws increasingly favorable to the production of art—many Americans still lamented and even resented the powerful influence of Europe. This chapter offers views on America's opportunity to become, at last, the dominant nation in the world for the arts.

OPPORTUNITY KNOCKS

✻ 1914 — *THE NEW YORK TIMES*

From "New York as an Art Center," *New York Times* (12 October 1914), 8.

Comments by William Sloane Coffin, Sr. (1879-1933), a respected business executive and president of the Metropolitan Museum of Art in New York City, prompted the following editorial concerning the obvious negative impact of the war in Europe on the creation of art and its implications for the United States.

In the opinion of Mr. William Sloan Coffin, which in all matters relating to art is worth heeding, the Great War in Europe gives New York an opportunity to become the great art center of the world. But that is an opportunity more difficult to turn to good account than the numberless trade opportunities which are so easily seen but not so easily realized. To be sure, the war in Europe has temporarily paralyzed artistic production, but the passions involved are so mighty and deep, the sacrifice is so enormous, that this very war may be, in the end, productive of ideals which will prove inspiring to art, and we may reasonably expect that a new race of poets, painters, composers, and sculptors will come into being after the tide of battle has subsided. . . .

We may hope that the setback to art in Europe will serve as an impetus to American artists, but in the future, as in the past, the great art centers will be where the artistic inspiration is most potent and the native art spirit strongest.

From "America Has Opportunity, Musical Supremacy May Be Won during War Abroad, Says Seagle," *New York Times* (13 October 1914), 11.

Oscar Seagle (1877-1945), a prominent singer and teacher, admitted that the War provided the United States with unprecedented musical opportunity, but he also remained cautiously guarded. Seagle believed that for America to become a world leader in music its citizens must cultivate a true appreciation of the art form.

Oscar Seagle, the American baritone, who has just returned from a summer of teaching in England, says that he and his students had no war experience and lived in such a calm atmosphere that they were sorry to depart. The war preparations were so quietly and methodically carried on, he says, that the peace of the Sussex villages was scarcely marred.

"The desired musical supremacy which has been claimed for America, and particularly for New York," says Mr. Seagle, "is now achievable, owing to the deplorable state of Europe, a condition that has driven both American and foreign musicians to these shores and has forced the return of hundreds of American students. If the presence of scores of teachers and thousands of students, together with the quantity of musical events that occur here, make for supremacy then the title is won, but there is an important factor too often overlooked. It is not the quality of the concerts and opera nor the ability of the teachers, nor is it the ability of the students; these cannot be questioned. It is the attitude of the students which so faithfully reflects the position of the public."

"Of course, that thing we call artistic atmosphere is at present smashed beyond hope of immediate recovery in Europe and America will have to furnish the available supply this year. Those who know what this atmosphere is talk about it often and long, while those who have not experienced it 'pooh-pooh' [it] often and long. It is not made up entirely of concerts and the number of persons engaged in the study of music, but depends upon a background supplied by people who know the worth of art and time, and have a high regard for the professions that require years to perfect."

"There are many favorable signs, but if we could only do something in this, the year of our greatest opportunity, if we could bring the American mind to understand that now is the time to place our imprint upon art, to make it as much our own as possible!"

* * * * *

✻ 1915 — JOHN GALSWORTHY, NOVELIST AND PLAYWRIGHT

From "Art and the War," *Atlantic Monthly* 116/5 (November 1915), 624-28.

In this essay British man of letters John Galsworthy (1867-1933) did not predict a coming musical windfall for the United States, but he pointed out eloquently the resilience of art during times of war. Born to wealth and social privilege, the well-travelled Englishman is best known for his trilogy of novels *The Forsyte Saga*.

Art is the universal traveler, essentially international in influence. Revealing the spirit of things lying behind parochial surfaces and circumstance, delving down into the common stuff of nature and human nature, and recreating therefrom, it passes ten thousand miles of space, ten thousand years of time, and yet appeals to the men it finds on those far shores. It is the one possession of a country which that country's enemies usually still respect and take delight in. War, [the] outcome of the side of man's nature which denies breadth of heart, can for the moment paralyze the outward activities of art, but can it ever chain its spirit, or arrest the inner ferment of the creative instinct? For thousands of generations war has been the normal state of man's existence, yet alongside war has flourished this art, reflecting man's myriad aspirations and longings, and by innumerable expressions of individual vision and sentiment, ever unifying human life, through the common factor of impersonal emotion passing from heart to heart by ways more invisible than the winds of travel, carrying the seeds and pollen of herb life. If one could only see those countless tenuous bridges spun by art, a dewy web over the whole lawn of life! If for a moment we could see them, discouragement would cease its uneasy buzzing. What can this war do that a million wars have not? It is bigger, and more bloody–the reaction from it will but be the greater. If every work of art existing in the Western world were obliterated, and every artist killed, would human nature return to the animalism from which art has in a measure raised it? Not so. Art makes good in the human soul all the positions that it conquers.

When the war is over, the world will find that the thing which has changed least is art. . . .

✻ ✻ ✻ ✻ ✻

✻ 1917 — OLIN DOWNES, MUSIC CRITIC AND JOURNALIST

From "Making a Singing Army," *The Musician* 22/12 (December 1917), 892-93.

New Yorker Olin Downes (1886-1955) saw in the Great War an opportunity for Americans to re-establish music as an integral part of their daily lives in a manner that he thought had been lost in the modern world. Here Downes documented the many and varied musical activities at one army base, Camp Devens in Ayer, Massachusetts.

One of the admirable and encouraging features of modern warfare has been the evident broadening of the conceptions of various governments as to their duties to their troops, and the realization of the practical value of all sorts of social and artistic stimuli in heightening the morale and the efficiency of the fighters.

The part that musical instruction and entertainment is playing in the camps in this country is a striking illustration. It has been many years since men have become aware of the value of song, of the absolute need of it, in fact, as they are now. Modern conditions and business had made us forget what primitive peoples knew so well: The heartening and communicative power of music.

So song has come back into the lives of a great many men who had forgotten all about it. It has come back, I think, to stay. . . .

I asked [at Camp Devens in Ayer, Massachusetts] whether there were any bands. "A good many," a soldier told me, "and more all the time. We need instruments more than anything else, for we have more players than we have brass."

Only now are the players and instruments sorted out and apportioned each to his or its place. They took a roster of all available music purveyors [players] in the camp. These were divided into three classes—good, indifferent, and poor. No one was turned away, though, and the result was that every bugler in Camp Devens took to departing into the hills and practicing in his off duty hours.

"It was the most horrible sound you ever heard," said the soldier, "for a while." Then it commenced to work out. The players were grouped together, given leaders, and rehearsed. Already, in this camp two and a half months old, we have bands that march before the troops, and many small bands who enliven their various battalions and divisions with their performances."

"There are a good many musicians among us, also speakers and vaudeville performers. It's astonishing what you find when you set out to look for it. Some of the companies have orchestras of a number of instruments. The bands of drum corps play at the football games. Forty percent of the barracks have pianos. The 30th company of the Springfield [battalion] has its orchestra play for several dances, the proceeds of which have been devoted to funds for war purposes. Practically all regiments and even smaller units have brass bands and drum corps. The orchestras may not measure up to the standard of the Boston Symphony, but they certainly make good. They play for singing. And when it comes to dancing they're right there with the *jazz band* stuff!" . . .

Efforts at entertainment are by no means limited to composing or singing songs. One sight that met my eyes as I passed through a corridor will long remain in my memory. One man was seated on a carpenter's bench, playing the mouth-organ [i.e., harmonica] for dear life. Another man, the cynosure of a dozen pairs of fascinated eyes, was "jigging it," for all he was worth in the middle of a circle. Mouth-organs are in great demand, and their popularity seems to be on the increase instead of on the wane. . . .

It seems to me that the thing music lovers, educators and sociologists have been wishing for these long years, an America that is musical, is being accomplished in a logical, evolutionary, widespreading manner in our military camps—that is, if the musical conditions in other camps are what they are at Ayer. [Camp singing director] Mr. [Vernon] Stiles believes that the men will not leave their music behind them in the camp. They will certainly carry it into the trenches, and those that come home—may they be many—will bring with them the airs that sustained hope and courage in the field. . . .

* * * * *

✻ 1918 — EDWIN LITCHFIELD TURNBULL, VIOLINIST, CONDUCTOR, AND COMPOSER

From "Musicians Needed to Help Win War," *New York Times* (20 January 1918), IV: 8.

> **During the early years of the twentieth century labor issues, including those that affected professional musicians, were at the forefront of many political agendas. Baltimore-based Edwin Litchfield Turnbull (1872-1927) noted the importance of music to the war effort but further observed that the musicians' union had hampered the ability of the government to provide music to soldiers and citizens alike. According to Turnbull, not only had morale been negatively affected, but the musicians' union had also slowed the dispersal of quality band music. With America's entry into the War, he expressed the hope that change was imminent.**

General [John J.] Pershing is evidently keenly alive to the power of martial music to arouse the patriotic emotions and has been quick to recognize the marked inferiority of American military bands as compared with those of France.

Recent dispatches from American Headquarters by Thomas Marion Johnson state that General Pershing desires to have American bands with an average of twenty-eight musicians patterned after the typical French army band containing fifty musicians, in addition to a field music corps of thirty-six drummers and trumpeters.

For years the work of our army and navy bands has been seriously hampered by legislation passed at the instigation of the labor unions in the interest of the American Federation of Musicians, an organization of some 80,000 professional band and orchestral players.

This organization has long dominated our orchestral and band music. They supply musicians for most of our symphony orchestras, theater and dance orchestras and bands. Through their affiliation with the American Federation of Labor they have secured legislation which has kept army and navy bands out of their legitimate sphere of supplying patriotic and martial music, and open air concerts for the great public of this country which is taxed so heavily for the support of our military and naval establishments.

Prior to the war the majority of state militia regiments hired civilian bands to furnish their music, and some of it was mighty poor music. In the eyes of the Musical Union all members are equal, and the man who worked all day at a trade and played a trombone horribly out of tune in some "jazz band" at night would receive the same compensation as a first-class player who devoted his entire time to music.

Army bands were limited to twenty-eight musicians, much too small a number to produce a satisfactory volume of tone when playing for large audiences in the open air. The compensation offered, which before the war was $36 per month for first-class musicians, even when taking into account all perquisites included . . . was not a sufficient inducement to attract really high-grade musicians, especially when Federal musicians were prevented, by the labor union legislation referred to, from adding to their income and improving their art by playing outside engagements in their free time.

And the narrow field of musical work to which our Government musicians have been restricted has not been such as to develop splendid concert bands of the kind one may hear in any part of Europe. . . . We have only one Government band which could be compared with these famous European bands—the Marine Band of Washington [D.C.]. This band was formerly permitted to take outside engagements and to make an annual concert tour, but these privileges were abolished at the request of labor unions, and, consequently, our finest band may now be heard only in Washington. But with the coming of the war a change for the better has come about. The Navy Department permitted Lieutenant [John Philip] Sousa and his band of 230 naval apprentices to make a concert tour, and many other army and navy bands have been permitted to march in civilian parades and to give patriotic concerts.

The outlook for American military music is now more encouraging, and I am hopeful that all the musical forces of the Government will be mobilized for the great cause of patriotic music and to help win the war "to make the world safe for democracy."

❊ ❊ ❊ ❊ ❊

THE GERMAN PROBLEM

By the start of the First World War American musical culture was deeply indebted to Germany not only for providing a large number of performers and conductors but also for lending the model on which American music pedagogy was based. But during a time of war with Germany, Americans naturally focused their biases against Germans living in the United States, and musical circles provided a rich arena for nationalist vitriol. If artists and conductors were often German, audiences and philanthropists most often were Americans, and usually very patriotic ones at that. These selections describe the wrangling that went on between Americans and Germans in America.

❊ 1914 — *THE NEW YORK TIMES*

From "Neutrality in Music," *New York Times* (7 October 1914), 8.

The issue of German musicians was discussed often in the pages of the *New York Times.* Closely scrutinized was the New York Symphony led by Walter Damrosch (1862-1950). Damrosch, himself a native German, had not only to convince audiences of his musicians' fealty to America, but he also had to keep politics out of the rehearsal and the concert hall.

Mr. Damrosch's plea to the members of his Symphony Orchestra to "forget the war" was happily inspired, and we trust that his advice will be taken to heart by all the musicians who are to provide Americans with the consolation and intellectual refreshment of good music this winter. A large proportion of our musicians are either German or of German ancestry, and . . . they must sit side by side and work in complete sympathy with Frenchmen, Russians, Englishmen, and Italians. There are, in fact, men of thirteen different nationalities in one orchestra. The Germans must lend their services to the performance of Russian, Italian, and French music, with some English music, too. It is most desirable, therefore, that all alike should dismiss from their minds all thoughts of the great conflict of the nations, except in their hours of leisure. As members of the great republic of music they must be friends and brothers, and they must remember, as Mr. Damrosch suggests, that they are Americans, for this is the great land of profit and fame for them, even if they are not as yet politically affiliated with us. . . .

It will not be easy for Frenchmen, Germans, and Russians to spend hours together and work in complete harmony, but they must do it. . . . The temperament of a competent interpreter of musical masters is often his best asset, and his natural tendency to emotional excitement is notorious. Mutual antagonism and distrust have arisen among musicians, before now, through a dispute about the relative merit of Niersteiner and Chablis [beer and wine]. The cause is greater now, [and] the greater need of severe self-restraint is obvious. . . .

❋ ❋ ❋ ❋ ❋

❋ 1917 — *THE NEW YORK TIMES*

From "Halt German Opera at Metropolitan," *New York Times* (2 November 1917), 13.

> Two topics that generated considerable discussion in musical circles were personnel and repertoire. The latter, especially in the opera house with its predominant use of the German language, caused alarm among American patrons, while many others wondered if orchestras were harboring spies.

The Metropolitan Opera Company . . . has suddenly been confronted with a difficulty in arranging for "a German opera" on the second night of the opening week, when it had been intended to have Olive Fremstadt return in her famous role in [Wagner's] *Tristan und Isolde*. . . .

A minority of the Board of Directors is understood to have opposed giving opera in German . . . for that reason the usual early announcement of the first week's bills is still delayed. . .

Mrs. William Jay, the only woman director of the New York Philharmonic Society, has written . . . : "I feel that to give German operas, particularly those of Wagner, at this time would be a great mistake. Given in the German language, and depicting scenes of violence and conflict, they must inevitably draw our minds back to the spirit of greed and barbarism which has led to so much suffering. Perhaps gala nights of German operas could be used as a political propaganda to imply a division of sentiment in this country. As the Metropolitan is practically a national institution, we should take into consideration the sensitiveness of all patrons, and especially the patriotic ones. There can be no imputation of bigotry, since Americans continue to welcome the instrumental music of the great Germans, in spite of the status of the war." . . .

❋ ❋ ❋ ❋ ❋

✻ 1917 — FRITZ KREISLER, VIOLINIST, COMPOSER, HUMANITARIAN

From "Fritz Kreisler in a Statement of Great Frankness Tells of His Conduct in the War," *New York Times* (25 November 1917), VIII: 5.

Like many European musicians of the era, violinist Fritz Kreisler (1875-1962) was looked upon by the American public—especially those unfamiliar with him and his art—with some contempt. Kreisler had moved to the United States with his American wife in 1914 following a brief tour of duty in the Austrian army. After the appearance of a number of printed attacks that questioned his allegiance to his new homeland, he was compelled to fight back. His modest humanitarian efforts were misconstrued by some as anti-American, an argument he vehemently rejected. This open letter marked Kreisler's withdrawal from the concert stage until after the War. He did not resume his brilliant career until 1919.

There have been continuous statements in Pittsburgh papers designed to prejudice and arouse public opinion against me. It has been said that I am an Austrian officer on furlough and that my funds were sent abroad to give comfort to enemy arms. In this morning's papers these statements are intensified by positive and violent accusations to that effect. These statements are utterly baseless and untrue.

I am not on furlough here. At the outbreak of the war in July, 1914, I served for six weeks as a reserve officer of the Austrian army on the Russian front and after receiving a wound was pronounced an invalid and honorably discharged from any further service. There has been no attempt whatever by my Government to recall me into service.

It is true that I sent money to Austria. I have sent a small monthly allowance to my father, a medical doctor and Professor of Zoology, who had lost everything during the Russian invasion of Austrian territory in October, 1914, and has been prevented by a subsequent paralytic stroke from exercising his profession. He is 74 years old.

I have sent monthly allowances to the orphan children of some artists, personal friends of mine who fell in the war.

In fulfillment of a pledge undertaken by my wife, at the deathbed of some Russian and Serbian wounded prisoners whom she nursed during my stay at the front, I have sent eleven individual monthly allowances to their destitute orphans in Russia and Serbia through the medium of the Red Cross in Berne, Switzerland.

The bulk of my earnings, however, has gone to the Brotherhood of Artists, founded by me for the purpose of extending help to stranded artists and their dependents regardless of their nationality. For full three years my contributions were the sole and unique support of seventeen British, Russian, French, and Italian artists and their entire families who found themselves stranded and utterly destitute in Austria at the outbreak of the war.

I have been bitterly and violently attacked by Chauvinists in Vienna for diverting my earnings to that channel. On the other hand, I am honor bound to state that I have never been rebuked for my actions by any official of my Government.

I have not sent a penny to Austria since the entrance of the United States in the war, and I have not had a word from abroad for fully eight months.

The ironical aspect of the situation is that some three-score of British, French, Russian, and Italian children may now actually be dying of want because I, technically their enemy, am prevented by the laws of this country, their friend and ally, from saving them.

During every minute of my three years' stay in this country I have been conscious of my duty to it in return for its hospitality. I have obeyed its laws in letter and in spirit, and I have not done anything that might be construed in the least as being detrimental to it. Not a penny of my earnings has ever, nor will it ever, contribute to the purchase of rifles and ammunition, no matter where and in whatsoever cause. The violent political issues over the world have not for an instance beclouded my fervent belief in true art as the dead center of all passions and strife, as the sublime God-inspired leveler of things, as the ultimate repacifier, rehumanizer, and rebuilder of destroyed bridges of understanding between nations.

It is to the cause of crystallizing and purifying this true vocation of art and to the preservation and marshaling of its forces, the brotherhood of artists all over the world against the coming day of their mission, that every penny of my earnings has been and shall be devoted as long as I shall be permitted to exercise my profession. No sordid consideration of my material welfare enters for a moment into my mind. After four years' successful tour of this country, I have less money to my name than many a prosperous bank clerk. I have no personal interests at stake. I shall serve the cause I am devoted to undismayed by personal attacks as long as I shall be permitted to and so long as the deep sentiment and feeling I bear this country will not be thrown into conflict with the fundamental and unalterable principles of my honor as a man and artist. I make no appeal for sympathy, but for justice and respect.

But come what may, my deep gratitude for past kindness, hospitality, and love shown me by the American public will forever be engraved in my heart.

* * * * *

✻ 1917 — *THE NEW YORK TIMES*

From "Philharmonic Facts," *New York Times* (9 December 1917), 9.

> **The New York Philharmonic, perhaps not wishing to suffer the problems experienced by Damrosch and his New York Symphony, made available personal facts about the members of the orchestra. The Philharmonic was also quick to publicize its musicians' financial contributions to the war effort.**

The orchestra members of The Philharmonic Society of New York responded loyally to the recent Second Liberty Loan. Although musicians can rarely be ranked among the wealthy classes, the men who play for the Philharmonic have contributed more than $12,000 to the purchase of Liberty bonds. It is generally believed that symphony orchestras in the United States are made up largely of German musicians. Although this was doubtless true some years ago, it is a fact that the present Philharmonic Orchestra is composed of entirely American citizens, and that by far the largest percent of them were born in this country. To speak in exact figures, there are forty-two native-born musicians in the orchestra. The naturalized citizens represent eleven nations, Russia, Italy, Holland, Hungary, Bohemia, France, England, Germany, Norway, and Belgium among them. Only fourteen men came originally from Germany or Austria, and their contributions to the orchestra's total bond subscription of $12,000 is ample testimony to their unqualified Americanism. . . .

* * * * *

✻ 1918 — *THE NEW YORK TIMES*

From "Philharmonic Bars German Composers," *New York Times* (22 January 1918), 9.

> Objections to performances of German opera quickly spilled over into the concert hall. New York Philharmonic conductor Josef Stransky (1872-1936), a Bohemian with strong German predilections, relented to the wishes of his board of directors and his audience by restricting performances of German music. He managed to save Beethoven and other acknowledged masters from banishment, but contemporary German composers were rejected. It was no accident that Richard Strauss's music was replaced in the first program by a work of Edward MacDowell (1860-1908), an American composer with a strong, obvious Germanic proclivity.

The Philharmonic Society announced last night that no more music by living German composers will be performed at the society's concerts in New York or elsewhere for the duration of the war. Conductor Stransky, whose programs had been carefully planned to represent all nations impartially even before America was actively engaged on the side of the Allies, agreed to this decision.

Under the Directors' rule, the first work to be barred will be Richard Strauss's *Till Eulenspiegel's Merry Pranks*, on the programs for Thursday and Friday this week. In its place . . . the orchestra will play an American symphonic work, *Hamlet and Ophelia*, by the late Edward MacDowell.

As the Philharmonic has just concluded a Beethoven-Brahms festival, and it is to give next Saturday a program of Bach and Wagner, it was explained that the Directors had decided to adopt the procedure followed in England and France since the war, whereby the "old masters" of music are not made to suffer for the acts of their countrymen today. . . .

* * * * *

THE CONTROVERSY SURROUNDING DR. MUCK

> In the autumn of 1917 Karl Muck (1859-1940), the German conductor of the Boston Symphony Orchestra, was falsely accused of failing to honor requests to perform "The Star-Spangled Banner" at concerts in Providence, Rhode Island. The discord this created soon spilled into Baltimore, the city where Francis Scott Key (1779-1843) had composed what would later

become the nation's official anthem in 1931. The controversy and threats that ensued are unlike anything else in American music history before or since. These selections chronicle one tumultuous week in the life of Muck based on reports from the *New York Times*. The *Times*, already a leading newspaper in the United States, was compelled by the city's large German population to address consistently matters of Germanism. As a center for music in America, the city naturally attracted German musicians in large numbers. In addition, the citizens of New York and Boston, then as now, were sometimes bitter rivals in an ongoing battle for supremacy in matters ranging from politics to the arts to baseball. Because of the incendiary nature of the Muck controversy and his close identification with the city, the coverage in the *Times* was scrupulous; its tone, however, often implied an artistic and cultural superiority to Boston.

❊ 1917 — *THE NEW YORK TIMES*

From "Orchestra and Muck Condemned," *New York Times* (1 November 1917), 10.

[Providence, Rhode Island, October 31] – Resolutions condemning the Boston Symphony Orchestra and Dr. Karl Muck, conductor, "for his deliberately insulting attitude" in failing to play "The Star-Spangled Banner" at a concert here last night after being requested to do so by a number of women, were adopted today by the Rhode Island Council of Defense. The Police Commission was requested by the council to refuse further permission for concerts here during the war "when conducted by Dr. Muck."

C. A. Ellis, manager of the orchestra, said he had received a telegram signed by a number of women of this city, asking that "The Star-Spangled Banner" be played, but that, as they were not subscribers to the concert, the request was ignored. Dr. Muck, he said, did not know that such a telegram had been received.

The telegram asking that the national anthem be played at the concert was signed by the Presidents of various local societies, all prominent in musical circles, and was supplemented by a similar message from the Liberty Loan Committee of Rhode Island. . . .

C. A. Ellis, manager of the orchestra, said: "The Boston Symphony Orchestra played 'The Star-Spangled Banner' every night for ten weeks during the 'pop' concerts in Symphony Hall, Boston, where it was appropriate."

To a question whether Dr. Muck led the national anthem at the "pop" concerts, Mr. Ellis replied that "Dr. Muck does not lead the pop concerts." Asked if the conductor had ever led "The Star-Spangled Banner," he replied, "I do not know."

From "Threat to Disband Boston Symphony," *New York Times* (1 November 1917), 10.

[Boston, Mass., October 31] – Major Henry L. Higginson, founder and patron of the Boston Symphony Orchestra, announced today that the orchestra would be disbanded and Symphony Hall sold if public clamor for "The Star-Spangled Banner" continued. . . .

Major Higginson said the anthem was out of place in purely harmonic [i.e., artistic] programs. It has no place in a program of artistic symphony music, he said. He added that the conductor, Dr. Karl Muck, a German, made up the programs in the Summer and that when the war started he addressed the orchestra and asked musicians to forget their racial differences. . . .

Dr. Muck said: "Why will people be so silly? Art is a thing by itself and not related to any particular nation or group. It would be a gross mistake, a violation of artistic taste and principles, for such an organization as ours to play patriotic airs."

From "A Musician Makes a Mistake," *New York Times* (2 November 1917), 14.

In ordinary times, the one reason avowed by Dr. Muck and Major [Henry] Higginson for not adding "The Star-Spangled Banner" to the programs of the Boston Symphony Orchestra probably would be accepted as adequate by most people, and probably should be so accepted, coming as it does from men with high authority to speak on musical subjects and the proper conduct as such organizations as this one. They say that in quality our national anthem is incongruous with the sort of music which it is the mission of the symphony orchestra to perform —the sort of music it is under an implied contract with its admirers and patrons to provide for them.

But these are not ordinary times. The nation is at war, and it happens to be at war with the only country whose antagonism to "The Star-Spangled Banner" as an expression of American policy and determination would be likely to be shared by Dr. Muck and a considerable number of his associated musicians. When he refuses, therefore, to obey an urgent popular demand that he and they do what anybody of their capacity who was not distinctly hostile to us would do without hesitation, the refusal is naturally and justly taken as a strong indication, if not absolute proof, that these men, so estimable and so esteemed as artists, are rather more Germans than musicians. . . .

From "An Artists Grave Indiscretion," *New York Times* (3 November 1917), 14.

However painful it may have been for Dr. Karl Muck to lead his admirable orchestra through the mazes of "The Star-Spangled Banner," and however sincerely as a musician he may disapprove of its progressions and as a German of its associated meaning, it would have been judicious for him, before refusing to play it, to consider the inevitable result of the refusal. Had he done so, a musician of his intelligence could not have failed to see that thus and now to offend and irritate the great mass of the American people would not only bring deep disfavor on himself, but would do a disservice of no small importance to every man, woman, and child of German birth or descent now living in the United States.

* * * * *

✻ 1917 — DAVID STANLEY SMITH, MUSIC THEORY TEACHER, CONDUCTOR, AND MUSIC ADMINISTRATOR

From "National Anthem's Place" *New York Times* (4 November 1917), II: 2.

After graduation from Yale University and study in Munich and Paris, David Stanley Smith (1877-1949) served as a member of the faculty of his alma mater for forty-three years, eventually as the Dean of the School of Music.

The present discussion concerning the wisdom of playing the national anthem at symphony concerts has resolved itself into much needless *argumentum ad hominem* [personal argument] at the same time failing to throw light on the actual justification of its appearance on a program.

"The Star-Spangled Banner" has been officially designated the symbol of our national unity, appealing to the ear as the flag appeals to the eye. To object to its performance at a serious concert on the ground of the impossibility of its fitting into the scheme of a program of orchestral music is not unlike a refusal to display the Stars and Stripes on our house because the striking colors "kill" the color arrangement of the flowers in the garden. Nor is it a question of the literary and musical value of the national anthem; scoffing on the part of professional critics is but futile. The emblem is there for us to accept in its real significance, transcending individual opinion.

To be sure, it is hard to determine just the proper amount of publicity which the song should have, to fix the point beyond which it loses its force through repetition and becomes merged in the general mass of popular music. But at least we may protect it from the odium implied in the published remark of one conductor to the effect that it is all very well to play "The Star-Spangled Banner" at popular concerts, but not at symphony concerts. Actually, the opposite is true. The national anthem is never presented with more appropriateness than before audiences that have gathered for serious reflection. It begins to offend only when it is used as a cloak of respectability over general cheapness of entertainment; and it is in the field of mere amusement that its use might well be curtailed.

Let us hope that the mutual recrimination and professional aloofness and hypersensitiveness may give way to a vision of the exalted symbolism which a thoughtful conception of the national anthem reveals.

* * * * *

✻ 1917 — *THE NEW YORK TIMES*

From "Muck Blameless, Higginson Insists," *New York Times* (5 November 1917), 13.

A statement absolving Dr. Karl Muck, conductor of the Boston Symphony Orchestra, and the men under him of disloyal or disrespectful intent to omit "The Star-Spangled Banner" from their programs was made tonight by Major Henry L. Higginson, sponsor for the orchestra. Major Higginson took upon himself blame for any mistakes made. . . .

"The first time Dr. Muck and the orchestra were asked to play the 'Star-Spangled Banner' they played it, and, still further, the request had never been refused.

"The original object and plan of these concerts was the enjoyment and education of our fellow citizens. On one point I may insist: The orchestra, under Dr. Muck, has given to the public from the Atlantic to the Pacific great comfort and happiness through many years, and this band of many nationalities has worked well and loyally under most trying circumstances for the good of us all. Each one of them deserves not abuse or suspicion but hearty thanks, and I ask it for them—thanks, not in words, but in deeds and in trust."

From "Ex-Gov. Warfield Would Mob Muck," *New York Times* (5 November 1917), 13.

[Baltimore, Maryland, November 4] — Ex-Governor Edwin Warfield, President of the Fidelity Trust and one of Baltimore's foremost citizens and financiers, who has arranged for a big patriotic meeting at the Lyric Theatre Tuesday afternoon to protest against Dr. Karl Muck leading the Symphony Orchestra at its concert here Wednesday evening, said today:

"Karl Muck shall not lead an orchestra in Baltimore. I told the Police Board members that this man would not be allowed to insult the people of the birthplace of 'The Star-Spangled Banner.' I told them that mob violence would prevent it, if necessary, and that I would gladly lead the mob to prevent the insult to my country and my flag. I told them that I knew of a thousand others who would gladly aid in leading the throng."

"This is a time when our government must stand endorsed. We should not and will not tolerate any dictation as to the patriotic feeling of our flag. Our people have only contempt for the man who utters a criticism of the demand to play our national anthem. We consider it a symphony incomparable at a time like this [and] greater than anything ever composed in Germany, more glorious and befitting the hearing of true Americans than the works of any composer living or dead. We deny that our anthem jars with any harmony or symphony to which the American people should listen. 'The Star-Spangled Banner' will be sung when the others are long forgotten." . . .

From "Baltimore Forbids Dr. Muck's Concert," *New York Times* (6 November 1917), 13.

[Baltimore, Maryland, November 5] — Dr. Muck and the Boston Symphony Orchestra have been barred from performing in Baltimore Wednesday night. As a result of threats of mob violence and indignant protests in which agitation former Governor Edwin Warfield . . . took a leading part, the Grand Jury today notified the Police Commissioners that, owing to the state of the public mind and the fact that the appearance of Dr. Muck might lead to grave disorder, even bloodshed, the Prussian conductor should not be permitted to appear before the public in Baltimore, and that the concert should be called off. . . .

On learning the action of the Police Commissioner former Governor Warfield, who has arranged a big patriotic meeting for tomorrow, said:

"The action of the commissioners follows, of course, upon a tremendous wave of popular sentiment against Muck, and is in the interest of peace and order. Whether the commissioners had acted or not, Muck would never have conducted the concert. He would never have reached the theater, and he will never conduct another concert in Baltimore. We never had any objection to the orchestra. We would have been willing for the concert to take place if somebody else had conducted. The man we were after was the Prussian who said, 'To hell with your flag and your national anthem.' We were after the man who said our 'Star-Spangled Banner' was not fit to be included in an artistic program. . . ."

From "Denounce Muck at Rally," *New York Times* (7 November 1917), 11.

[Baltimore, Maryland, November 6] – A big crowd turned out this afternoon to attend the meeting called by ex-Governor Warfield to protest against Dr. Muck's being allowed to lead the Boston Symphony Orchestra. A regimental band from Camp Meade was present and fifty men from Company I marched into the hall.

When the resolutions were read declaring that Dr. Muck should not be allowed to lead the orchestra in this city whether he played "The Star-Spangled Banner" willingly or unwillingly, the applause was deafening. When ex-Governor Warfield, in referring to the musician, said "he should be in an internment camp," the applause lasted almost a minute. At its end a woman who had been waving a flag from a box near the stage shouted: "Muck should have been shot when he said that."

After the anthem was sung Mr. Warfield shouted: "The day is coming when that anthem will be sung by every nation on the globe. Talk about your musical art—what does art amount to when it is in competition with patriotism?" . . .

Then Mr. Warfield read a few out of a sheaf of letters written to him, commending his stand. He read this communication from Cardinal [James] Gibbons:

"I regret that I cannot attend the meeting arranged in honor of 'The Star-Spangled Banner,' but shall be with you in spirit, and approve with all my heart of the efforts being put forth to surround this sacred emblem of our country with all the respect which it should command. In the first place, the anthem was composed in Baltimore. Secondly, it is the national song of the Republic. Thirdly, the flag itself is the embodiment of our political faith, and he who sings this anthem is making a profession of fidelity to the country. As with the Ark of the old covenant, he who touches it with profane hands shall suffer."

From "Dr. Muck, Citizen of Switzerland," *New York Times* (8 December 1917), 13.

[Washington, D. C., Dec. 7] – Dr. Karl Muck, director of the Boston Symphony Orchestra, is a citizen of Switzerland, and not a German subject, was the statement made at the Swiss Legation today in response to an inquiry. . . .

In line with the disclosure of Dr. Muck's Swiss citizenship, Charles A. Ellis, manager of the Boston Symphony Orchestra, has sent to friends of Dr. Muck in Washington the following letter:

"For the information of subscribers to concerts by the Boston Symphony Orchestra and to correct the impression made by assertions concerning Dr. Karl Muck widely circulated by publication in newspapers and in other ways, I beg to submit the following statements, which can be verified by any one who cares to make inquiries to the proper authorities:

"Dr. Muck is not a Prussian. He is not an enemy alien of the United States. He is not an official of the German government. He is not a citizen of Germany. While he was born in Bavaria, he is a citizen of Switzerland, as was his father. After careful investigation of many fantastic and pernicious rumors about Dr. Muck that have been brought to their attention, the Federal authorities have found nothing to incriminate him as a German agent or as having performed any act which is prejudicial to the interests of our country. Dr. Muck is a man of high attainments, and his unusual gifts as a musical director are well known. During the more than seven years he has been in America he has respected our laws and has complied with them in letter and spirit. For three years of the war he has directed our cosmopolitan orchestra with rare tact in almost daily rehearsals and concerts. He has permitted no discussion of political affairs and there has not been the slightest friction among our musicians of many nationalities. The membership of the Boston Symphony Orchestra comprises 54 American citizens (17 native-born), 22 Germans, 8 Austrians, 2 Italians, 2 British, 6 Dutch, 2 Russians, 3 French, 2 Belgians, 2 Bohemians."

* * * * *

Before the rise of modern technologies, making music at home was a popular pastime for many American families. It was enjoyed and shared between the generations, as depicted in this photoprint (ca. 1905) of an elderly gentleman and a young girl.

Courtesy of the Prints and Photographs Division, Library of Congress: LC-USZ62-77011.

❊ 13 — American Musical Culture: Traditions, Conditions, and Outlook

1902 – Henry C. Lahee
From "Opera in English,"
Grand Opera in America

1915 – Arthur Farwell,
Introduction to *The Art of Music: Music in America* [vol. 4].

1915 – John Wesley Work, "Characteristics and Peculiarities"
From *Folk Song of the American Negro*

This chapter presents a number of topics that do not neatly fit into the other areas of this book. They have been selected for a variety of reasons; some present important but little-explored topics; others express points of view well removed from the beaten path; some are merely interesting or entertaining and deserve to be read.

❊ 1861 — JOHN SULLIVAN DWIGHT, MUSIC CRITIC AND JOURNAL EDITOR

From "Popular Concerts," *Dwight's Journal of Music* 18/19 (9 February 1861), 367.

Today critic John Sullivan Dwight (1813-1893) is often chided for his perceived contempt of popular music, but in fact his views were not far removed from those of other consumers and producers of music. One example, conductor Theodore Thomas, refused to "water down" his programs with lighter fare, and today he is highly regarded for upholding stringent standards. Although Dwight merely attempted to maintain high standards himself, he suffered in two ways: his views were constantly barraging the public through his *Journal of Music*, and he had little patience or respect for the uneducated "masses." The following selection is an early example of a plea for musical excellence.

There is a large class of persons, who either from a natural defect, or want of practice in listening to the *best*, or from a habit of listening to bad music, are unable to find enjoyment in what some people sneeringly term "classical" or "scientific" music. We almost wish those terms had never been employed. They are so often used as an excuse for disliking good music, that it would have been better had such people been left in ignorance of the distinction between compositions conveyed in those words. . . . In short, we cannot expect people as a mass to like what is best, to have a tendency for the ideal. The mass of people, on the contrary, have a tendency to what is mediocre or commonplace, and so we have flourishing "opera houses," nightly thronged by "appreciative audiences," places that derive a principal attraction from the fact that the natural color of the face and hands is changed to a more sable hue [i.e., black-face minstrelsy]. And therefore we have no orchestral concerts, no [Boston] Philharmonic Society this winter, because there is not interest enough in the mass of the people to pay $2.50 for six concerts.

There is demand for music that is of a low or at least commonplace character, and therefore that demand must be satisfied. And it will be satisfied. But this is a fact so well understood that it [would be] hardly worth the ink shed in writing these paragraphs, if there were not people who conceive it to be their especial duty, to put in a plea for such music. It is scarcely a twelve month since a musical paper, not far from the town where we are writing, was inaugurated by a leader setting forth that the concerts in Boston had been of too elevated a character; that they needed to be popularized; [that] the public desired another class of music; and that therefore the programs in [the] future ought to be of a mixed character so as to attract large (mixed?) audiences. This reminds me of the preface to an instruction book, in which the author alleges that the majority of persons that learn music do not desire or comprehend good music, and that in view of this fact (undeniable, to be sure) pleasing music ought to be put in instruction books. Which the good man did, and thus supplied the "longfelt want." There is no danger, therefore, of that want for music of a lighter character ("Dixie," etc., etc.) being unsupplied. It is taken care of in the places proper for it. But where it ought *not* to be supplied is just in the [Boston] Music Hall or any other place where good concerts are given. We know there is music of a lighter kind which is not as bad as "Dixie"; quite good in fact, of its kind, such as good waltzes and polkas and other dances [and] a number of operatic songs, without much lasting value, but as useful as candy or checkerberry lozenges. That, too, is furnished generally in its proper place by bands, in afternoon concerts, etc. We have not the least objection to its being performed at its proper time and place. But to advocate the introduction of lighter music in [Boston] Philharmonic concerts proves the incapability of such persons or papers to take an intelligent part in the discussion of musical matters.

The mass of the people remain children, intellectually and morally. And therefore they ought to be treated as such. Generally speaking we have the idea that in the case of children a progressive course of instruction is best, proceeding from the rudiments up to the higher branches. Well then, if the public be like children, let them be musically instructed, proceeding from the ABCs among musical compositions to the nobler effusions of the human heart, from the simplest national air or waltz and polka up to "classical' or "scientific" music.

* * * * *

⁕ 1872 — F. N. S.

From "American Choral Societies," *Church's Musical Visitor* 1/5 (February 1872), 5.

> America's veneration of Europe as the musical center of the world held well into the twentieth century. But this writer indicated that by the year 1872 America had already achieved an important place among musical nations, especially with regard to vocal music.

The resources of the American people for the formation of societies for the performance of the choral works of the masters are inferior to that of none among the family of nations. This fact, till recently not generally known or even suspected, has at last dawned upon our musical authorities, and is practically conceded both at home and abroad. In the resources for vocal music, we can boast a supply, excellent in quality too, adequate to any emergency. As a nation, we are essentially a singing people, and of no mean order of excellence either. In every community, in proportion to its population, may be found a liberal *pro rata* of musicians, varying in excellence, of course, in a degree corresponding with their facilities, but in all cases keeping well up with them, and averaging far ahead of all other nations in this particular. This is more particularly true of vocal culture, and is true also, to a lesser extent, of instrumental music as well.

From time out of mind, it has been customary to decry all and everything of mature growth and cultivation, in matters pertaining to art music more particularly. "Can any good thing come out of Nazareth," has been the sarcastic question, even at home, and the sneer has not wanted [for] an echo on the other side of the ocean, when interest plainly pointed to such a course. As long as America furnished a ready market for everything that bore a foreign stamp, it would have been inevitably suicidal to admit the existence of anything that pertained to, or even gave promise, however remote, of a home talent. And so it was perfectly natural for foreigners to decry our musical resources, and their fiat was accepted as gospel, and re-echoed by our people, who, it must be admitted, are much addicted to worshiping false gods, particularly if said gods are imported, until the verdict becomes so widespread and confirmed that it had been very difficult to reverse it. But each succeeding year has seen American artists graduating with high honors from the leading musical conservatories in the Old World, and winning high places upon the lyric stage and in concert, until today the Old World accords to our representatives a place second to none in the temple of fame. So it has been triumphantly shown that a good thing can, and has, come out of our western Nazareth. And so vocal culture has progressed, commencing in our public schools, where infant lips first lisp out childish songs, and imbibe the primary elements, continuing thus upward through the singing school, the vocal class, the musical academy, the conservatory, with their useful accessories, the choir, the glee club, and the choral society, until at last we have emerged from all these a nation of singers, strong, and knowing our strength. In our incipient days, we were wont to look with veneration to Germany, to Italy, and with bated breath fear[ed] to use what powers we did possess, because these ancient lands were fabled as the home of music, and we feared our efforts would be sacrilege. But that flimsy veil has been rent away, and now we dare claim for America that today she stands foremost as a land of vocal music, her choral organizations and resources standing preeminent. Hereafter I may continue this subject, and furnish the data upon which this claim is founded.

* * * * *

✻ 1872 — *THE ATLANTIC MONTHLY*

From "Music," *Atlantic Monthly* 30/181 (November 1872), 635-38.

In the days before recorded sound was available for the cinema, live music pervaded America's many theaters. This writer lamented the selections performed at most theaters and berated one of the genre's leading instruments.

Among other questions of more or less vital importance to the musical cultivation of our people, there is one which forces itself irresistibly upon our notice, namely, the musical performances at our theaters. There is probably not a theater in the country that does not boast something in the shape of an orchestra, which, besides furnishing such occasional music as may be required in the course of the drama itself, regales the audience with "choice and varied selections of new and popular music" between the acts. As a subject for aesthetic contemplation, the theater "orchestra" is at best a dispiriting one; but in spite of the fact that it is, at present conducted and constituted, in nine cases out of ten an almost unmitigated evil, we are not inclined to look upon it as a wholly hopeless case. The question whether music ought or ought not to be introduced between the acts of a play is an interesting one for abstract aesthetic discussion, but it is unfortunately of no practical value. Whatever may be our opinion as to what ought or ought not to be is little to the purpose in this case, as playwrights, managers, and orchestral players have long since settled what *shall be*. . . . With lamentably few exceptions the musical interludes at our theaters are very poor, both as to the music performed and the manner of performance. To be sure the management of the theater has, at the outset, little reason to suppose that the audience is of a particularly musical cast. They have not come together with any distinctly musical intent, and whatever of music is introduced during the evening will no doubt be regarded by most listeners as merely a conventional make-weight in the entertainment. But yet it may be fairly supposed that a certain proportion of the audience are in some measure musically cultivated, or, at the very least, musically disposed, and we cannot see how the theater management would lose by furnishing music that would be enjoyed by the more cultivated portion of the public, instead of more than boring them by such musical trash as is merely tolerated by the unmusical portion to whom good and bad music are equally indifferent. . . .

To look at once at the darkest side of the picture, there is one point in our theater orchestras about which the many are unfortunately *not* indifferent, and that is the *cornet á pistons*. It would be difficult to estimate the harm that has been done to the popular musical taste and to musical performances in general by this, we had almost said diabolical, little instrument. Through its great popularity with the masses it has gradually crept from the lowest place in the orchestra up to the first and highest. It dominates the whole orchestra, and everything has to give way before it. A good cornet soloist draws a higher salary at some of our theatres than any but the leading violinist. As a solo instrument, the cornet has the smallest pretensions to anything beyond a certain penetrating brilliancy of tone, fascinating at first, but inexpressive and, after a while, most tediously monotonous. . . .

* * * * *

✻ 1874 — CONSTANCE F. WOOLSON, AUTHOR OF SHORT STORIES AND TRAVEL SKETCHES

From "Euterpe in America," *Lippincott's Magazine* 14/40 (November 1874), 627-33.

Constance F. Woolson (1840-1894) regarded America as a musical country with appreciative audiences and talented performers, but she lamented the lack of artistic sentiment in American men.

Music is a real pleasure to the large majority of our population. Those who cannot enjoy it are to be pitied as having lost a sense. If these unfortunates are wise, they will not obtrude their deficiencies, but devote themselves to cultivating their other talents—and they generally have others—as a compensation. But when they persist in talking during the performance of a perfect sonata, or rustling in and out of a concert hall when the audience [is] listening in breathless delight to some enchanting voice, then they should be regarded as disturbers of the public peace, and put under bonds. The real music lovers, however, so far outnumber those who have no "ear"—as the popular phrase clearly expresses it—that Americans may be called a musical people. Not only do they freely lavish money to attract the stars of other skies, but they have some promising young starlings of their own, asteroids in numbers, and a milky way of lesser lights extending from Maine to California. . . .

American gentlemen are agreeable; and even chivalrous, but they are, alas! deficient in sentiment. They cannot design and execute a real serenade; they have neither the romance nor the musical ability. Their imagination soars not beyond a brass band in an omnibus wagon at so much an hour, whereas an ideal serenade is a very romantic and even mysterious affair. It requires a [moonlit] night, a solitary cavalier wrapped in a mantle, a tenor voice mingling with the tones of a guitar, a vine-draped casement above, disclosing an outline, a white hand and two starry eyes. In the hearts of our young girls, even the much-maligned girls of the present day, lingers a genuine love of romance. They would willingly supply the vine-draped casement, the starry eyes, and even furnish the guitars, if cavaliers could be found to enact the rest of the scene. But the cavaliers of the period are not skilled in guitar accompaniments; . . . The old-fashioned serenade, therefore, is no longer heard save on the operatic stage. Its successors are the brass band and occasional merry excursions from house to house, when the moonlight calls young hearts abroad, and music bursts forth involuntarily, the language of the summer night.

* * * * *

✻ 1878 — HENRY T. FINCK, MUSIC CRITIC AND WRITER ON MUSIC

From "Music in America," *Lippincott's Magazine* 22/41 (November 1878), 630-35.

Critic Henry T. Finck (1854-1926) painted a conflicted picture of the state of music in the United States. While performers, especially instrumentalists, were excellent and available to the American public, activity in composition was so far unimpressive. Finck looked to American philanthropists to solve some of opera's problems.

England and America have long been classed among the unmusical countries of the world, and for good reasons. Their history so far records the names of no composers of a high rank; and although in both countries there are plenty of amateurs and minor musicians who fully appreciate the best there is in the art, yet the people as a whole are not influenced by it in the same way as the Germans and the Italians, to whose hungry souls music is as necessary as is oxygen to their lungs. . . .

Perhaps there is no better way of arriving at a just estimate of the present state of general musical culture in this country than by looking at what may be called the creative department, and examining the vocal and instrumental sheet music of native composers continually issued in such large quantities by our publishers. Were we to follow an old maxim, that the best way of judging the inner life of a nation is to listen to its music, and accordingly judge of the sentiments and emotions of Americans by their sheet music, we should arrive at very discouraging results. The characteristics of our sheet music, briefly summed up are: (1) trite and vulgar melody, devoid of all originality, repeating what has already been heard a thousand times already; (2) equally trite and monotonous accompaniments, the harmony limited to a half dozen elementary chords, the rhythm mechanical and commonplace, and the cadences as unchanging as the laws of Nature; (3) insipid, sensational titles; (4) words usually so silly that a respectable country newspaper would refuse to print them in its columns—true to the French *bon mot*, that what is too stupid to be spoken or read must be sung.

This may seem too sweeping a condemnation, but it is not. . . .

If we turn from this aspect of music in America to our concert halls, the prospect is much brighter. In this department we have achieved more than in any other, and no one is now obliged to go abroad in order to hear a good concert, as he is if he wishes to enjoy a respectable operatic performance. . . .

Of the condition of our operatic affairs it is impossible to speak in the same terms of self-congratulation as of our concerts, and will remain impossible as long as our opera troupes differ in no essential respects—except in being less sure of their parts—from traveling bands of Negro minstrels. An orchestra may with impunity travel from one city to another; it always remains the same, and only needs a good hall to appear to advantage. But an operatic performance is such a complicated affair that excellence can only be attained after years of constant practice under the same conditions . . . . European experience seems to show that without government assistance good dramatic and operatic performances are not possible. In France and Germany, where such assistance is given, the theaters are good; in England and America, where none is given, they are bad. Perhaps in the course of time our national or city governments will come to recognize and support the theater as an educational institution, or at least as a good means of suppressing intemperance and other vices by supplying a harmless mode of amusement. There is little prospect, however, that this will happen soon. It is more likely that some of our rich men will at last come to see the folly of founding so many new colleges, and devote their money to other uses.

. . . . Formerly, some of the great *prime donne* used to pay us an occasional visit, but now even they have learned to avoid us, because we are no longer willing to pay five dollars for an evening's amusement. London, Paris and St. Petersburg [Russia] are at present the headquarters of the costly "stars." Nor is this fact to be regretted. The decline of the star system is rather to be greeted as the dawn of a better era. It has always been the curse of the opera and the greatest obstacle to improvement. There was a time when the *prima donna* was so omnipotent that even the composers were her slaves, being frequently obliged to alter passages to suit the taste of the stage goddess; and there are instances on record of whole operas having been composed in vain because she did not happen to be pleased with them, and [therefore] refused to sing. This evil period we have happily outgrown, but an equally great nuisance remains. The exorbitant prices still demanded by the "stars" are all out of proportion to their desserts, and show that even if the composers are their slaves no longer, the spectators and managers still are so.

* * * * *

❋ 1878 — *THE ATLANTIC MONTHLY*

From "The Contributor's Club," *Atlantic Monthly* 42/254 (December 1878), 769-70.

> The Bostonian writer of this essay did not consider America's musical progress impressive and noted that music was not a natural pursuit for Americans.

A good deal has been written, of late, to show that Boston's claim to musical culture and taste is not quite so valid as had been supposed. Exactly what claims to such culture we Bostonians have made and still make I do not know; but they are probably not so large as have been imputed to us. I would by no means try here to gauge the musical culture of Boston, but humbly beg to suggest to those who have recently expressed such grave doubts as to its extent that the line of argument they have hitherto pursued does not in the least serve to invalidate any claim to musical culture, taste, or discrimination we might be pleased to make for ourselves.

It is a sufficiently notorious fact that for the last few years the Boston public has given very meager support to worthy concert enterprises, both of our own artists and musical organizations, and of various celebrated performers who have visited our city. . . . We have not shown sufficient enterprise to admit of an efficient and permanent orchestra's being formed, so that the cream of our orchestral players have been forced to form private clubs for the performance of chamber music, and to travel through the country on concert expeditions in order to gain a decent livelihood.

. . . As Anglo-Saxons we must say that what may be called the necessity of art, the natural hunger and thirst for the beautiful, the *desiderium pulchri* [desire for beauty], is not born in us. We have applied ourselves to music as an item of culture; we have, to the best of our abilities, refined our taste and sharpened our judgment; but we have not made music, good or bad, a necessary of life. . . . Music is not a natural appetite with us. . . .

* * * * *

❋ 1883 — FRANK L. BRISTOW, COMPOSER OF POPULAR SONGS AND COMMUNITY MUSIC TEACHER

From "Lady Orchestras," *Church's Musical Visitor* (1 August 1883), 210.

Long before the women's suffrage movement had reached Kentucky, Frank L. Bristow (1845-1914) was giving encouragement to talented young ladies there.

Allow me to call your attention to a "new departure" on my part, in the musical instruction at our female boarding school, which, if introduced into other schools by my brother teachers, will not only enthuse the young lady pupils, but will also relieve the weary monotony of a music professor's daily life. About the last of February, this year, I recommended to one of my pupils –who was suffering from weak lungs–that she should learn the cornet. She accepted my advice and in a short time developed such wonderful proficiency that I suddenly conceived the idea of organizing a female orchestra from among the most talented young ladies of my piano and vocal class. As the result of my new idea I organized the Millersburg [Kentucky] Female College Orchestra . . . .

The proficiency of these young ladies, on these instruments, proved to me beyond a doubt that, by judicious training, on the part of competent professors, orchestras can be organized in all of our schools for the gentler sex. The executive power of Misses Kirkpatrick on the cornet, Miller on the [clarinet] and McLendon on the double bass, I consider the greatest wonder of my twenty-two years of musical instruction.

* * * * *

* 1884 — HENRY EDWARD KREHBIEL, MUSIC CRITIC AND WRITER ON MUSIC

From *Notes on the Cultivation of Choral Music and the Oratorio Society of New York* (New York: E. Schuberth, 1884), 55-57.

In his important history of choral music in New York Henry Krehbiel (1854-1923) documented the many failures to establish excellent vocal societies in the city. Here he outlined the requirements for the success achieved by the founders of the New York Oratorio Society, who ostensibly applied lessons learned in Germany.

We have now reached the period which saw the birth of the [New York] Oratorio Society. It was eleven years ago [1873]. The only society that was keeping up even the semblance of an active existence was The Church Music Association, which, as has been indicated, had no artistic *raison d'etre*. The Harmonic Society, not yet out of existence, had fallen into a sad somnolency, from which it was aroused once a year in order that it might scramble through a performance of [Handel's] the *Messiah* at Christmas. The situation was one which could give only sorrow to genuine lovers of chorus singing. There were such in the city, but the experiences of a decade back had been of a kind that did not encourage further attempts at reorganization or original construction. So far as musical leaders were concerned the number of singers in the city was sufficiently large to enable them, when it was desired to introduce a choral work into a concert scheme, to get together a choir. The nature of the German societies, in which the social element, beautiful and praiseworthy in itself, was cultivated more assiduously than the musical, prevented them from becoming the energetic public cultivators of choral music which were needed. In their way they were as exclusive as The Church Music Association. To make a new venture, and give it the foundation that would assure success and permanency, was a formidable thing, and challenged a careful study of the lessons of the past. Those lessons were chiefly warnings. How not to do it any thinking man familiar with music and musical people might have learned had he had the story of which I have given the outlines before him. But an equally important question was how to do it; and this called for cooperation of elements which might fairly have been described at that time as novel. Let us glance at these elements; we can draw most of them from the story of the Berlin *Singakademie*.

First, singers with a real love for music, and a devotion to their work so great that they are willing to put their hearts into it; that being the case, the putting of their bodies into it becomes a pleasure, not a task.

Second, a director actuated by a burning zeal for his art, and not by mercenary considerations; a man of broad sympathies and liberal tastes; one who can win the affectionate regard of his singers, while commanding their respectful obedience. To do this high aims must be associated with thorough knowledge and that magnetic quality which is possessed by leaders of men. He must be such a teacher that study under him becomes exhilarating intellectual and emotional exercise, instead [of], as is the rule, wearying, soul-killing drudgery. . . .

Third, a wise, discreet, confidence-inspiring, and confidence-possessing business administration. Here must be, ultimately, the strong props that give the society permanency. Here must be the inspiriting influence of a love for art equal to that of the singers and the conductor, yoked with a willingness to bear a burden greater than that of either of the other factors. Here must lodge a sense of discipline, business ability, a willingness to make sacrifices of self, and a wisdom great enough to perceive the inevitability of annoyance and to discover the remedy, coupled with a spirit that can thrust itself between chafing elements, and take off the friction upon itself.

* * * * *

* 1888 — WILLIAM H. NEAVE, BANDMASTER AND COMPOSER

From "Concerning 'An American School of Musical Composition,'" *American Art Journal* 49/10 (23 June 1888), 145-46.

> As the American band movement grew, so too did controversy over the artistic value of its most important instrument, the cornet. A prominent bandleader and composer in the Confederacy, William H. Neave (1821-1902) was clearly a fan of the instrument when it was played by trained musicians.

. . . In this connection, I feel constrained to say, positively, that in one point of musical advancement–of far more vital musical significance than most musical people have any conception of–Americans are far ahead of all other nations; I mean in the true knowledge of tone production and artistic performance, [and] in velocity, on the cornet. The tubular metallic wind instruments are the source from which was evolved all knowledge of the laws of sound, by which I mean musical theory, harmony and acoustics generally. This statement will startle some and may evoke protests. If so, I will gladly present, clearly and fully, indisputable data and logical deductions therefrom, that every earnest musical student should have cognizance of. No mere solo instrument capable of producing only one line of sound, such as flute, voice, etc., is comparable to cornet in artistic resources. But it having been used, until recently, mainly for making "outdoor" music, it has been, very generally, played by only uncultured, illiterate men, by mere muscular force; and those who have come from Europe to this country as experts—or artists (?)—have been mere graduates of army band rooms, as common soldiers, many of them also deserters. A true musical artist, allied to illiteracy, is an impossibility on cornet, delusive appearances to the contrary; for while no instrument, on the one extreme, can be made to produce sounds so mellifluous, so, on the other extreme, no instrument can be made to produce sounds so superlatively abominable. . . .

* * * * *

✻ 1892 — LOUIS C. ELSON, MUSIC HISTORIAN, MUSIC EDITOR, AND MUSIC CRITIC

From "Our National Anthem," *The Realm of Music* (Boston: New England Conservatory of Music, 1892), 290-92.

Critic Louis C. Elson (1848-1920) voiced concerns about the national anthem, many of which linger to the present day.

In Europe they have about decided that "Hail Columbia" is the National tune of America. When [Thomas] Edison entered the Grand Opera House in Paris recently, the band played this as the most fitting American air, and in the French Exposition as well as in Germany the tune has been similarly honored. This is quite as it should be, for "Yankee Doodle" is not dignified for a National anthem. "America" is entirely British in its musical part, and the "Star-Spangled Banner" was at first but an English drinking song. The last-named melody went through many odd phases; it was a great favorite in England in the last century [the 1700s], and even in the beginning of this century it was so popular that [John] Braham, the great tenor, made it one of the regular pieces of his repertoire. . . .

On the other hand, both the march tune which became the melody of "Hail Columbia" and the words of the anthem are American in origin, and it is quite fitting that this should be, for the present, our National tune. Yet it is not to be ranked, in artistic worth, with the national tunes of England, France, Germany, or Austria, and the need of the hour is a great American National Anthem, which shall be native in both its words and melody, and which shall be worthy of the vast and free nation it represents.

* * * * *

✻ 1896 — DUDLEY BUCK, COMPOSER AND MUSIC EDUCATOR

From "The Future of Musical Art in America," *Musical Visitor* 25/6 (June 1896), 154.

By 1896 composer Dudley Buck (1839-1909) could note the rapidly changing demographics of the nation and eschew the current trend toward musical nationalism. Although many feared the wave of immigration, for Buck it was enthralling: he sensed optimism and a renewed vigor in American life, traits that portended, he thought, a bright future for music in America, one based on the best traditions from around the world.

The measurement we give ourselves today is not the measurement of nationality. We have got past that. But in almost every branch of the musical art we have men and women who are the equal and match of any you find in the old country. There may be yet a certain halo of romance about Europeans, but going abroad you will find they are not so immeasurably high as we fancied they were. All we need is the opportunity, and we will find some one who will rise equal to it. The old New England stock, with consumption and too much pie and too little blood, is dying out. We will find that good art is always a product of good blood. We are finding it in the West, with the mingling of the Norwegians, Swedes, and Germans with the Americans. There is a champagne effervescence in this country, a progress which absorbs the best of all nationalities which come here. This will do much for music in this country. To be good in art, as in anything, people must be robust and healthy. I believe the musical outlook for our coming race to be great. . . . America has already reversed the musical record of its early history. See how many great artists we have in this country who are constantly singing and playing. You will not find more good artists in any nation of the old world. We have great concerts going on all over the country. We want only the best, and are very critical. There is such a thing as hypercriticism. We are apt to be spoiled by only wanting the best, and not arriving at the stage of culture by slow, digestive degrees. We have the money, are willing to pay, and want only the best, although it may spoil our taste for what is good. All the big foreign artists are glad to come here and to return here. . . .

✻ ✻ ✻ ✻ ✻

✻ 1902 — HENRY C. LAHEE, WRITER ON MUSIC

From "Opera in English," *Grand Opera in America* (Boston: L. C. Page, 1902), 308-39.

Music historian Henry C. Lahee (1856-1953) was not alone in his plea for opera in English. His argument—that Americans flocked to opera to hear celebrities rather than to experience the art form itself—resonated among those who resented the large salaries commanded by predominantly European "stars." Many hoped that, by presenting opera in English, it would become more accessible and encourage attendance. For that to happen,

Lahee contended, opera in English would require the imprimatur of European audiences.

If there are outcries against the "star" system, there is much to justify these outcries, but the star system seems to be the only predictable one in the conditions now prevalent in America. As long as Americans are obliged to look to Europe for that which is the highest in the musical art, so long will the people neglect opera in English, operatic stock companies, and all those things which appeal to common sense and moderate means. Musical taste has developed wonderfully during the last half century, but, until America stands on an equal footing, artistically, with Europe, it is unlikely that the public will be contented with what they are educated to believe is not "the best." When American and English operas are produced in Paris, Italy, and the musical centers of Europe, the American public may be induced to believe that it is the correct thing to hear opera in English.

[When] American singers, who have won recognition in the great art centers of Europe, are worth as much to American audiences as foreign singers—the public will flock as eagerly to hear them. But American opera [?] We are going along very nicely, and American composers are doing better work every year, but a long way off—perhaps about the middle of this century—there may be a day when an American composer may produce a work which can be performed in English at Paris, or Berlin, or Milan. When that day arrives, American opera will probably be good enough for American audiences, and by that time the musical conditions will have changed to such an extent that stock companies will make a profit, and opera will be enjoyed for the music rather than for the excitement of hearing celebrities of worldwide reputation, or for the opportunity of exhibiting a wealth of jewelry.

* * * * *

* 1915 — ARTHUR FARWELL, COMPOSER, MUSIC CRITIC, AND MUSIC EDITOR

From "Introduction," *The Art of Music: Music in America* [Vol. 4], ed. Arthur Farwell and W. Dermot Darby (New York: The National Society of Music, 1915), vii-xxiii.

Arthur Farwell (1877-1952), in the introduction to his important volume on American music history, contradicted the widely-held notion that democracy is bad for music. He cited several positive trends that were bringing music to "the people," including the rise of community choruses and pageants, the availability of cheap concert tickets, and the utilization of public buildings as performance venues. But Farwell had to admit that the democratization process had changed the old aesthetic of music in America, one that revered the accepted masters, to one that forced modern composers to write for an increasingly diverse audience.

The true condition of affairs is made evident today by the fact that when a resident of any moderate-sized prosperous American city starts to inaugurate some local musical enterprise for the benefit of the whole community, and calling for the entire community's support, he learns that the concert and recital life of his city, its "musical world," reaches and is supported by but from 3% to 5% of the entire population. The other 95% to 97% find the regular musical events beyond their means, as well as beyond the facts of their culture, though in the latter respect America is now rapidly learning that the enjoyment of the best music is far less dependent upon special education than has commonly been supposed.

Meanwhile, by phonograph and player piano, by newspaper and magazine, by high-class municipal concerts and occasional chance glimpses into the world of greater musical possibilities, the mass of the people have begun to become awakened to the existence of the larger musical world which they do not see and the larger musical life which they do not share, and to crave participation in it. Finally, therefore, we have the spectacle of an American "musical world" which is no longer true to American conditions and which does not serve the people. In short, we have finally come face to face with the problem of reactions [to] musical art and democracy.

With this question the nation has of late begun to deal in no half-hearted or uncertain manner. In fact, the national response to this situation involves the greatest American musical movement of the day. In its earlier phase the question asked was: Will the people, under democracy, rise to the accepted standards of musical culture? A negative answer to this question has been generally entertained, and among cultured people it has been commonly supposed that democracy would drag down the standards of musical culture. That a wholly new and multifold phase of musical life would arise to meet the requirements of a civilization such as that of America seems to have been earlier suspected or foreseen only by a few thinking students of conditions, who recognized the fact that the exact meeting of the mass, as it became more enlightened, with the conditions of traditional musical culture was not the solution which was to be expected or even desired. The plain fact was that the people at large were not enjoying the benefits, the pleasure, recreation, or inspiration, as the case might be, of all that the world prizes as music in any of its forms above that of popular songs and dances. Neither the educational system, on the one hand, nor the cultural system, on the other, provided them with it. One merely gave a little elementary training of the most primitive sort, and for a short time, to children, and the other did not reach beyond the extremely restricted sphere of culture and wealth. A movement was needed which should bring music in all of its forms directly to the masses of the people, and in the nationwide campaign for what may be termed "music of the people" such a movement has arisen. Experiments on every hand have shown that the people have needed only to be brought in contact with the higher forms of music, under advantageous conditions, to rise spontaneously to the enjoyment of it. The movement, in its activities, has assumed no particular form, but has taken a variety of forms according to the possibilities of local conditions. . . . The musical phase of the social center movement has assumed vast and national proportions, making use of the public school halls for concerts and recitals for thousands of persons who were previously without musical opportunities. Certain towns . . . have established choral enterprises which include in the choruses practically the entire population. In two years the custom of [singing] Christmas trees with music, free to the people, has become almost a national movement. The "community chorus," such as that established in Rochester, N. Y., with a membership of nearly one thousand drawn from the people at large, and singing in the public parks and school halls, should prove a desirable form of people's musical enterprise in many places. Standard symphony orchestras in various cities are branching out extensively in the direction of giving concerts involving the highest order of music to the people at popular prices, and in some cities the organization of symphony orchestras for popular price concerts is threatening the existence of the regular orchestra. And well-nigh surpassing in significance most other phases of the general movement, and certainly in their popular inclusiveness, are the pageants or "community dramas" with music, which are now constituting a feature of community life throughout the country.

If, then, the appreciative epoch along the older lines, is concluded in America, it may be said that the nation is coming to a new appreciation of music, as a whole, in relation to humanity. The new movement will call forth new and larger efforts on the part of American composers, who, with their present thorough assimilation of the various musical influences of the world, will lead the nation into a new and mature creative epoch.

* * * * *

✻ 1915 — JOHN WESLEY WORK II, COMPOSER, CONDUCTOR, AND MUSIC EDUCATOR

From "Characteristics and Peculiarities," *Folk Song of the American Negro* (Nashville: Press of Fisk University, 1915), 35-42.

> John Wesley Work II (1873-1925), an African-American composer and conductor, was an early authority on the Negro spiritual. Here Work discussed the important role of religion in black music, as well as its melodic structure and rhythmic appeal. He naturally attributed many peculiarities to the African-American experience in the New World but went out of his way to downplay animosity between the races.

In spite of the continued contact with whites, the Negro melodies as we have them today still retain their exotic traits. It is the aim of this chapter to point out these exotic traits and other elements which give individuality to our Folk Song and as far as possible to give the reason or reasons for these characterizing and peculiarizing features. By far the most prominent and weighty influence in this music, as we have often reiterated, is its religious element. . . .

The reason why the Negro songs are so full of scripture, quoted and implied, is that for centuries the Bible was the only book he was allowed to "study," and it consumed all his time and attention. This reason finds added strength in the Negro's religious nature. . . .

The rhythm of this music is the element which has been most generally imitated and appropriated by the composers of today. Especially is this true of those who write popular music, both secular and sacred. This rhythm is a distinguishing feature of many of our most effective gospel hymns, and with heightened syncopation, another idiomatic peculiarity of Negro Folk Song, it gives "ragtime" it currency and popularity. "Ragtime" is an ingenious and fitting appellation for the music to which it gives a name, for it is time torn to tatters, but in such a rhythmically fascinating manner as to arouse every single motor nerve of our being. That is why we like it, say what we may. The element of ragtime which makes it objectionable is the language and thought, not the vehicle, for were the vehicle objectionable we would discard some of the choicest music we now possess and cherish. Against the words and moral ideas of ragtime songs, all respectable people, those who love aright, have just complaint; but let the spirit of ragtime be changed and let the writers of it express high ideals, instead of the low ones they now use, and the public, all, would welcome it, and hail it as a new development of the musical art. In the simple music of ragtime is a naturalness that appeals to nature. This rhythm in folk music, as hinted before, is idiomatic and is as essential to the body of our music as pure red blood is to the human body. A fresh, vigorous flow carries the life-giving forces to all parts of the system. In the Negro's character there is a quality which rhythm alone expresses. This quality is as striking and as characteristic as rhythm is in his music, and, furthermore, it is as evident in his life as rhythm is in his songs. . . .

That the life of the Negro is rhythmic is an uncommon blessing. It is an ever-increasing wealth of happiness. . . .

Finally, the very foundation of this music is of the Negro's building. The scale is peculiarly his own, and consequently satisfies his nature. Through it this nature manifests itself to the world. The spirit of the music is a common possession which takes outward form according to the nature of the possessor. The Negro in his primitive nature expressed his musical scale 1-2-3-5-6. Why? That was all the world meant to him. But the American Negro has gone one step further and added one more note, flat seven, an addition which goes a long way toward expressing the effect of added experience brought to him by a new life in a New World. This flat seven expresses a wild and overwhelming surprise at the utter strangeness of things. Who can describe the feelings of the African slave as he beheld this great American civilization unfolding itself? What are the feelings of an infant as the big world gradually opens itself up? What would be the feelings of a black boy who had been born and reared in a cabin of the black belt, if suddenly he should be placed in the palace of a king? Compared to the feelings of the African in the presence of this new American civilization, these are as the gentle ripple on the calm bosom of the lake to the boisterous billows of the deep. All this feeling of the African's awe was injected into that little flat seven, America's contribution to the Negro's scale. . . .

The folk song of the American Negro, then, is characterized by the elements of religion, rhythm, syncopation, spontaneity, and the sexatonic [or hexatonic, six-tone] scale with the flat seven expressing surprise and the absence of any feeling of hatred or revenge.

* * * * *

Buildings such as Boston's Symphony Hall were temples of art, culture, and education. Pictured here shortly after its completion (ca. 1904), it remains a symbol of the era's devotion to music and one of the great orchestra halls in the world.

Courtesy of the Detroit Publishing Company Photograph Collection, Prints and Photographs Division, Library of Congress: LC-D4-17045.

❊ 14 — Quotations and Miscellany

The publication of astute observations about music and culture proliferated in the United States during the years between 1860 and 1918, which, in retrospect, has been identified as a "golden age" of American music criticism. The following excerpts—some pensive, some amusing, but all insightful—are only representative of a wealth of such commentary and opinion.

✻ 1874 — THOMAS WENTWORTH HIGGINSON, HISTORIAN, ESSAYIST, AND EDITOR

From "A Plea for Culture," *Atlantic Essays* (Boston: James R. Osgood, 1874), 22.

Every form of human life is romantic; every age may become classic. Lamentations, doubts, discouragements, all are wasted things. Everything is here, between these Atlantic and Pacific shores, save only the perfected utterance that comes with years. Between Shakespeare in his cradle and Shakespeare in Hamlet there was needed but an interval of time, and the same sublime condition is all that lies between the America of toil and the America of art.

✻ ✻ ✻ ✻ ✻

✻ 1877 — *THE ATLANTIC MONTHLY*

From "The Contributors' Club," *Atlantic Monthly* 40/237 (July 1877), 106-07.

I like critics, especially musical critics. Audacity in any form always has a certain charm. A man who will go to a concert or opera at eight p.m., stay there until ten or half past eleven, and then evolve from his own brain (and the program) half a column of infallibility for the next morning's newspaper before he goes to bed is certainly an object for admiring wonder. But why, oh why, should he, living as he does in an English-speaking community, not write English? . . . A Western critic once wrote that "Miss [Christine] Nilsson sang as if she had a nightingale in her throat." Now that is good straightforward English, besides being poetic, and to a certain extent Shakespearian. To be sure, one may, not unreasonably, be in doubt as to how a person would sing under such circumstances. I by no means ask critics to write intelligibly; that would be going too far; but it would be gratifying to find them couching their unintelligibility in language that one can at least read without the aid of a polyglot slang dictionary.

✻ ✻ ✻ ✻ ✻

✻ 1882 — PROTEUS [LOUIS C. ELSON], MUSIC HISTORIAN, MUSIC EDITOR, AND MUSIC CRITIC

From "Music in Boston," *Church's Musical Visitor* (November 1882), 383-84.

Verily, music is getting so low-priced in Boston that the poorest man can have his little symphonic enjoyments.

✻ ✻ ✻ ✻ ✻

⁕ 1882 — MAX MARETZEK, IMPRESARIO, CONDUCTOR, AND COMPOSER

From "Musical Critics and Criticisms in America," *American Art Journal* 37/14 (29 July 1882), 289-90.

Sound and scientific criticism promotes and elevates art; impartial criticism, such as tries to guide and instruct, but not to cavil and ridicule, encourages artists and incites them to more energy and ambition; but what effect can criticism have upon art, artists and the public, which in quality and quantity is dealt out by many newspapers according to the amount of advertisements sent previously to them? Unfortunately, four-fifths of the newspapers in America, and among them some very influential ones, act on the principle of "no advertisement, no notice," or "for each square of advertising, a certain limited space of criticism and no more."

⁕ ⁕ ⁕ ⁕ ⁕

⁕ 1896 — RUPERT HUGHES, COMPOSER, NOVELIST, FILM MAKER, AND WRITER ON MUSIC

From "Music in America–Homer N. Bartlett," *Godey's Magazine* 133/798 (December 1896), 640-45.

The notoriously low average of American musical taste is chiefly due to the Yankee fondness for trash by bad composers. Put not your trust in cadenzas; neither yet in "variations." What the American public accepts as variations would smell as bad by any other name, but could hardly be more inaccurately titled. Instead of the real variation and diversifying of a set theme–sort of a game of solitaire with which musicians sometimes amuse themselves—Yankee "variations" keep the original air pitilessly unchanged and swaddle it in far-soaring arpeggios and gaudy decorative figures.

⁕ ⁕ ⁕ ⁕ ⁕

⁕ 1897 — BLISS CARMAN, CANADIAN POET

From "The Artist and His Critic," *Boston Evening Transcript* (2 January 1897), 18.

Our critical journals are neither many nor good.

⁕ ⁕ ⁕ ⁕ ⁕

⁕ 1898 — WILLIAM FOSTER APTHORP, MUSIC AND DRAMA CRITIC AND WRITER ON MUSIC

From *By the Way* (Boston: Copeland and Day, 1898), ix.

To write with any approach to finality on Music and Art in general is a task fit for no one to attempt today. To write what may be suggestive of, and stimulating to, further thinking on these subjects is the best that any of us can hope to do.

* * * * *

✻ 1900 — RUPERT HUGHES, COMPOSER, NOVELIST, FILM MAKER, AND WRITER ON MUSIC

From *Contemporary American Composers* (Boston: L. C. Page, 1900), 447.

In the ninth century Iceland was the musical center of the world; students went there from all Europe as to an artistic Mecca. Iceland has long lost her musical crown. And Welsh music in its turn has ceased to be the chief on earth. Russia is sending up a strong and growing harmony marred with much discord. Some visionaries look to her for the new song. But I do not hesitate to match against the serfs of the steppes the high-hearted, electric-minded free people of our prairies; and to prophesy that in the coming century the musical supremacy and inspiration of the world will rest here overseas, in America.

* * * * *

✻ 1912 — GEORGE WHITEFIELD CHADWICK, COMPOSER, TEACHER, AND MUSIC ADMINISTRATOR

From "Orchestral Conductors & Conducting," (Boston: New England Conservatory, 18 January 1912), 11-12. [Unpublished manuscript reprinted courtesy of the New England Conservatory]

The salary of a conductor depends partly on the amount of time and labor involved, but to a greater extent on his ability and prestige. Generally speaking, they earn rather more than a college professor and not as much as a successful plumber or commercial traveler [i.e., traveling salesman].

* * * * *

✻ 1902 — MABEL W. DANIELS, COMPOSER AND MEMOIRIST

From a letter (4 October 1902), *An American Girl in Munich* (Boston: Little, Brown, 1912), 47.

Today, while we were waiting in the salon for dinner to be announced, I chanced to play a few bars from a piece by [Edward] MacDowell.

"Is that by your national composer, Sousa?" inquired Herr Doktor.

I hastily informed him that it was not.

"Why! I didn't know you had any other composers of importance," he remarked, with interest.

It is a sad but true fact that American music has, as yet, no footing in Germany.

* * * * *

✻ 1913 — JAMES GIBBONS HUNEKER, MUSIC CRITIC AND JOURNALIST, WRITER ON MUSIC

From "Four Famous Virtuosos," *Old Fogy: His Musical Opinions and Grotesques* (Philadelphia: Theodore Presser, 1913), 69-77.

Such a month of dissipation! You must know that at my time of life I run down a bit every spring, and our family physician prescribed a course of scale exercises on the Boardwalk at Atlantic City, and after that—New York, for Lenten recreation! Now, New York is not quiet, nor is it ever Lenten. A crowded town, huddled on an island far too small for its inconceivably uncivilized population, its inhabitants can never know the value of leisure or freedom from noise. Because he is always in a hurry a New York man fancies that he is intellectual. The consequences artistically are dire. New York boasts—yes, literally *boasts*—the biggest, noisiest, and poorest orchestra in the country. I refer to the Philharmonic Society, with its wretched woodwind, its mediocre brass, and its aggregation of rasping strings. All the vaudeville and lightning-change conductors have not put this band on a level with the Boston, the Philadelphia, or the Chicago organizations. Nor does the opera please me much better. Noise, at the expense of music; quantity, instead of quality; all the *tempi* distorted and *fortes* exaggerated, so as to make an effect. Effect, effect, effect! That is the ideal of New York conductors. This coarsening, cheapening, and magnification of details are resultants of the restless, uncomfortable, and soulless life of the much overrated Manhattan.

Naturally, I am a Philadelphian, and my strictures will be set down as old fogyism. But show me a noise-loving city and I will show you an inartistic one. Schopenhauer was right in this matter; insensibility to noise argues a less refined organism. And New York may spend a million [dollars] of money on music every season, and still it is not a musical city. The opera is the least sign; opera is a social function—sometimes a circus, never a temple of art. The final, the infallible test is the maintenance of an orchestra. New York has no permanent orchestra; though there is an attempt to make of the New York Symphony Society a worthy rival to the Philadelphia and Boston orchestras. . . .

* * * * *

※ A Timeline of Landmarks in American Music, 1860-1920

Prepared by the Editor[1]

1862 ※ Composition of the patriotic concert piece *Union* by pianist Louis Moreau Gottschalk, who championed the Northern cause during his first extended American recital tour after spending years in Cuba and the West Indies

※ Passage of two bills by the U. S. Congress concerning the disposition and standards of bands in the Union Army

※ Publication of "Battle Hymn of the Republic," a setting of poetry by Julia Ward Howe to the tune "Glory, Hallelujah" (based on a Methodist hymn tune already familiar as "John Brown's Body")

1867 ※ Performance of the first major work by an American composer in Europe to critical acclaim: Mass in D (1866) for vocal soloists, chorus, and orchestra by John Knowles Paine at the Berlin Singakadamie (with the composer conducting)

1869 ※ Extravagant commemoration of the Civil War in Boston with the National Peace Jubilee organized by bandmaster Patrick S. Gilmore (with nearly 1,000 singers and instrumentalists participating)

1871 ※ First tour of the Jubilee Singers of Fisk University (Nashville, TN)

※ First reported written use of the term "vaudeville" in the context of American variety entertainment (Louisville, KY)

1873 ※ Publication of *Sacred Songs and Solos*, first collection of gospel songs by the partners Ira David Sankey (singer/composer) and Dwight C. Moody (evangelist)

1875 ※ Appointment of John Knowles Paine to first full professorship in music (Harvard University)

[1]The portion of this timeline for the years between 1870 and 1920 first appeared in the editor's article on "Music," *American History through Literature 1870-1920*, 3 vols., ed. Tom Quirk and Gary Scharnhorst (Detroit: Charles Scribner's Sons / Thomson Gale, 2006), II, 721-30.

1876 ❋ First publication in Germany of a symphony written by an American composer: Symphony No. 1 in C Minor by John Knowles Paine

1877 ❋ Development by Thomas A. Edison of first commercially viable sound recording mechanism

1879 ❋ Performance in America of as many as 100 productions of Gilbert & Sullivan's *H.M.S. Pinafore* (including one all-Black, one all-children, and one Yiddish)

❋ Affiliation of James A. Bland, composer of "Carry Me Back to Old Virginny" (1878), with Haverly's Genuine Colored Minstrels, an early all-Black troupe

1881 ❋ Founding of the Boston Symphony Orchestra

❋ The demise of the influential, Boston-based *Dwight's Journal of Music* after espousing "good music" based on German principles for 29 years

❋ Opening in New York City of the first vaudeville house conceived for men and women by Tony Pastor

❋ Establishment in New York City of T. B. Harms, the publishing firm that revolutionized the popular song industry

1883 ❋ Opening of the Metropolitan Opera House in New York City

❋ Most geographically extensive tour of the Theodore Thomas Orchestra, led by Theodore Thomas—from Baltimore to San Francisco and then back across the Upper Midwest

1884 ❋ First issue of *The Etude*, monthly periodical directed to piano teachers and their students (Theodore Presser, Lynchburg, VA)

1886 ❋ Founding of the National Conservatory of Music in New York City by Jeanette Thurber

1891 ❋ Founding of the Chicago Symphony Orchestra

1892 ❋ Arrival in New York City of Antonín Dvořák to direct the National Conservatory of Music

❋ First public concert of the Sousa Band (in Plainfield, NJ)

1896 ✻ Composition of Symphony No. 1 in E Minor ("Gaelic") by Mrs. H. H. A. Beach, the first symphony by an American to quote folk tunes as thematic material and the first symphony written by an American woman

✻ Composition by Edward MacDowell of the suite of character pieces for piano *Woodland Sketches*, containing "To a Wild Rose"

✻ Formation of the American Federation of Musicians, trade union for professional musicians

1897 ✻ Publication of "On the Banks of the Wabash," best-known song of Paul Dresser

✻ Premiere of "Stars and Stripes Forever" by John Philip Sousa (Philadelphia, PA)

1898 ✻ Founding of the National Federation of Musical Clubs, a network of women societies advocating the performance and study of fine-art music

1899 ✻ Publication of Scott Joplin's "Original Rags" and "Maple Leaf Rag" (John Stark, Sedalia, MO)

1900 ✻ Founding of the Philadelphia Orchestra

1901 ✻ Founding of the Wa-Wan Press by Arthur Farwell (Newton Center, MA)

1903 ✻ American debut of Italian tenor Enrico Caruso in Verdi's *Rigoletto* with the Metropolitan Opera Company

1904 ✻ Opening of *Little Johnny Jones* (with "The Yankee Doodle Boy" and "Give My Regards to Broadway") written, composed, staged, and choreographed by its star George M. Cohan

1905 ✻ Founding of the Institute of Musical Art in New York City by Walter Damrosch (after 1924 The Juilliard School of Music)

1906 ✻ First American radio broadcast of both live and recorded music–both fine-art selections (Brant Rock, MA)

1907 ✻ First season of *The Ziegfeld Follies* produced by Florenz Ziegfeld (annual productions until 1925, with four more ending in 1931)

✻ Publication in Germany of *Early Concert-Life in America, 1731-1800* (Breitkopf & Härtel, Leipzig) by Oscar Sonneck, early landmark scholarship on the history of American music

1909 ✻ First printing of *Songs of the Workers to Fan the Flames of Discontent: The Industrial Workers of the World Songbook* ("The Little Red Songbook")

1910 ✻ Premiere of the *The Pipe of Desire* (1906) by Frederick Shepherd Converse, first opera by an American composer to be mounted by the Metropolitan Opera Company

1911 ✻ Publication of the song "Alexander's Ragtime Band," which made Irving Berlin a household name

1912 ✻ First reported appearance of the blues in European notation: W. C. Handy's "The Memphis Blues"

1913 ✻ Opening of the Palace Theatre at Broadway and 42nd Street in New York City, in its time the most prestigious booking for vaudeville performers (two shows a day until 1932)

✻ First appearance of the word "jaz" in print (in the *San Francisco Bulletin*)

✻ Release of the first recordings by Black musicians: ragtime arrangements by James Reese Europe and His Society Orchestra (New York City)

1914 ✻ Formation of the American Society of Composers, Authors, and Publishers (ASCAP)

1915 ✻ Completion by Charles Ives of Sonata No. 2 ("Concord, Mass., 1840-60") for piano with its tributes to Emerson, Hawthorne, the Alcotts, and Thoreau

✻ Opening of *Nobody's Home*, first of a series of so-called "Princess Theatre musicals" created by Jerome Kern and Guy Bolton, later with P. G. Wodehouse

✻ First issue of *The Musical Quarterly* (edited by Oscar Sonneck), a periodical devoted to musicological scholarship (G. Schirmer, New York City)

✻ Distribution of silent film *The Birth of a Nation* by D. W. Griffiths with a "live" orchestral soundtrack of original music by Joseph Carl Breil and quotations of music by Grieg and Wagner and of patriotic tunes

✻ Premiere performance of John Alden Carpenter's orchestral suite *Adventures in a Perambulator* by the Chicago Symphony

1916 ✻ Publication of *Jubilee Songs of the United States of America*, collection of folk song and spiritual arrangements by Harry T. Burleigh

1917 ⁕ First recording of jazz, "The Dixie Jazz Band One-Step" / "Livery Stable Blues" by the Original Dixieland Jazz Band

⁕ Publication of *English Folk-Songs from the Southern Appalachians* by Olive Campbell and Cecil Sharp (G. P. Putnam's Sons, New York City)

⁕ Beginning of the diaspora of jazz musicians from New Orleans because of the closing of the notorious Storyville district

1918 ⁕ Ballet performance to the symphonic poem *Dance in the Place Congo* (1908) by Henry F. B. Gilbert at the Metropolitan Opera House in New York City

⁕ Premiere of Charles Wakefield Cadman's *Shanewis, or the Robin Woman*, the first opera with a contemporary American setting presented by the Metropolitan Opera Company (partly based on the life of a Creek Indian woman and including an onstage jazz band)

⁕ Composition of *Poem* for Flute and Orchestra by Charles Tomlinson Griffes

1919 ⁕ Formation of the Radio Corporation of America (RCA) by General Electric

⁕ Widely heralded assessment of jazz musician Sidney Bechet as a "genius" by Swiss conductor Ernest Ansemet (published in *Revue Romande*)

⁕ First "million-selling" recording: "Japanese Sandman" / "Whispering" by Paul Whiteman and His Orchestra

1920 ⁕ Emergence of earliest commercial radio stations (WWJ in Detroit, MI, and KDKA in Pittsburgh, PA)

Cited Sources and Recommended Readings

Books

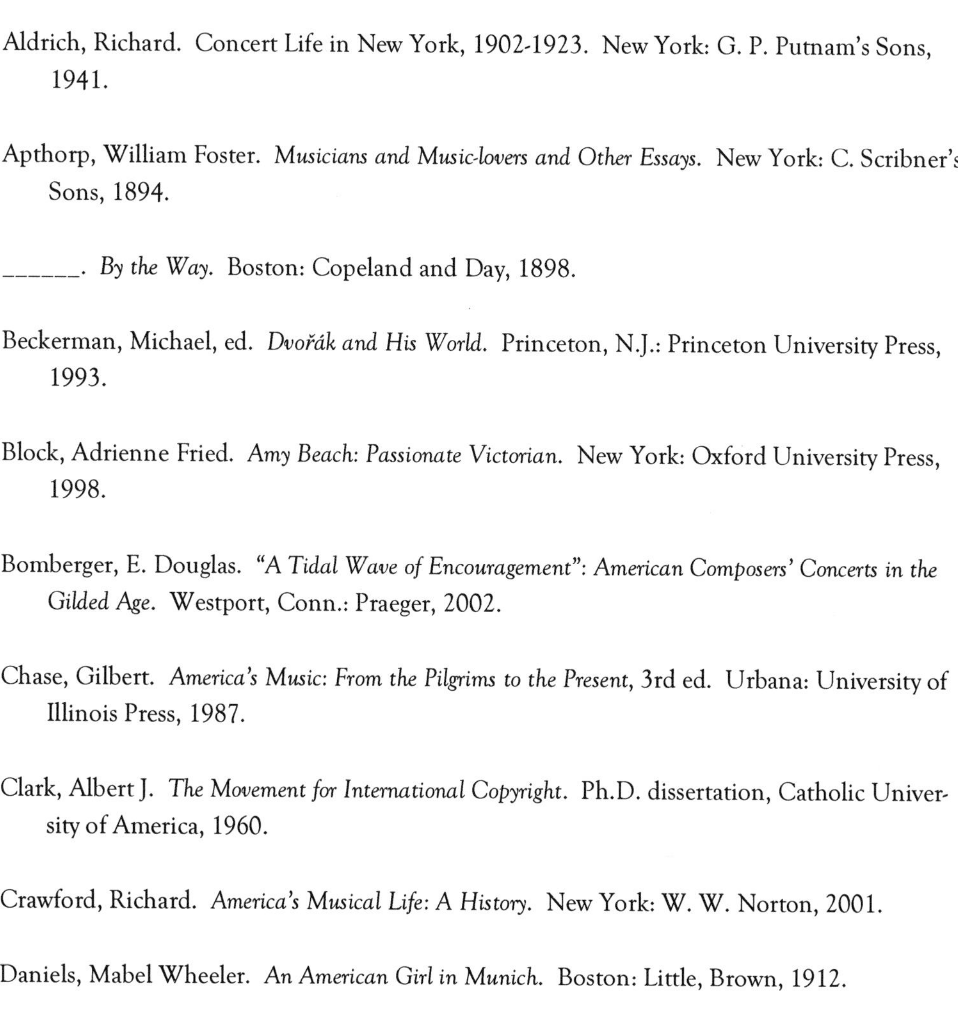

Aldrich, Richard. Concert Life in New York, 1902-1923. New York: G. P. Putnam's Sons, 1941.

Apthorp, William Foster. *Musicians and Music-lovers and Other Essays.* New York: C. Scribner's Sons, 1894.

______. *By the Way.* Boston: Copeland and Day, 1898.

Beckerman, Michael, ed. *Dvořák and His World.* Princeton, N.J.: Princeton University Press, 1993.

Block, Adrienne Fried. *Amy Beach: Passionate Victorian.* New York: Oxford University Press, 1998.

Bomberger, E. Douglas. *"A Tidal Wave of Encouragement": American Composers' Concerts in the Gilded Age.* Westport, Conn.: Praeger, 2002.

Chase, Gilbert. *America's Music: From the Pilgrims to the Present*, 3rd ed. Urbana: University of Illinois Press, 1987.

Clark, Albert J. *The Movement for International Copyright.* Ph.D. dissertation, Catholic University of America, 1960.

Crawford, Richard. *America's Musical Life: A History.* New York: W. W. Norton, 2001.

Daniels, Mabel Wheeler. *An American Girl in Munich.* Boston: Little, Brown, 1912.

Elson, Arthur. *Woman's Work in Music.* Boston: The Page Company, 1903.

Elson, Louis C. *The Realm of Music.* Boston: New England Conservatory of Music, 1892.

______. *European Reminiscences.* Philadelphia: T. Presser, 1896.

Farwell, Arthur, and W. Dermot Darby, eds. *The Art of Music: Music in America*, Vol. 4. New York: The National Society of Music, 1915.

Fay, Amy. *More Letters of Amy Fay: The American Years, 1879-1916*, ed. Margaret William McCarthy. Detroit: Information Coordinators, 1986.

Finck, Henry T. *Songs and Song Writers*. New York: Charles Scribner's Sons, 1900.

Gilman, Lawrence. *Edward MacDowell: A Study*. New York: John Lane Company, 1908.

______. *Phases of Modern Music*. New York: Harper & Brothers, 1904.

Gilmore, Patrick S. *History of the National Peace Jubilee*. Boston: Lee & Shepard, 1871.

Gottschalk, Louis Moreau. *Notes of a Pianist*, ed. Jeanne Behrend. New York: Alfred A. Knopf, 1964.

Hamm, Charles. *Music in the New World*. New York: W. W. Norton, 1983.

Higginson, Thomas Wentworth. *Atlantic Essays*. Boston: James R. Osgood, 1874.

Horowitz, Joseph. *Classical Music in America: A History of its Rise and Fall*. New York: W. W. Norton, 2005.

Howells, William Dean. *Suburban Sketches*. Boston: Houghton, Mifflin, 1901.

Hughes, Rupert. *Contemporary American Composers*. Boston: L. C. Page, 1900.

Huneker, James. *Mezzotints in Modern Music*. New York: Charles Scribner's Sons, 1899.

______. *Old Fogy: His Musical Opinions and Grotesques*. Philadelphia: Theodore Presser, 1913.

Jones, F. O. *A Handbook of American Music and Musicians*. Canaseraga, N.Y.: F. O. Jones, 1886.

Kowalski, Henry I. *National Conservatory: Educate Americans in America and Establish a Standard of Art*. San Francisco: Meese Print, [ca. 1900].

Krehbiel, Henry E. *Notes on the Cultivation of Choral Music and the Oratorio Society of New York*. New York: E. Schuberth, 1884.

______. *Afro-American Folksongs: A Study in Racial and National Music*. New York: G. Schirmer, 1914.

Lahee, Henry C. *Grand Opera in America*. Boston: L. C. Page, 1902.

Levy, Alan Howard. *Musical Nationalism: American Composers' Search for Identity.* Westport, Conn.: Greenwood Press, 1983.

MacDowell, Edward. *Critical and Historical Essays.* Boston: Arthur P. Schmidt, 1912.

Marsh, J. B. T. *The Story of the [Fisk] Jubilee Singers with their Songs.* Boston: Houghton, Mifflin, 1881.

Mason, Daniel Gregory. *Contemporary Composers.* New York: Macmillan, 1918.

Mason, William. *Memories of a Musical Life.* New York: The Century Company, 1901.

Mathews, W. S. B. *The Great in Music.* Chicago: Music Magazine Publishing Company, 1902.

Miller, Delavan S. *Drum Taps in Dixie: Memories of a Drummer Boy, 1861-1865.* Watertown, N.Y: Hungerford-Holbrook Company, 1905.

MTNA *Official Report of the Eighth Annual Meeting.* Cincinnati: Music Teachers National Association, 1884.

MTNA *Studies in Musical Education, History and Aesthetics.* Cincinnati: Music Teachers National Association, 1906.

Patterson, Lyman Ray. *Copyright in Historical Perspective.* Nashville: Vanderbilt University Press, 1968.

Perry, Bliss, ed. *The Life and Letters of Henry Lee Higginson.* Boston: Atlantic Monthly Press, 1921.

Ritter, Frederic Louis. *Music in America.* New York: Charles Scribner's Sons, 1890.

Root, George F. *The Story of a Musical Life.* Cincinnati: John Church, 1891.

Ryan, Thomas. *Recollections of an Old Musician.* New York: E. P. Dutton, 1899.

Samuels, Edward. *The Illustrated Story of Copyright.* New York: St. Martin's Press, 2000.

Sonneck, Oscar G. *Suum Cuique: Essays in Music.* New York: Schirmer, 1916.

Starr, Frederick S. *Bamboula!: The Life and Times of Louis Moreau Gottschalk.* New York: Oxford University Press, 1995.

Thomas, Theodore. *A Musical Autobiography*, Vol. 1. Chicago: A. C. McClurg, 1905.

Tischler, Barbara. *An American Music: The Search for an American Musical Identity*. New York: Oxford University Press, 1986.

Van Vechten, Carl. *Music after the Great War and Other Studies*. New York: Schirmer, 1915.

______. *Interpreters and Interpretations*. New York: Alfred A. Knopf, 1917.

______. *Red: Papers on Musical Subjects*. New York: Alfred A. Knopf, 1925.

Work, John Wesley II. *Folk Song of the American Negro*. Nashville: Press of Fisk University, 1915.

Zuck, Barbara. *A History of Musical Americanism*. Ann Arbor: UMI Research Press, 1981.

PERIODICALS

American Art Journal
American Musician and Art Journal
Appleton's Magazine
The Atlantic Monthly
Boston Evening Transcript
Century Magazine
Church's Musical Visitor
The Dial
Dwight's Journal of Music
The Etude
Godey's Magazine
Harper's Bazaar
Harper's Magazine
Harper's New Monthly Magazine
Harper's Weekly
Lippincott's Magazine
Manufacturer and Builder
Musical America
Musical Courier
The Musical Visitor
The Musician
New England Conservatory Magazine
New England Magazine
The New Republic
The New York Herald
The New York Times
North American Review
The Outlook
Puck
Scientific American
Scribner's Magazine
Scribner's Monthly Magazine
Variety
Yale Review

INDEX